Advance praise for *Strategy and Organization*

"In this refreshingly lucid book on *Strategy and Organization: Realizing Strategy Management* Professor Loizos Heracleous applies organizational theory to strategic management. In the process, he critically reviews conventional strategic thought and develops the many building blocks of an 'organizational action' view of strategic management, providing a valuable reference for students of both strategic management and organization theory. But his greatest contribution is the analytical synthesis of strategy and organization theory, which he accomplishes in a systematic and methodical yet easily accessible writing."

THEODORE PANAYOTOU Harvard University and Cyprus International Institute of Management

"At last! A clear, concise and convincing exposition that integrates strategy formation with organizational behavior and action. Drawing on recent developments and applications in social action theory, and his own extensive research, Professor Heracleous introduces an 'organization action' perspective for understanding the interdependencies among the social processes of organizations and strategy and change. This is a superb book for those interested in new and different ways of thinking about organization strategy, change and behavior. It would be an excellent addition to graduate courses in strategic management, organization theory and behavior, and organizational change."

ROBERT J. MARSHAK Distinguished Adjunct Professor, School of Public Affairs, American University

"Rarely has a book offered such an effective bridge between two distinct discourses as this one. Dr Heracleous opens the wide vista of strategic management to the large numbers of theorists of organization who view it as a foreign country, showing how current thinking on strategy grows organically out of insights on the nature of organizations, leadership, environment, politics and culture. A remarkably erudite book which is going to become a standard reference for many years to come."

YIANNIS GABRIEL Professor of Organizational Theory, Imperial College, London

"For a consultant and practitioner in strategy implementation and the management of organisation change, this book provides valuable challenges to some aspects of conventional thinking, and fascinating insights into the reality of strategic management. It provides a holistic and integrative route through the complexity and confusion of diverse academic thinking on the subject matter. The second and third sections, with their case studies and examination of highly topical issues, demonstrate the richness, excitement and problematic nature of working in this area. This book has motivated me to redouble my efforts to understand the what, why and how managers do what they do, and given me further clues about how they can increase their chances of strategic success."

BRIAN LANGHAM Hay Group

"It is rare to see a book on strategy that engages so well with the field of organization studies. All too often books on strategic management, especially those aimed at practitioners and students, treat strategy as a self-contained phenomenon that is primarily, if not purely, a managerial challenge. By integrating strategy with a wider understanding of the organizational literature, such as culture, leadership and organizational development, the book succeeds in providing a more substantive basis for strategy making, which enriches our understanding of the practicalities of strategic change, as well as linking strategy to some of the broader debat͏͏ ͏͏͏
It should prove a rewarding read for researchers, student͏

CYNTHIA HARDY Professor, Department of Managemer
Director of the International Centre for Research in Org͏
Strategy and Change

D1516891

"This book is a timely and relevant look at the links between organizational behavior, corporate governance and business strategy, and offers material both for 'experts' and the generalist alike. The researcher or academician will find value in the comprehensive review and elucidation of the theoretical and practical implications of organizational theory in considering strategy, a new frontier of management. Heracleous then applies his theory to several areas of emerging business importance, including ICT and 'best practices' in corporate governance – and thereby reaches out to the generalist and business practitioner audience in a step that too few academicians take. As a scholar writing in Asia, his choice of 'applications' is timely indeed, as the region's companies search for the paths and structures that will provide business growth and sustainability for the coming years."

PAMELA C. M. MAR Associate Director – China, World Economic Forum

"Heracleous employs an accessible style in his book and brings a remarkable range of sources in social theory and organization studies to his argument for a new 'organization action' view of strategic management. Highly original and inspirational, this book will be of invaluable interest to researchers, postgraduate and advanced undergraduate students in the fields of strategy and management, organization theory, and organizational behaviour."

ANDREW CHAN Associate Professor, City University of Hong Kong

"Strategy is a serious business and this is one of those rare books that treats it in a fittingly serious way. Heracleous provides an authoritative overview of a lively and central discipline. His book will be valued by all serious students of strategy and by teachers and researchers wanting to understand where the discipline has come from and where it is going today."

RICHARD WHITTINGTON Professor of Strategic Management, Said Business School, University of Oxford

"The 'soft' aspects of strategy, that is primarily organizational culture and politics, have at long last found their ways into strategy textbooks and this is to be welcomed. In this fine textbook Loizos Heracleous goes further: by making agency and discourse the central organising principles of his argument he tackles strategy from a performative, as opposed to a representationalist, point of view. Strategy making is a creative activity par excellence, he argues, deeply entangled with language and discourse, and in this book he shows us how and why. His analysis is well embedded in the fine tradition of hermeneutical organization theory and, furthermore, Heracleous usefully extends his theoretical excursions in social theory, searching for better ways of making sense of strategy. This book has all the things I admire in good organizational scholarship: it is grounded in a process epistemology, it explicitly focuses on agency and praxis, and adopts a dynamic view of how organizations behave and strategies are made."

HARIDIMOS TSOUKAS The George D. Mavros Research Professor of Organization and Management, Athens Laboratory of Business Administration (ALBA), Greece Professor of Organization Theory and Behaviour, University of Strathclyde Editor-in-Chief of *Organization Studies*

"*Strategy and Organization* is a theoretically rigorous examination of current issues and debates in strategy. Dr Heracleous does an excellent job in combining organization theory with existing theories on strategy to develop a new perspective on strategy and produce a very readable and useful book."

CONSTANTINOS MARKIDES Robert P. Bauman Professor of Strategic Leadership, London Business School

Strategy and Organization

Examining some of the new and emerging issues in strategic management, Loizos Heracleous offers a fresh approach to the established ideas of strategy. Beginning with the historical development of the strategy field, including the influence of industrial organization and the resource-based view, he develops a new perspective labeled an "organizational action" view of strategy. This approach is theoretically underlain by organization theory and takes seriously such issues as the role of agency, the need for a longitudinal focus on process, the complexities of strategy implementation, and organizational facets such as strategic choice, organizational culture, organizational discourses and learning. Combining theoretical subtlety with an applied orientation, Heracleous examines topical areas such as corporate governance, inter-organizational networks, and organizing for the future. With original research and extensive surveys of the strategy literature, combined with a strong practical orientation, this book is ideal for MBA students, strategy researchers, and the more thoughtful practitioner.

Dr. Heracleous is Associate Professor of Corporate Strategy at the School of Business, National University of Singapore.

Strategy and Organization

Realizing Strategic Management

LOIZOS HERACLEOUS

CAMBRIDGE
UNIVERSITY PRESS

PUBLISHED BY THE PRESS SYNDICATE OF THE UNIVERSITY OF CAMBRIDGE
The Pitt Building, Trumpington Street, Cambridge CB2 1RP, United Kingdom

CAMBRIDGE UNIVERSITY PRESS
The Edinburgh Building, Cambridge, CB2 2RU, UK
40 West 20th Street, New York, NY 10011–4211, USA
477 Williamstown Road, Port Melbourne, VIC 3207, Australia
Ruiz de Alarcón 13, 28014 Madrid, Spain
Dock House, The Waterfront, Cape Town 8001, South Africa

http://www.cambridge.org

First published 2003

Printed in the United Kingdom at the University Press, Cambridge

Typeface Sabon 10/13 pt. *System* LaTeX 2_ε [TB]

A catalogue record for this book is available from the British Library

Library of Congress Cataloguing in Publication data

ISBN 0 521 81261 5 hardback
ISBN 0 521 01194 9 paperback

To my parents, whose unconditional and loving support
made my work possible

Contents

Figures

Tables

Preface

The first books on organization theory I read were Burrell and Morgan's (1979) *Sociological Paradigms* and *Organizational Analysis*, and Morgan's (1986) *Images of Organization*. These works explored the conceptual and methodological pluralism of the social sciences and in particular organization theory, and made clear that the dominant positivist mode of inquiry was just that: a mode of inquiry, that taken to extremes, could hinder the knowledge-generation process. Pettigrew's (1985) and Johnson's (1987) in-depth studies of the strategy process, in addition, shaped my early understanding of strategy. They emphasized that we cannot hope to understand sufficiently the complex processes related to strategic management unless we take a good look at the *internal functioning* of organizations. This entails getting one's hands dirty in the field, gathering nuanced data on actors' first-order perceptions through hermeneutically oriented methodologies.

These initial orientations enabled me to view strategy as inextricably linked to organization, and as such processual rather than static, messy and ambiguous rather than clear-cut, socio-political rather than simply "technological" or sanitized, and located within local conditioned rationalities rather than universal rationalities. I became convinced that carrying out my doctoral research on the topic of how organizational discourse and culture influence strategic change processes (Heracleous 1997) using ethnographic methodologies would be useful in terms of contribution to knowledge (even though it would also be pretty hard work).

My research work over the last few years has revolved around themes whose common thread was the attempt to understand what is actually going on in organizations, or how social theory can contribute to such understanding, rather than what classical theories tell us should go on. When asked to explain what my research is about, I say that at the most basic level I am interested in how people in organizations think, how they interpret things, and why they choose to act as they do. This is certainly a tall order, and perhaps unacceptably broad and subjectivist from the positivist's perspective. Yet, the alternative risks micro-defining issues out of relevance or substantive interest, and constructing "objective" surveys that could tell us a lot about correlations between variables yet precious little about whether these variables matter to, and are meaningful to, actors, whether they can actually describe what is going on, or how they were developed in the first place.

Conducting hermeneutically oriented research entails a mainly positive rather than normative orientation, even though these cannot be neatly separated, since useful organization change and development prescriptions should be based on a robust understanding of the organizational setting. In a similar vein, strategic management itself cannot be separated from organization change and development since the realization of strategic goals often involves the effective implementation of significant organizational change (Heracleous and Barrett 2001; Tan and Heracleous 2001).

In my research I have tried to understand issues such as the relationship between organizational culture and change (Heracleous and DeVoge 1998; Heracleous and Langham 1996); the complementarity between strategic management and organizational development (Heracleous 1998, 2000); the relevance of organizational discourse to the functioning of organizations (Heracleous 2002, 2003; Heracleous and Barrett 2001; Heracleous and Hendry 2000) and how applications of social theory can contribute to more nuanced understanding of issues such as processes of globalization (Barrett and Heracleous 1999) or organizational controls (Jacobs and Heracleous 2001).

In the context of my doctoral and subsequent research, the genesis of this book is rooted in my interest in how organization theory can engender a new paradigm in strategic management, that takes seriously such issues as the role of agency; how the world is meaningful to organizational actors; a longitudinal focus on process rather than on static cross-sectional analyses; and pays due attention to organizational facets such as strategic choices, culture, discourse, and learning. I have labeled this an "organizational action" view of strategic management, in order to highlight the relevance of such organizational issues, and perhaps to invoke Silverman's (1970) challenge to positivism in the form of his "action frame of reference." There are already several scholars contributing to this emerging paradigm, often labeled as "strategy as practice" (e.g. Hendry 2000; Jarzabkowski and Wilson 2002; Whittington 2002).

Part I of the book, on "Bases of strategic management" outlines the literature in the field; develops the organizational action view; applies organizational learning theory to the concepts of strategic thinking and planning; and explores how leadership research can improve our understanding of boards of directors.

Chapter 1, entitled "The strategic management field," opens the scene by briefly addressing the historical origins of strategy, the writings of classic authors and the entry of consulting firms; it then considers the industrial organization model with a look at the work of Michael Porter, organizational economics and the resource-based view. The chapter ends by noting the disenchantment with the traditional planning paradigm, the fragmentation of the strategic management field, and the need for a new, more organizationally informed paradigm.

Chapter 2 locates the dominant strategic management approaches outlined in chapter 1 in the functionalist paradigm, notes their main critiques, and discusses the emergence of what may be labeled the "organizational action" view of strategic management in terms of applications of interpretive sociology and organization theory to strategy. It then discusses the conceptual building blocks of the organizational action view and their interrelationships, and concludes with some key theoretical features of this emerging view.

Chapter 3 aims to disentangle the relationship between the terms "strategic thinking" and "strategic planning" as found in the literature; to develop the analogy of strategic planning as single-loop learning and strategic thinking as double-loop learning; to propose a dialectical view of the relationship between strategic thinking and strategic planning; and to offer examples of strategic thinking and planning and the dialectical process involved. This discussion illustrates the general orientation of the organizational action view, the application of organization theory to strategic management issues, in this case using organizational learning concepts to clarify the nature and interrelationship between strategic thinking and strategic planning. It can also potentially contribute to a deeper understanding of strategic choice, a key facet of the organizational action view, by exploring the nature and complementarity of these two concepts.

Chapter 4 explores the relevance and applicability of leadership research in enhancing our understanding of boards of directors'

functioning and effectiveness. Secondly, it discusses methodological issues with respect to board research and indicates potentially fruitful
methodological approaches. Consistent with the organizational action
view of strategic management, this chapter aims to gain a deeper understanding of the dominant coalition, and shares the methodological
perspective of this view.

Part II of the book, on "Realizing strategy," is concerned in various
facets of strategy implementation within an organizationally informed
perspective. Chapter 5 sets the scene, by highlighting the turbulence
of the competitive environment, which makes capabilities for strategic
thinking and successful realization of strategy even more critical. It
addresses the high costs of failed implementation efforts, as well as
the reasons for which strategy implementation efforts can fail. Finally,
it outlines various concepts and frameworks that can aid successful
strategy implementation.

Chapter 6 goes in depth into one facet of the organizational action view, the organizational paradigm, which provides the context for
strategic choices and actions. It employs a processual approach to examine the nature of organizational culture and its effects, focusing on
the close interrelationship between culture and strategic change. The
case discussion illustrates how a strategic re-direction involving market
repositioning and substantial growth, can also entail significant cultural and organizational changes. The discussion suggests that rather
than aiming for wholesale cultural change, an organization should recognize what aspects of the culture need to change and what aspects
need to be nurtured. The cultural web is employed as a useful framework for understanding the cultural and organizational situation of the
firm, and identifying relevant changes. A typified framework for strategic decision-making is also presented as a useful tool for managing the
change process, and some important issues of change management arising at each stage are discussed.

Continuing chapter 6's focus on the ideational aspects of the organization and a change perspective, chapter 7 emphasizes that effective
change management is not just about the "hard" structural aspects of
organizations; it requires an in-depth appreciation of the cultural and
human aspects of organizations, and taking actions based on this understanding. This chapter suggests that organizational discourse can
provide access to this conceptual world of organizations and can also
be used as an avenue for influencing it. Use of metaphor by change

agents is discussed as a prime example of how discourse can help to achieve effective organizational change.

Chapter 8 describes an organization development (OD) approach to managing strategic change processes, based on an "integrated organizational model" developed for this purpose, and illustrates its use through an empirical example. The process of applying the model and learning from this and other OD interventions, indicates how closer integration between the fields of OD and strategic management can help to bridge the gap of relevance between academic and practitioner concerns. The findings also highlight useful lessons which merit careful consideration by top management teams when developing strategy, and planning and leading strategic change. In terms of the organizational action view, this chapter exemplifies a processual approach to strategic choice and implementation that takes into account key organizational factors in planning for and implementing change. In addition, it presents an organization development-oriented decision process that can support strategic choices by the dominant coalition; in doing so, it emphasizes the value of integrating organizational development with strategic management, in terms of enhanced practitioner relevance and more effective strategy implementation.

Part III of the book, entitled "Current themes and applications," discusses selected topical issues in strategic management. Chapter 9 outlines global privatization trends and the impact of privatization programs. Using a variant of the organizational action view as a theoretical framework, Singapore Telecom is analyzed as a case where state ownership combined with several contextual and firm-related factors, especially firm strategy, has led to sustained world-class performance relative to its peers. This analysis challenges the widely held position that public ownership is associated with inferior performance and points to the importance of strategy as a key factor in aiding superior performance even under public ownership. Some theoretical and practical implications of the analysis are then outlined.

Research on the importance of generally accepted "best practices" in corporate governance has generally failed to find convincing connections between these practices and organizational performance. Chapter 10 discusses research outcomes on the relationship between two such "best practices" (CEO/Chair duality and insider/outsider composition) and organizational performance, that find this relationship to be insignificant. Four possibilities are proposed for this tenuous relationship, that are not mutually exclusive. The methodological and substantive implications of each of these possibilities are then addressed. This chapter suggests that in order to gain an understanding of the strategic role and impact of boards, studies of structural board factors are insufficient; we must rather use in-depth qualitative methodologies to explore actual board functioning, and track the board's role in specific strategic decisions and actions. This shares the methodological perspective of the organizational action view, its focus on strategic choices by the dominant coalition, and the importance of following through the decisions' impact on realized strategy and performance.

Chapter 11 develops a typology of inter-organizational networks based on the key dimensions of organizational interdependence and network durability. This helps to place the network literature in context by suggesting that network features and processes vary in different types of networks, and have different implications for performance. This chapter includes an extended discussion of "embedded" networks found in East Asia. A "micro-typology" of such embedded networks is developed, based on the dimensions of formalization of ties and networking scope. Thirdly, taking a strategic perspective on the role of the board of directors, it is suggested that in the context of achieving more effective governance, (interlocking) directors' roles should differ based on the type of network in which they are engaged. This chapter represents an attempt to operationalize a key conclusion of chapter 10, on the need to better understand directors' strategic roles, rather than the mostly fruitless attempt so far of attempting to relate structural board features to organizational performance.

Chapter 12 begins by addressing the characteristics of the shifting competitive landscape, significantly influenced by the forces of globalization and information and communication technologies. It expands on the crucial role of leadership for guiding organizations towards competitive success, especially the ability to effectively balance strategic and organizational tensions and paradoxes. The implications of the new competitive environment for organizational design are then addressed, especially how firms can develop strategic flexibility. Intensified competitive churning leads to higher levels of uncertainty and risk. The chapter suggests that even though structured tools exist to help managers deal with such risk, the most effective defense at a strategic level is building sound strategic thinking and implementation capabilities. The chapter ends by suggesting that notwithstanding the hype and popular assertions that the old rules of strategy are not applicable any more, the opposite is true. Strategic clarity based on established principles is now more crucial than ever.

Without Fiona's unceasing encouragement this book might not be a reality. I would also like to thank Chris Harrison and his colleagues at Cambridge University Press for their professional and outstanding work on all aspects of publishing this book.

Bibliography

Barrett, M. and Heracleous, L., 1999. Understanding globalization as a structurational process in the context of the London Insurance Market, *Academy of Management Best Papers Proceedings*, OCIS: A1–A6, Best Paper Award

Burrell, G. and Morgan, G., 1979. *Sociological Paradigms and Organizational Analysis*, Aldershot: Gower

Hendry, J., 2000. Strategic decision making, discourse, and strategy as social practice, *Journal of Management Studies*, 37: 955–977

Heracleous, L., 1997. *Strategic Change, Discourse and Culture: Conceptualizations and Interconnections*, unpublished doctoral thesis, Judge Institute of Management, University of Cambridge

1998. Strategic thinking or strategic planning, *Long Range Planning*, 31: 481–487

2000. The role of strategy implementation in organization development, *Organization Development Journal*, 18(3): 75–86

2001. An ethnographic study of culture in the context of organizational change, *Journal of Applied Behavioral Science*, 37(4): 426–446

2002. The contribution of discourse in understanding and managing organizational change, *Strategic Change*, 11: 253–261

2003. A comment on the role of metaphor in knowledge generation, *Academy of Management Review*, 28: 190–191

Heracleous, L. and Barrett, M., 2001. Organizational change as discourse: communicative actions and deep structures in the context of IT implementation, *Academy of Management Journal*, 44: 755–778

Heracleous, L. and DeVoge, S., 1998. Bridging the gap of relevance: strategic management and organizational development, *Long Range Planning*, 31: 732–744

1998. Budging the gap of relevance: strategic management and organizational development, *Long Range Planning*, 31, 732–744

Heracleous, L. and Hendry, J., 2000. Discourse and the study of organization: towards a structurational perspective, *Human Relations*, 53: 1251–1286

Heracleous, L. and Langham, B., 1996. Strategic change and orga-
    nizational culture at Hay Management Consultants, *Long Range
    Planning*, 29: 485–494
Jacobs, C. and Heracleous, L., 2001. Seeing without being seen: to-
    wards an archaeology of controlling science, *International Studies of
    Management and Organization*, 31(3): 113–135
Jarzabkowski, P. and Wilson, D. C., 2002. Top teams and strategy in a
    UK university, *Journal of Management Studies*, 39: 355–381
Johnson, G., 1987. *Strategic Change and the Management Process*,
    Oxford: Blackwell
Morgan, G., 1986. *Images of Organization*, Beverly Hills, CA: Sage
Pettigrew, A., 1985. *The Awakening Giant: Continuity and Change in ICI*,
    Oxford: Blackwell
Silverman, D., 1970. *The Theory of Organizations*, London: Heinemann
Tan, T. K. and Heracleous, L., 2001. Teaching old dogs new tricks: imple-
    menting organizational learning at an Asian National Police Force,
    Journal of Applied Behavioral Science, 37: 361–380
Whittington, R., 2002. Practice perspectives on strategy: unifying and de-
    veloping a field, paper presented at the Academy of Management
    Meeting, Denver, August 9–14

I *Bases of strategic management*

1 | *The strategic management field*

Historical origins of the term "strategy"

Strategy as a term was coined in Athens around 508–7 BC, where ten *strategoi* comprised the Athenian war council and yielded both political and military power. Etymologically, *strategos*, or general, derives from *stratos* (the army) and *agein* (to lead). So, in this original sense, "strategy" is "the art of leading the army." Concerns of early writers on strategy such as Aenias Tacticus, Pericles, and Xenophon included the qualities of effective *strategoi*, principles of employing the troops, and wider strategic goals such as Pericles' admonition about the "need to limit risk while holding fast to essential points and principles." According to Xenophon, moreover, a commander "must be ingenious, energetic, careful, full of stamina and presence of mind, loving and tough, straightforward and crafty, alert and deceptive, ready to gamble everything and wishing to have everything, generous and greedy, trusting and suspicious." An essential attribute of aspiring strategoi was "knowing the business which [they] propose to carry out." A general was expected not only to plan for battle, but also to lead the troops into battle himself (Cummings 1993).

Parallel developments in Asia included Sun Tzu's *Art of War*, dated to around the 5th century BC (Sawyer 1996). Sun Tzu emphasized meticulous planning, the ideal of vanquishing the enemy indirectly without the need to fight, the qualities of effective generals, advice on managing the troops, and general principles and tactics of engaging with the enemy.

While strategy has originated in the military sphere, since the 1960s it has risen into prominence in the business world. Top executives of multidivisional corporations such as Chester Barnard of AT&T (1938) and Alfred Sloan of General Motors (1963) were among the first to draw attention to the need for strategy within a business context. Drucker (1954) argued for an active approach to management which entailed

planning and actions intended to shape a firm's environment as opposed to simply reacting passively to it. The sociologist Philip Selznick
(1957) at around the same time proposed the notion of an organization's "distinctive competence," which would become a central concept
of the resource-based view of the firm (Wernerfelt 1984).

There are indeed good reasons for positing effective strategy as a cornerstone of high-performing organizations. Research has shown that
a firm's strategy is the most important determinant of its performance;
industry context is important to performance, but not as important as
firm strategy (Bowman and Helfat 1998; McGahan and Porter 1997;
Rumelt 1991). Some companies in very tough industries consistently
deliver higher performance than their competitors, and this is because
of the particular strategies they adopt at the global, corporate, business,
and functional levels.

Classic authors on strategy

In 1912, the Harvard Business School began offering a course in "Business Policy," intended to be a capstone course integrating the functional knowledge that the students had gained in earlier study. Alfred
Chandler of the Harvard Business School, in his classic *Strategy and
Structure* (1962), explored how large businesses adapted their administrative structures to accommodate strategies of growth. In this work
he gave a basic definition of strategy and structure which would have
long-lasting resonance in the field: "strategy can be defined as the determination of the basic long-term goals and objectives of an enterprise,
and the adoption of courses of action and the allocation of resources
necessary for carrying out these goals...Structure can be defined as
the design of organization through which the enterprise is adminis-
tered" (1962: 15–16). Chandler also suggested, based on his data, that
"structure follows from strategy and that the most complex type of
structure is the result of the concatenation of several basic strategies"
(1962: 16).

Learned *et al.*, also at Harvard, in their *Business Policy: Text and
Cases* (1965–9) echoed Chandler when they defined strategy as "the
pattern of objectives, purposes, or goals and major policies and plans
for achieving these goals, stated in such a way as to define what business the company is in, or is to be in and the kind of company it is or
is to be" (1965–9: 15). They viewed strategy formulation as a process

interrelated but practically distinct from strategy implementation, a distinction that has been questioned by strategy scholars, even those aligned with industrial organization economics such as Michael Porter, who has asserted that "there is no meaningful distinction between strategy and implementation, because strategy involves fine-grained choices about how to configure particular activities and the overall value chain" (1999: 25). In formulating strategy, Learned *et al.* proposed that managers should balance external market opportunity with internal firm competence and resources, managers' personal values and aspirations, and obligations to stakeholders other than the stockholders. Strategy could then be implemented through mobilizing resources, exhibiting leadership, and configuring the appropriate organization structure, incentives, and control systems. This broad approach was consistent with that of Chandler, and incorporated Selznick's concept of "distinctive competence" as well as the idea of an uncertain environment.

Also in the mid-1960s, Igor Ansoff, in his *Corporate Strategy* (1965) argued that strategy provided a "common thread" for five interrelated issues – (1) product-market scope, (2) growth vector, (3) competitive advantage, (4) internally generated synergy, and (5) make or buy decisions – and stressed the need for mutual reinforcement among these choices. Ansoff proposed the well-known product – mission matrix as a way for firms to define the common thread of their own strategy. This framework has nevertheless been popular as a means of identifying avenues for growth (figure 1.1).

	Present product	*New product*
Present mission	**Market penetration**	**Product development**
New mission	**Market development**	**Diversificaition**

Figure 1.1 Ansoff's product/mission matrix
Source: Ansoff (1965).

The major pedagogical approach to the study of strategy at Harvard consisted of case studies combined with industry notes, an approach followed later by most other business schools. This approach reinforced the notion that strategy had to be determined inductively on a case-by-case basis, depending on both the specific internal capabilities of each company and its particular external environment. This approach assumed that the complexity of strategic decisions meant that it would be difficult if not impossible to establish useful generalizations.

Strategic decisions such as divestments, new product launches, acquisitions, and overseas expansions do involve what has been referred to as "wicked" problems (Mason and Mitroff 1981). Strategic decisions involve issues that are inherently ambiguous and unstructured, complex, have organization-wide implications and interconnections, are fundamental to the welfare of the organization, and often involve significant organizational change. By comparison, operational decisions are routinized, operationally specific, and may involve smaller-scale change.

Work by these early authors established the main parameters for how the subject of strategy would be understood and researched in the next few decades. These parameters included the link between strategy and performance, the importance of internal capabilities and resources as well as external environment, the distinction between formulation and implementation, and the active role of managers in setting and realizing strategy.

The entry of consulting firms

While academics determined how strategy was to be taught in business schools, their insistence that strategy was idiosyncratic to each individual firm, meant that the growing business demand for standardized strategic frameworks could be addressed by consulting firms, who used this opportunity to exercise substantial influence on the practice of strategy.

The Boston Consulting Group (BCG), founded in 1963, for example, was a pioneering consultancy that introduced influential concepts such as the "experience curve" and the "growth-share matrix" (Stern and Stalk 1998). The experience curve concept held that total costs would decline by a certain percentage every time cumulative production doubled. This idea spurred corporations to expand aggressively their capacity, focus on cost minimization, and seek higher demand, often by keen price competition. However, when inevitable market downturns occurred or innovative products were introduced, the flaws of this approach became apparent. Companies found themselves with excess capacity and outdated product designs, as well as reduced capacity for innovation given their previous focus on cost-cutting. More criticism ensued. According to Ghemawat (2000: 9), "the concept of the experience curve was also criticized for treating cost reductions as automatic rather than something to be managed, for assuming that most experience could be kept proprietary instead of spilling over to competitors, for mixing up different sources of cost reduction with very different strategic implications (e.g., learning vs. scale vs. exogenous technical progress), and for leading to stalemates as more than one competitor pursued the same generic success factor."

The growth-share matrix viewed companies as a portfolio of businesses and was intended to help senior managers identify the cash-flow requirements of different businesses and take resource allocation decisions about them. When using the growth-share matrix, businesses are grouped in strategic business units (SBUs) (a term introduced at a later stage by the CEO of General Electric for use in their own portfolio analysis tools) and are mapped on a matrix along two dimensions: industry growth rate and relative market share. The SBUs are then divided into "stars," "question marks," "cash cows," and "dogs" (figure 1.2).

BCG assumed that competitors with larger market shares would have the lowest costs and highest profits, and that in growing markets

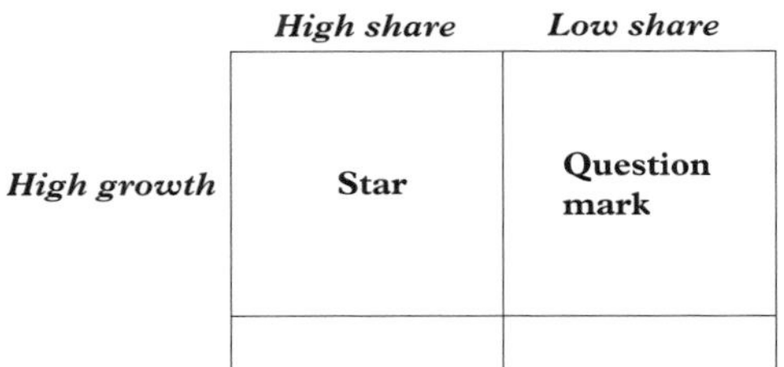

	High share	Low share
High growth	Star	Question mark
Low growth	Cash cow	Dog

Figure 1.2 Boston Consulting Group's growth-share matrix
Source: Boston Consulting Group.

a company should try to capture most of the growth by growing faster than its competitors, so that when growth slowed down, it would emerge as the highest-share competitor. Based on these assumptions, the strategic implications of the BCG matrix were that cash from "cash cows" should be used to support selected "question marks" and to strengthen emerging "stars," the weakest "question marks" should be divested or liquidated, the company should exit from "dog" industries, and that the company should have a balanced portfolio of "stars," "cash cows," and "question marks."

Companies that followed these recommendations blindly made important strategic errors. One reason is that it is too simplistic to take important investment decisions based on just two, historically oriented dimensions. The historical performance of business or the historical growth pattern of markets were not guaranteed to continue along the same trajectory in future. Secondly, the relationship between market share and cost savings is not as straightforward as assumed by the growth-share matrix, for example in industries using low-share technologies such as mini-mills or micro-breweries, and in industries benefiting from computer-assisted manufacturing (CAM). Thirdly, even "cash cows" may require substantial investment to be kept competitive; for example, the motor vehicle industry is indeed low-growth and relatively consolidated, but it is also characterized by cut-throat competition. If the leading competitors reduce their investment in new vehicle designs, and product or process innovations in general, they are likely to be quickly overtaken by other more capable competitors. Lastly, portfolio planning techniques tend to view businesses as free-standing entities, and thus ignore any potential or actual synergies between them.

Improved models of portfolio planning techniques have been developed, which address some of the above flaws, one example being the McKinsey/GE matrix. Even though such models are definite improvements over the BCG matrix, in that they address a much higher number of relevant dimensions of industry attractiveness and business strength, they still have some drawbacks. They still tend to regard businesses as independent, downplay diversification as a strategy for creating value since they focus on existing businesses, and undervalue the need to leverage distinctive competencies and resources across business units to achieve synergies.

A significant alternative approach is Hamel and Prahalad's view of the corporation as a portfolio of *core competencies* as opposed to a portfolio of businesses (Hamel and Prahalad 1994). Building on the resource-based view of the firm (Wernerfelt 1984), this view has important implications for investment decisions that are quite different from the implications arising from using portfolio tools such as the BCG matrix. The aim shifts from strict maximization of financial performance of SBUs in the short term, to longer-term investment in the nurturing and creation of core competencies across SBUs that can enable the company to be a winner in the future; they thus focus on "opportunity share" rather than simply market share.

The industrial organization model

Meanwhile, developments in the academic sphere continued. Two streams of strategy research are particularly worth noting because of their significant influence on the field: the industrial organization model, and the resource-based model. The industrial organization (IO) model focuses on the industry structure or attractiveness of the external environment, suggesting that the performance of any firm is largely determined by market characteristics (Porter 1980). Economists have traditionally assumed a situation of perfect competition, where several equally capable competitors would gradually eliminate super-normal profits, and the choice of competing firms would be either to produce efficiently and price at cost, or exit the industry. This emphasis has downplayed the empirically differential internal capabilities of firms, and focused on market structure, leading to the Structure–Conduct–Performance (S–C–P) paradigm (that market structure would determine firm conduct which would determine performance). This was based on research by Edward Mason (1939) and Joe Bain (1951, 1956), two Harvard economists. Bain (1956) identified three main barriers to entry to an industry as a means of explaining why some industries are more profitable than others: absolute cost advantages, product differentiation, and economies of scale. These entry barriers are linked with two out of three "generic" strategies subsequently proposed by Michael Porter, then a joint economics/business doctoral researcher at Harvard: cost leadership, differentiation, and focus (Porter 1980). Michael Porter proposed his well-known "five

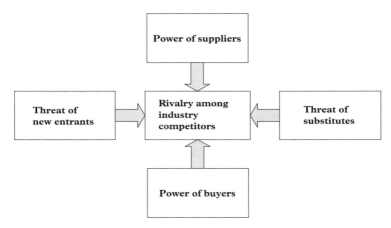

Figure 1.3 Porter's five forces framework for industry analysis
Source: Porter (1980).

forces" framework for industry analysis as a more structured way to evaluate industry attractiveness and to explain the differential performance of industries (figure 1.3). Porter's model was an advance over existing understandings of the market in that it emphasized extended competition rather than simply current competitors, in the form of threat from substitute products, as well as offering a memorable, structured framework that could be easily applied.

One subsequent development is the introduction of the concept of "complementors" (Brandenburger and Nalebuff 1996), firms from which customers buy, or suppliers sell, complementary products or services. Porter, however, believes that the relationship of complementors to industry profitability is not "monotonic," and that it has to be analyzed not as a force in its own right but through its effects on the five forces. He made similar arguments for the role of government, that some have proposed as a sixth force (Porter 2002).

This early research set the foundations for the IO paradigm of strategic management; this includes using the industry as the unit of analysis, addressing the content rather than the process of strategies, methodologically employing archival data longitudinally, and posing the dominant inference pattern that industry structure sets limits on firm performance (Jemison 1981).

The realization that profitability differences within industries can be even greater than across industries, led to research on strategic groups

(Hunt 1972) that aimed to explain this differential. Companies within the same strategic group follow the same or similar strategies along certain dimensions (Porter 1980: 129), and movement from one strategic group to another is hindered by so-called "mobility barriers" (Caves and Porter 1977), a similar concept to "barriers to entry."

Another aspect of industries highlighted by IO research is that they can be fragmented or consolidated to various degrees. Fragmented industries are often characterized by low entry barriers and commodity-like products. Consolidated industries, on the other hand, have higher entry barriers and are composed of interdependent firms. Industry structure is dynamic; industries can move from being fragmented to more consolidated after an industry shakeout; or they can become fragmented after the entry of new competitors enabled by environmental shifts such as deregulation or the availability of new technologies or new distribution channels.

Porter's value chain and generic strategies

Michael Porter also developed the value chain as a tool for analyzing an organization's internal activities. This represents the flow of activities that results in a product or service of value to the customer. "Primary" activities relate to manufacturing, marketing, sales, and service, and "support" activities relate to infrastructure (structure and leadership), human resources, research and development, and materials management. Use of the value chain can enable a company gain a deeper understanding of where its distinctive value-adding competencies lie, or identify problems with its functioning. Porter has shown how successful strategies involve clear choices as well as mutual reinforcement among a firm's internal activities (Porter 1996). For example, a successful strategy of cost leadership involves cost control in all of a firm's activities which are mutually reinforcing to deliver a product or service of sufficient quality at a lower cost than most or all competitors.

With regard to generic strategies, Porter argues that "the fundamental basis of above-average performance in the long run is sustainable competitive advantage ... there are two basic types of competitive advantage a firm can possess: low cost or differentiation ... combined with the scope of activities for which a firm seeks to achieve them lead to three generic strategies ... Each of the generic strategies involves a fundamentally different route to competitive advantage" (Porter 1985: 11). Porter believes that a company should not try to follow more than one generic strategy, otherwise it risks being "stuck in the middle," achieving neither cost leadership nor differentiation: "achieving competitive advantage requires a firm to make a choice... Being 'all things to all people' is a recipe for strategic mediocrity and below-average performance, because it often means that a firm has no competitive advantage at all" (Porter 1985: 12). Porter believes that it is possible for a firm to achieve both cost leadership and differentiation, but only where its competitors are stuck in the middle, cost is greatly affected by market share or firm interrelationships, or a firm pioneers a major innovation (1985: 19–20). All of these situations, however, are seen as temporary, and there will come a time when a firm has to make a choice: "A firm should always aggressively pursue all cost reduction opportunities that do not sacrifice differentiation. A firm should also pursue all differentiation opportunities that are not costly. Beyond this point, however, a firm should be prepared to choose what its ultimate competitive advantage will be and resolve the tradeoffs accordingly" (1985: 20).

Whether cost leadership and differentiation are compatible or not has been a point of controversy. Hill (1988), for example, has argued that it is possible to have both, under certain conditions. He argues that investment to increase differentiation can improve brand loyalty and expand sales, in turn reducing the long-run average costs. In this way, differentation allows a firm also to attain a low-cost position. This proposition holds, however, only when expenditure on differentiation significantly increases demand, and the extent to which significant reductions in unit costs arise from increasing volume.

Generic strategies can be seen as a first step in deciding on business-level strategies. A company has also to decide on its particular image or positioning in the market and on its sales appeal to customers. For example, differentiators in the vehicle industry may choose to be principally differentiated in terms of luxury (Rolls-Royce), speed and styling (Ferrari), engineering excellence (Mercedes, BMW), and/or safety (Volvo). Companies can also attempt to reposition themselves if they believe that this will lead to competitive advantage. For example, Volvo attempted to reposition not only as a brand associated with safety, but also associated with speed, and aired advertisements portraying a race between a Volvo and a BMW vehicle, with the Volvo winning. BMW complained to the US advertising authorities, who ruled that the advertisement was not misleading because, taking into account the particular models shown, Volvo was indeed the faster. The point is, however, that not many consumers were ultimately convinced of the Volvo brand's sportiness, illustrating how difficult it is to alter an already diffused brand image.

Organizational economics

Two branches of organizational economics, transaction costs economics and agency theory, have been particularly influential in the strategic management field. Transaction costs economics (Williamson 1975, 1985) seeks to explain the existence of organizations (hierarchies) based on their higher efficiency in carrying through certain transactions, as compared to markets. The goal is minimization of transaction costs and the unit of analysis is firm-level dyadic transactions. Transaction cost logic can explain the widespread adoption of the multi-divisional form, as well as the potential benefits that accrue to firms undertaking related diversification (through economies of scope) or unrelated diversification (through financial economies within an internal capital market).

Agency theory (Jensen and Meckling 1976; Fama and Jensen 1983) suggests that the separation of ownership and control in modern corporations leads to a divergence of interest between the principals (shareholders) and the agents (managers). It is assumed that the agents will act in a self-interested and opportunistic way to maximize their own interests at the expense of the principals. Governance mechanisms thus become necessary. Internally they include the board of directors and configuration of executive compensation, and externally the market for corporate control and the market for managerial talent. Agency theory has been particularly influential in research on corporate governance, diversification, and firm innovation.

The resource-based view

While the traditional IO paradigm downplays internal firm capabilities and resources that can lead to competitive advantage, the resource-based view suggests that above-average returns for any firm are largely determined by characteristics inside the firm. This view focuses on developing or obtaining valuable resources and capabilities which are difficult or impossible for rivals to imitate, because their link with the firm's competitive advantage may be causally ambiguous or the resources themselves may be socially complex. Thus, capabilities and resources that are valuable, rare, imperfectly imitable, and not substitutable can enable a firm achieve sustainable competitive advantage (Barney 1991).

While the concept of firms as sets of resources was originated by Penrose (1959), it was Wernerfelt (1984) who more formally formulated the resource-based view of the firm. He suggested that most economic tools were relevant to the product/market domain, whereas the traditional view of strategy was more concerned with a firm's resource position in terms of strengths and weaknesses. He suggested that some resources can lead to higher profitability because they pose "resource position barriers" (Wernerfelt 1984: 172), that a firm should strike a balance between exploiting existing resources and developing new ones, and that acquisitions could be seen as purchasing a set of resources. His definition of resources was "anything that could be thought of as a strength or weakness of a given firm. More formally, a firm's resources at a given time could be defined as those (tangible and intangible) assets which are tied semipermanently to the firm... Examples of resources are: brand names, in-house knowledge of technology, employment of skilled personnel, trade contracts, machinery, efficient procedures, capital, etc." (1984: 172). Barney *et al.* (2001: 625) echoed this definition when they defined resources and capabilities as "bundles of tangible and intangible assets, including a firm's management skills, its organizational processes and routines, and the information and knowledge it controls."

The resource-based view of the firm has had immense influence on strategic management theory and practice since the late 1980s. It has contributed to fields as diverse as human resource management, economics, finance, entrepreneurship, marketing, and international business. Further potentially useful contributions can be made to the areas of organizational adaptation in fast-moving environments (in the form of "dynamic capabilities"), corporate governance, management buyouts or venture capital financing (Barney *et al.* 2001).

The substantial influence of the resource-based view was partly because of its consonance with ongoing research at the time, as well as its consonance with the classic Harvard business policy model (Wernerfelt 1995). With regard to theory, subsequent studies focused on specific resources such as culture (Barney 1986), the dynamics of resource acquisition and shedding (Montgomery 1995), and the potential inertial effects of certain resources (Leonard-Barton 1992). In spite of all the research, however, we still know more about markets than about resources: "we have a rich taxonomy of markets and substantial technical and empirical knowledge about market structures. In contrast, 'resources' remain an amorphous heap to most of us" (Wernerfelt 1995: 172). For this reason, scholars have called for more in-depth, qualitative studies (Rouse and Daellenbach 1999) that can more effectively capture the nature and functioning of intangible resources such as organizational culture or innovation capability.

Hoskisson *et al.* (1999), using the metaphor of a pendulum, argue that strategic management research began inside the firm, with the classical Business Policy approach at Harvard in the 1960s. It then swung outside to the market through the influence of IO economics (encompassing research under the S–C–P paradigm, strategic groups, and competitive dynamics), began to swing back towards the firm under the influence of organizational economics (encompassing transaction cost economics and agency theory), and in the 1990s returned inside the firm, with the popularity of the resource-based view.

Sustainability of competitive advantage and dynamic capabilities

According to Hoskisson *et al.* (1999: 444):

from an IO economics perspective, mobility barriers or market positions are the critical sources of competitive advantages that lead to superior performance. Organizational economics is more concerned with devising appropriate governance mechanisms or contracts to help reduce transaction or agency costs. However, the advance of the resource based view has refocused the field of strategic management on the firm's internal characteristics and views firms' internal resources as the source of competitive advantage. While all three theoretical perspectives have significantly advanced our understanding of the sources of competitive advantage and hence firm performance, the sustainability of firms' competitive advantages has increasingly become an important question.

Sustainability of competitive advantage is fleeting. A study by McKinsey Consultants found that out of 208 companies in various industries, only three could sustain their competitive advantage (in terms of above-average profitability and growth) over a ten-year period (Ghemawat 2000). In addition, analysis of 700 business units showed that 90 percent of the profitability differentials between above-average and below-average performers disappeared over a ten-year period (Ghemawat 1986). This was referred to as the "Red Queen" effect, where companies have to deal with continually improving competitors and therefore have to "keep running" as fast in order just to stay in the game.

Factors that influence the sustainability of competitive advantage include the extent to which a company's competencies are valuable, rare, imperfectly imitable and non-substitutable, the dynamism of the industry context, and the capabilities of competitors. Tangible resources, such as production facilities, are the easiest to imitate. Intangible resources such as brand name and trademarks are harder to imitate. Capabilities such as innovation capability or absorptive capacity (Cohen and Levinthal 1990) are the hardest to imitate, because they do not reside in any one individual, but in the routines and culture of the organization as a whole.

A company without sustainable competitive advantage is in danger of imminent failure, in terms of sustained below-average performance and finally bankruptcy. Companies can fail for several reasons, including organizational inertia that hinders change (Kelly and Amburgey 1991), misplaced prior strategic commitments (Ghemawat 1991), or the "Icarus paradox" (Miller 1992) – being so content with their success that they lose touch with their customers and the shifts in their competitive environment.

Disenchantment with the traditional planning approach and fragmentation in the strategic management field

The "planning view" of strategy developed at Harvard in the 1960s holds that strategy is a rational, top-down, structured process that involves clear steps of establishing mission and goals, conducting internal and external analyses, choosing strategies at the corporate, business and functional levels, and then implementing these strategies through changes in the organizational structure and control systems. This traditional view has been criticized on various grounds, however, including the fact that it downplays the existence of unintended consequences of actions and the inherent unpredictability of the environment, sees

Table 1.1 *History lessons on the future*

"I think there is a world market for maybe five computers"
(Thomas Watson, Chairman of IBM, 1943)

"Nobody wants to watch a box night after night"
(Daryl F. Zanuck, Chairman of 20th Century Fox, rejecting television, 1949)

"We don't like their sound, and guitar music is on the way out"
(The Decca Recording Company, rejecting the Beatles, 1962)

"This 'telephone' has too many shortcomings to be seriously considered as a
  means of communication"
(Western Union internal memo, 1896)

"Whatever could possibly be invented, has now been invented"
(The head of the US Patent Office, 1899)

"There is no reason anyone would want a computer in their home"
(Ken Olsen, President and founder, Digital Equipment Corp., 1977)

strategy as an exclusively top-down process, and ignores the role of emergent strategy.

Global trends such as inter-organizational networking, accelerated product and process innovations, new technologies, deregulation and liberalization, globalization of product and financial markets, higher consumer sophistication, and intensifying competition, spurred the development of more flexible planning approaches such as "scenario planning" (Wack 1985a, 1985b). Since the traditional planning paradigm was based on the assumption that the future can be reasonably predictable, or at least that the firm can make plans and allocate resources in fixed ways that will not be negated by environmental changes, it was soon realized that this approach was not feasible. Managers realized that attempts to predict the future were doomed to failure. Some high-profile misjudgments are illustrated in table 1.1.

A trenchant critic of the traditional planning paradigm is Henry Mintzberg (1987), who argues that strategy is a multi-dimensional concept and that at least five different views of strategy are required; *intended* strategy, which may remain unrealized; *deliberate* strategy, where resources are invested in the intended strategy; *realized* strategy, either intended or not; strategy that is intended but remains *unrealized*; and *emergent* strategy, which arises from the grass roots of the organization.

Other critics include Hamel and Prahalad (1994), who argue that the traditional planning model of strategy focuses too much on the concept of "fit" between environmental conditions and organizational capabilities and resources. This focus on fit and the present, however, could prevent a company from thinking about how to develop its capabilities for creating winning products for the future. Managers were therefore advised not to think just in terms of market share, but also in terms of "opportunity share." Companies should create new competitive space through introducing groundbreaking new products, as opposed to fighting for incremental slices of the same pie.

These criticisms led to a "behavioral" view of strategy, where strategy is seen as a pattern of decisions and actions at the organizational level (Mintzberg 1978). These decisions and actions are not always "rational" (in the classical sense of being solely based on structured and objective analysis), in that they are influenced by the socio-political climate and the existing routines, structure, and systems of the organization.

A related "interpretative" view of strategy has also emerged. In this view, strategy is the product of the minds and ideologies of individuals and groups in the organization. This view emphasizes the fact that the relation between the organization and its competitive environment is always mediated by how individuals in the organization interpret both its environment and capabilities. In turn, strategic decisions and actions are based on these interpretations, and an adequate understanding of the strategy of the organization must include the particular interpretations of actors in the organization (Chaffee 1985). Mintzberg *et al.* (1998) present a useful overview of the fragmentation of the strategy field, identifying ten schools of strategic thought (table 1.2).

Despite the fragmentation of the strategy field, there are some areas of agreement; strategy concerns both the organization and its environment, and an effective strategy is important for the welfare of the organization. The substance of strategy is complex, non-routine and unstructured, and its study involves issues of content, context and process (Pettigrew 1987). Lastly, strategies are not purely or simply deliberate; they can be intended but unrealized, or emergent; strategies exist on different levels – the corporate, business, and functional levels; and their development involves various thought processes, including both analytical and creative ones (Chaffee 1985).

Table 1.2 *Ten schools of strategic thought*

Strategy school	View of strategy (strategy formation as)
Design school	A process of *conception*
Planning school	A *formal* process
Positioning school	An *analytical* process
Entrepreneurial school	A *visionary* process
Cognitive school	A *mental* process
Learning school	An *emergent* process
Power school	A process of *negotiation*
Cultural school	A *collective* process
Environmental school	A *reactive* process
Configuration school	A process of *transformation*

Source: Mintzberg *et al.* (1998).

Dominant strategic management approaches based on industrial organization and organizational economics, however, and even the resource-based view that at face value looks inside the firm, tend to neglect social and organizational factors in the strategy process. In particular, the role of human agency (the strategists who form the dominant coalition, and how they make strategic choices), as well as the organizational paradigm within which strategic decisions and actions take place, are rarely seriously analyzed. Chapter 2 develops an organizational action (OA) view of strategic management that incorporates these aspects, and integrates them with the traditional concerns of the S–C–P paradigm. But this integration occurs in the context of a different set of guiding assumptions, that acknowledge multi-directional, systemic effects on the strategy process, conditioned rationalities of agents, and messy socio-political organizational processes that nevertheless have an important bearing on strategic decisions and actions.

Bibliography

Ansoff, H. I., 1965. *Corporate Strategy*, New York: McGraw-Hill

Bain, J. S., 1951. Relation of profit to industry concentration: American manufacturing, 1936–1940, *Quarterly Journal of Economics*, 65: 293–324

  1956. *Barriers to New Competition*, Cambridge, MA: Harvard University Press

Barnard, C. I., 1938. *The Functions of the Executive*, Cambridge, MA: Harvard University Press

Barney, J. B., 1986. Organizational culture: can it be a source of sustained competitive advantage?, *Academy of Management Review*, 11: 656–665

    1991. Firm resources and sustained competitive advantage, *Journal of Management*, 17: 99–120

Barney, J. B., Wright, M. and Ketchen, D. J., Jr., 2001. The resource-based view of the firm: ten years after 1991, *Journal of Management*, 27: 625–641

Bowman, E. H. and Helfat, C. E., 1998. Does corporate strategy matter?, Working Paper, University of Pennsylvania

Brandenburger, A. M. and Nalebuff, B. J., 1996. *Co-opetition*, New York: Currency/Doubleday

Caves, R. E. and Porter, M. E., 1977. From entry barriers to mobility barriers: conjectural decisions and contrived deterrence to new competition, *Quarterly Journal of Economics*, 91: 241–261

Chaffee, E. E., 1985. Three models of strategy, *Academy of Management Review*, 10: 89–98

Chandler, A. D., 1962. *Strategy and Structure*, Cambridge, MA: MIT Press

Cohen, W. M. and Levinthal, D. A., 1990. Absorptive capacity: a new perspective on learning and innovation, *Administrative Science Quarterly*, 35: 128–152

Cummings, S., 1993. The first strategists, *Long Range Planning*, 26: 133–135

Drucker, P., 1954. *The Practice of Management*, New York: Harper & Bros

Fama, E. F. and Jensen, M. C., 1983. Separation of ownership and control, *Journal of Law and Economics*, 26: 301–325

Ghemawat, P., 1986. Sustainable advantage, *Harvard Business Review*, September–October: 53–58

    1991. *Commitment: The Dynamic of Strategy*, New York: Free Press

    2000. Competitive and business strategy in historical perspective, *Harvard Business School Note*, 9-798-010

Hamel, G. and Prahalad, C. K., 1994. Strategy as a field of study: why search for a new paradigm?, *Strategic Management Journal*, 15: 5–16

Hill, C. W. L., 1988. Differentiation versus low cost or differentiation and low cost: a contingency framework, *Academy of Management Review*, 13: 401–412

Hoskisson, R. E., Hitt, M. A., Wan, W. P. and Yiu, D., 1999. Theory and research in strategic management: swings of a pendulum, *Journal of Management*, 25: 417–456

Hunt, M. S., 1972. *Competition in the Major Home Appliance Industry, 1960–1970*, unpublished PhD dissertion, Harvard University

Jemison, D. B., 1981. The contributions of administrative behavior to strategic management, *Academy of Management Review*, 6: 633–642

Jensen, M. C. and Meckling, C., 1976. Theory of the firm: managerial behavior, agency costs and ownership structure, *Journal of Financial Economics*, 3: 305–360

Kelly, D. and Amburgey, T. L., 1991. Organizational inertia and momentum: a dynamic model of strategic change, *Academy of Management Journal*, 34: 591–612

Learned, E. P., Christensen, C. R., Andrews, K. R. and Guth, W. D., 1965–9. *Business Policy: Text and Cases* (revised edn.), Homewood, IL: Irwin

Leonard-Barton, D., 1992. Core capabilities and core rigidities: a paradox in managing new product development, *Strategic Management Journal*, 13 (Special Issue): 111–125

Mason, E. S., 1939. Price and production policies of large scale enterprises, *American Economic Review*, 29: 61–74

Mason, R. O. and Mitroff, I. I., 1981. *Challenging Strategic Planning Assumptions*, New York: Wiley

McGahan, A. M. and Porter, M. E., 1997. How much does industry matter, really? *Strategic Management Journal*, 18: 15–30

Miller, D., 1992. The Icarus paradox: how exceptional companies bring about their own downfall, *Business Horizons*, January–February: 24–34

Mintzberg, H., 1978. Patterns in strategy formation, *Management Science*, 24: 934–948

　1987. Planning on the left side and managing on the right, *Harvard Business Review*, July–August: 49–58

Mintzberg, H., Ahlstrand, B. and Lampel, J., 1998. *Strategy Safari*, Englewood Cliffs, NJ: Prentice-Hall

Montgomery, C. A., 1995. Of diamonds and rust: a new look at resources, in C. A. Montgomery (ed.), *Resources in an Evolutionary Perspective: A Synthesis of Evolutionary and Resource-Based Approaches to Strategy*, Norwell, MA and Dordrecht: Kluwer Academic

Penrose, E. T., 1959. *The Theory of the Growth of the Firm*, New York: Wiley

Pettigrew, A. M., 1987. Context and action in the transformation of the firm, *Journal of Management Studies*, 24: 649–670

Porter, M. E., 1980. *Competitive Strategy: Techniques for Analyzing Industries and Competitors*, New York: Free Press

　1985. *Competitive Advantage: Creating and Sustaining Superior Performance*, New York: Free Press

1996. What is strategy?, *Harvard Business Review*, November–December: 61–78

1999. A conversation with Michael E. Porter: a significant extension toward operational improvement and positioning (interviewed by R. M. Hodgetts), *Organizational Dynamics*, 28(1): 24–33

2002. An interview with Michael Porter (interviewed by N. Argyres and A. M. McGahan), *Academy of Management Executive*, 16(2): 43–52

Rouse, M. J. and Daellenbach, U. S., 1999. Rethinking research methods for the resource-based perspective: isolating the sources of sustainable competitive advantage, *Strategic Management Journal*, 20: 489–494

Rumelt, R. P., 1991. How much does industry matter?, *Strategic Management Journal*, 12: 167–185

Sawyer, R. D., 1996. *The Complete Art of War*, Boulder, CO: Westview Press

Selznick, P., 1957. *Leadership in Administration: A Sociological Interpretation*, New York: Harper & Row

Sloan, A. P., 1963. *My Years with General Motors*, New York: Doubleday

Stern, C. W. and Stalk, G., 1998. *Perspectives on Strategy*, New York: Wiley

Wack, P., 1985a. Scenarios: uncharted waters ahead, *Harvard Business Review*, September–October: 73–89

1985b. Scenarios: shooting the rapids, *Harvard Business Review*, November–December: 2–14

Wernerfelt, B., 1984. A resource-based view of the firm, *Strategic Management Journal*, 5: 171–180

1995. The resource-based view of the firm: ten years after, *Strategic Management Journal*, 16: 171–174

Williamson, O. E., 1975. *Markets and Hierarchies*, New York: Free Press

1985. *The Economic Institutions of Capitalism*, New York: Free Press

2 | *An organizational action view of strategic management*

The dominant strategic management approaches discussed in chapter 1 have been criticized on various grounds, leading to the emergence of what may be called an "organizational action" (OA) view of strategic management. This chapter locates dominant strategic management approaches in the functionalist paradigm, outlines their main critiques, and discusses the emergence of the OA view in terms of applications of interpretive sociology and organization theory to strategic management. It then discusses the conceptual building blocks of the OA view and their interrelationships, and concludes with some key theoretical features of this emerging OA view.

Theoretical antecedents of the organizational action view

Functionalist and interpretive paradigms

The theoretical antecedents of the OA framework can be traced to applications of the interpretive sociological paradigm to strategic management (Chaffee 1985; Smircich and Stubbart 1985), as well as critiques of dominant strategic management approaches as deterministic in their assumptions, reductionist in their models, and insufficiently relevant to practice (Bettis 1991; Bourgeois 1984). Dominant strategic management approaches are located within the functionalist paradigm of social science (Burrell and Morgan 1979; Morgan 1980). This paradigm assumes that social phenomena have a concrete, solid reality underlain by a systemic orderliness; the goal of research is to understand the machine-like interactions of variables within this reality, so that one can ideally and ultimately control and predict them. Social scientists in this perspective aspire to the natural science positivist model; they imagine themselves to be outside and separate from their subject matter, and aspire to value free, "pure" science.

The influence of the interpretive paradigm in social science has constituted a potent critique of the functionalist paradigm. Finding

expression in such theoretical domains as hermeneutics, ethnomethod-
ology or phenomenological symbolic interactionism, the interpretive
paradigm assumes that social reality is far from concrete, solid and
"out there." It is, rather, malleable and inter-subjectively negotiated,
the product of patterned social interaction influenced by discursive
fields, legitimating values and power struggles, as the theory of structuration highlights (Giddens 1984). Social interaction draws from conditioned rationalities based on interrelated bodies of discourse that encourage relative stability in social life through their deep structures;
but are also amenable to change over the longer term (Heracleous and
Barrett 2001). Social scientists in the interpretive tradition do not impose *a priori*, second-order conceptual frameworks on their research
programs and observations (as for example the S–C–P paradigm in
strategic management), but rather aim to understand the agents' first-
order perspectives and build inductive frameworks in accordance with
these perspectives. They seek to understand agents' *actions* based on
actors' own interpretations, as opposed simply to their observable behavior (Weber 1991). They understand that social science is not and
cannot be value-free; and that it is more important to make one's assumptions and values explicit rather than hide behind the imaginary
cloak of "pure" social science.

Critiques of dominant strategic management approaches

Bettis (1991) has forcibly argued that even though strategic management as a field has experienced substantial growth since the 1960s, it
has not influenced management practice or public policy to any significant extent because it has been "prematurely stuck in a 'normal science
straitjacket'" (Bettis 1991: 315), drawing from Daft and Lewin's
(1990) similar observation about organization studies. Seminal studies in strategy such as Chandler (1962), Learned *et al.* (1965–9) and
Ansoff (1965) have defined the parameters of the field. The constrain-
ing manner through which many strategic management researchers
have built on these studies, however, has led to a situation where accepted paradigms "do not seem to capture, nor be capable of being
extended to capture, much of what is actually happening today and
what may happen tomorrow" (Bettis 1991: 316).

Bettis laments the fact that large sample multivariate statistical studies can lead to findings of statistical but not substantive significance, so

that "the bad money of statistical methodology [is] driving out the good money of strategic substance" (Bowman 1990: 26). Bourgeois (1984: 592) expressed similar feelings when he argued that "economists, psychologists, and organization theorists are all victims of linear thinking, in which the reduction of a chaotically large number of phenomena into a one-way sequence of cause and effect allows the psychological security of the illusion of 'prediction,' but which disallows the strategist as a 'cause' and ignores the real possibility of a cycle in which cause and effect are mutually interacting." The structure–conduct–performance paradigm of industrial organization economics is a prime example of such reductionist, linear uni-directional causality.

Bourgeois (1984) further criticized dominant strategic management approaches as being deterministic, implicitly assuming that strategy could be predicted or predestined. He argued that this assumption was inconsistent with the concept of strategy itself, which assumes a human agent (the strategist) who takes decisions and actions intended to distinguish a particular firm from competing firms (1984: 589). If the assumptions of the dominant approaches were valid, management would have no active role in guiding organizations but would instead "resign itself to succumbing to the matrix of deterministic forces presented by environmental, technical, and human forces that impinge on its freedom of choice" (1984: 586). If anything, successful organizations are those that reinvent their industries and create new pies, rather than keep fighting for incremental slices of existing shrinking pies (Hamel and Prahalad 1994). This shows a situation far from the environmental determinism implied by dominant approaches; one where the organization's dominant coalition can make strategic choices that are creative and unique, that can have an impact on industry structure and the rules of the competitive game, rather than the other way round. Examples include Dell Computers, Singapore Airlines, and Swatch watches.

Applications of interpretive perspectives to strategic management

Chaffee (1985) was among the first to sketch the emergence of an "interpretive model" in addition to the dominant "linear" and "adaptive" models in strategic management. The "linear" model was associated with the classic business policy approach at Harvard, which was oriented to the achievement of goals through formulating and implementing strategic plans. The "adaptive" model aimed towards achieving a match between external conditions and internal capabilities to align the organization with its environment. The "interpretive" model viewed strategy as an "orienting metaphor" (1985: 94) aimed towards guiding agents' perceptions of the organization and its context and motivating them to act in particular directions. Chaffee summarized the three models as follows: "In linear strategy, leaders of the organization plan how they will deal with competitors to achieve the organization's goals. In adaptive strategy, the organization and its parts change, proactively or reactively, in order to be aligned with consumer preferences. In interpretive strategy, organizational representatives convey meanings that are intended to motivate stakeholders in ways that favor the organization" (1985: 94). Drawing from Boulding's (1956) hierarchy of systems complexity, Chaffee (1985) represented the three models as involving progressively higher levels of complexity that were not necessarily mutually contradictory but could even be complementary. In this sense, the adaptive model could be extended to include the linear model, and the interpretive view could be extended to include the linear and adaptive models.

Smircich and Stubbart (1985) presented an alternative interpretive view of strategy characterized by a more ideational, voluntarist slant. They suggested that organizations are socially constructed systems of shared meanings, where agents enact their environments and their social reality through social interaction. This view is grounded in the social constructionism (Berger and Luckmann 1966) and enactment perspectives (Weick 1977), as well as research on the symbolic, ideational aspects of organizations, especially from the angle of organizational culture (Smircich 1983). The task of strategists in this sense is "to create and maintain systems of shared meaning that facilitate organized action" (Smircich and Stubbart 1985: 724). The research focus shifts from how organizations accomplish tasks efficiently to the very nature of organization and its meanings for the actors involved.

Another theoretical antecedent of the OA view is the field of "administrative behavior" (Jemison 1981a, 1981b), characterized by a higher focus on the firm rather than the industry, on strategy process rather than its content, and on managerial action rather than industry constraints. These original foci developed over time, to what March (1996) has aptly referred to as "action, ambiguity and interpretation" in theories of organizational action:

the premises of action are socially constructed. Preferences, expectations, identities, and definitions of situations are seen as arising from interactions within a social system, thus as embedded in social norms and cultural conventions of discourse. In this view, explanations of action gain legitimacy by invoking shared understandings or proper narrative. Shared understandings are the result of social exchange mediated by a panoply of social elements – social structure, language, myth, resource distributions. (1996: 285)

Conceptual building blocks of the organizational action view

The OA view is constituted operationally by the combination of a handful of central ideas; the concept of organizational paradigm (Johnson 1988; Litterer and Young 1984; Morgan 1980), the strategic choice perspective (Child 1972, 1997), distinctions between intended, realized, unrealized, and emergent strategies (Mintzberg 1978), a strategic choice view of the environment, and the strategic management field's concern with firm performance (Rumelt *et al.* 1994). The conceptual building blocks of the OA view, and their interrelations, are portrayed in figure 2.1.

Organizational paradigm

Paradigms can be defined as particular views of social reality that include assumptions about entities in the social world, their interrelations, legitimate avenues of enquiry, and implicit guidelines for

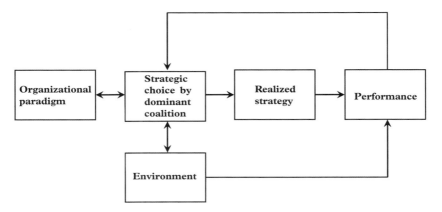

Figure 2.1 An organizational action view of strategic management

interpretation and action (Burrell and Morgan 1979; Litterer and Young 1984; Morgan 1980). At the descriptive level, paradigms include epistemological considerations (knowing what to know), and methodological considerations (knowing how to know). At the normative level, they include values (end purposes) and moral systems justifying these values (Litterer and Young 1984: 249–250). Steffy and Grimes (1986) have described four models of organization science (natural science, phenomenology, hermeneutics, and critical theory) that can be seen as apt examples of theoretical paradigms. Each is grounded in different theoretical domains, employs a different ontology, accepts a different epistemology, and supports a different methodology.

The concept of an organizational paradigm was explicitly employed in strategic management by Johnson (1987, 1988), who defined it as "the set of beliefs and assumptions, held relatively common through the organization, taken for granted, and discernible in the stories and explanations of the managers, which plays a central role in the interpretation of environmental stimuli and configuration of organizationally relevant strategic responses... both intended and realized strategy are likely to be configured within the parameters of the paradigm" (Johnson 1988: 84–85).

Michael Porter's (1999) comments point to the realization that the traditional business policy approach needs to be complemented by a focus on organizational issues: "I was trained to think in terms of the classic Alfred Chandler – a company had a strategy and that strategy should then determine the kind of organizational structure, incentives, norms, and so forth that enterprises would adopt. There was always the acknowledgement of a feedback from structure to strategy, but this was a dotted line. I've come to see that, in many companies, what actually happens occurs in *reverse order*" (1999: 25, emphasis in the original).

The paradigm can be more concretely and operationally represented, within an organizational context, in terms of a "cultural web," where the core beliefs and assumptions that constitute the paradigm are interrelated, rationalized, and mutually supported with several organizational elements. These include symbols, power structures, organizational structures, control systems, routines, and rituals, and myths (see chapter 6 for a portrayal of the cultural web). This Gestalt of cultural, behavioral, systemic, processual, and structural elements is self-perpetuating, self-preserving, and self-legitimizing (Heracleous and Langham 1996, 2001; Johnson 1987, 1988).

One key implication of the proposition that strategic choice is influenced by the organizational paradigm is that the notion of objective rationality underlying dominant functionalist strategic management approaches is both theoretically and empirically flawed. It cannot account for the fact, for example, that the same environmental stimulus can be interpreted differentially by different dominant coalitions, and consequently lead to different strategic choices and actions. Even within the same organization, different stakeholders can both share elements of the dominant paradigm, as well as having idiosyncratic values and beliefs relevant to their perception of their own position within the social organization. It is more accurate to speak of conditioned rationalities, therefore, rather than a single, "objective" rationality (Heracleous and Barrett 2001; Shrivastava *et al.* 1987). If the crucial relationship between the ideational world of the organization and strategic choices is ignored we, as students of organizations, cannot hope to gain a sufficiently robust understanding of why organizations act as they do, or even offer recommendations of sufficient relevance to practitioners' concerns.

Understanding and dealing with organizational culture, for example, is a key factor in successful strategic change programs (Heracleous 2001); yet, in-depth studies of culture in mainstream strategy journals are rare, and "culture" has been subsumed in the resource-based view of the firm in line with Smircich's (1983) outline of culture as a variable rather than as a root metaphor. Cultures that can contribute to sustainable competitive advantage and therefore performance have been described as those that are valuable, rare, and imperfectly imitable (Barney 1986). This is a useful perspective, but we need to complement it by understanding the particular values and beliefs enshrined in specific organization cultures and their links to strategic choices and organizational actions.

Strategic choice by the dominant coalition

The "strategic choice" perspective (Child 1972, 1997) has been extremely influential on the study of organizations (Lemke *et al.* 1999: 4), especially in the areas of agency and choice, the nature of organizational environments, and the relationship between organizational actors and their environment (Child 1997). As a broader organizational analysis perspective, strategic choice is relevant to individual organizations at a micro level, and exhibits a voluntarist orientation (Astley and Van de Ven 1983). It was originally introduced as a reaction to the dominant structural determinist view in sociology at the time, which held that contextual factors such as size, technology, or ownership imposed deterministic constraints on the structural arrangements of organizations. According to the strategic choice perspective, on the other hand, the structural determinist view ignored the fact that organizations were not at the mercy or their environments, and that the dominant coalition of the organization had the power to decide on structural arrangements and courses of strategic action. The dominant coalition are the *de facto* influential actors who are located within the organizational paradigm, and thus perceive strategic issues, and configure intended strategy, within the paradigm's parameters.

As Child's (1972) outline of the strategic choice perspective was focused on strategic choices regarding organizational structure, Child argued that "environmental conditions cannot be regarded as a direct source of variation in organizational structure, as open systems theorists often imply. The critical link lies in the decision-makers' evaluation of the organization's position in the environmental areas they regard as important, and in the action they may consequently take about its internal structure" (1972: 10). A lot of research has subsequently focused on improving understanding of the role of the dominant coalition in strategy-making processes (e.g. Hambrick and Mason 1984; Pettigrew 1992).

Bourgeois' (1984) trenchant critique of dominant strategic management theories echoed the strategic choice perspective, when he argued that dominant theories downplay the substantial and unpredictable influence of human agency on an organization's strategic actions. The OA view takes agents' local, tacit knowledge seriously, and focuses on the process of strategizing rather than on impersonal, acontextual and static strategies (Whittington 1996). Serious attention is given to strategic management as a social practice: to strategists, their conceptual tools and how they develop and use them (Whittington 2002).

The OA view portrays strategic choice as being influenced by the organizational paradigm, environmental factors, and the organization's actual performance, itself based on the organization's structural arrangements, competencies, and strategic positioning, which find expression in "realized strategy."

Realized strategy

The next component of the framework is Mintzberg's (1978) concept of "realized strategy." This concept draws attention to the fact that strategies may be intended by the dominant coalition but may not be ultimately realized, while other strategies that were originally not intended may emerge and be realized over time in an incremental fashion (Quinn 1978). The strategies that are bound to have the highest influence on performance, however, are the *realized* strategies. Strategy was shown to have a higher effect on performance than industry or corporate parentage factors (McGahan and Porter 1997; Rumelt 1991).

On the other hand, it may be argued that an organization may be successful partly because it has been fortunate. For example, Pfizer discovered the blockbuster Viagra drug by chance, when a drug intended for other ailments had rather unusual side effects. Bill Gates' access to and purchase of QDOS (which stood for Quick and Dirty Operating System) was also based on luck. He heard that IBM was looking for an operating system, found out that a Seattle firm owned one (this firm had not heard of IBM's search), borrowed money from his father, and bought the rights to the system. After making some incremental improvements, he licensed it to IBM and the rest is history. Fortuitous factors, however, will have only a limited effect on performance and solid strategizing is required to capitalize on chances and to sustain competitive advantage. On the other hand, unrealized strategies will not only be largely irrelevant to achieving superior performance, but they may also potentially lead the organization to disastrous underperformance. For example, this can happen when reckless and ill-conceived diversification efforts ultimately lead to fatal financial underperformance.

The environment

The environment from a strategic choice perspective presents certain constraints as well as opportunities for organizations, which shape strategic choices. While organizational actors can enact their environments (Weick 1977), this does not mean that environmental conditions can be fully reduced to subjective or even inter-subjective perceptions. "Enactment" within the strategic choice perspective refers to the process by which environments become relevant to organizations through the choices made by organizational actors. Environmental aspects are subjectively interpreted by actors, but environments contain objective features which cannot be simply "wished away" by organizations (Child and Smith 1987). Child (1997) has emphasized that the original sharp distinction between organizations and their environments has to be softened, because "organization and environment... permeate one another both cognitively and relationally – that is, both in the minds of actors and in the process of conducting relationships between the two" (1997: 58). The relationship between organization and environment is a dynamic and changing one.

The OA view portrays the environment as both influencing the strategic choices of the dominant coalition (for example, how the macro-environmental trend of deregulation can prompt organizational actors to consider market development), and being influenced by their strategic choices (for example how an innovative strategy can redefine the rules of competition). The dominant coalition can decide on the environmental domains that the organization will engage with (Child 1972) as well as initiate strategic actions that may exert market power through, for example, product or technological innovation and therefore alter industry structure. The environment in the OA view is portrayed as influencing both strategic choice and organizational performance, which is itself also influenced by realized strategy.

Performance

Lastly, the concern with superior performance has been a basic theme of the strategic management field (Rumelt *et al.* 1994), characterizing the field from its early days. This is implicit, for example, in Chandler's classic historical studies of how firms progressively adapted their structures to respond to new strategic imperatives (Chandler 1962); in Andrews' (1971) discussion of the need to identify core competencies and match these to environmental success factors; and in Ansoff's (1965) view of the role of strategy as providing a common thread between such elements as product/market scope, firm growth vector, and internal synergies. The OA view draws attention to the fact that *performance is ultimately rooted in strategies that are successfully realized,* whether intended or emergent. Organizational performance influences subsequent strategic choices of the dominant coalition, which in turn lead to realized strategies and to performance in a recursive cycle.

Conclusion

The OA view developed here incorporates the *elements* of the dominant S–C–P model, but not its *assumptions*. Market characteristics (S) are incorporated in the "environment," conduct (C) is incorporated in "realized strategy," and Performance (P) is common in both. However, the OA view does not accept the S–C–P's deterministic assumptions of uni-directional influence (from market structure to organizational conduct to performance), or its narrow scope of relevant variables. It includes, in addition to the above, the crucial influence of the dominant coalition and its strategic choices, as well as the paradigm within which the dominant coalition operates. This approach can thus help to address widespread concerns about the (lack of) relevance of a lot of mainstream strategy research (Bettis 1991; Bourgeois 1984; Heracleous and Devoge 1998), by focusing on how strategy is enacted in local contexts by knowledgeable agents in the context of local rationalities (Hendry 2000; Heracleous and Barrett 2001; Jarzabkowski and Wilson 2002).

The OA view thus brings agency back into the picture, highlights recursive and multi-directional rather than linear relationships, encourages processual, interpretive, and inductive inquiry rather than cross-sectional, positivist, and deductive research; and is holistic rather than reductionist. In these senses, it is a "framework" rather than a "model," in terms of Porter's (1991) discussion of alternatives to theory building. Models test relationships between a limited set of variables; their findings are sensitive to the models' assumptions and different models may be difficult if not impossible to integrate in a general framework. Models are useful in teasing out interrelations between a limited set of variables, but they downplay the complexity of actual situations and thus their potential usefulness for practice can be seriously compromised. On the other hand, frameworks incorporate several key variables within a particular organization or pattern, and portray their potential interactions, based on both theory and practice. The use of models and frameworks is not necessarily contradictory: "Models should challenge the variables included in frameworks and assertions about their link to outcomes. Frameworks, in turn, should challenge models by highlighting omitted variables, the diversity of competitive situations, the range of actual strategy choices, and the extent to which important parameters are not fixed but continually in flux" (Porter 1991: 98). This standpoint is consistent with scholars supporting the complementarity rather than opposition of qualitative and quantitative research approaches (Hari Das 1983; Jick 1979). The OA view underlies and informs the work reported in this book in different ways, as the preface outlined.

Bibliography

Andrews, K., 1971. *The Concept of Corporate Strategy*, Homewood, IL: Dow Jones-Irwin

Ansoff, H. I., 1965. *Corporate Strategy*, New York: McGraw-Hill

Astley, W. G. and Van de Ven, A., 1983. Central perspectives and debates in organization theory, *Administrative Science Quarterly*, 28: 245–273

Barney, J. B., 1986. Organizational culture: can it be a source of sustained competitive advantage?, *Academy of Management Review*, 11: 656–665

Berger, P. and Luckmann, T., 1966. *The Social Construction of Reality*, London: Penguin

Bettis, R. A., 1991. Strategic management and the straightjacket: an editorial essay, *Organization Science*, 2: 315–318

Boulding, K. E., 1956. General systems theory – the skeleton of science, *Management Science*, 2: 197–208

Bourgeois, L. J., 1984. Strategic management and determinism, *Academy of Management Review*, 9: 586–596

Bowman, E. H., 1990. Strategy changes: possible worlds and actual minds, in J. W. Fredrickson (ed.), *Perspectives on Strategic Management*, New York: Harper & Row: 9–37

Burrell, G. and Morgan, G., 1979. *Sociological Paradigms and Organizational Analysis*, London: Heinemann

Chaffee, E. E., 1985. Three models of strategy, *Academy of Management Review*, 10: 89–98

Chandler, A., 1962. *Strategy and Structure: Chapters in the History of American Industrial Enterprise*, Cambridge, MA: MIT Press

Child, J., 1972. Organizational structure, environment and performance: the role of strategic choice, *Sociology*, 6: 1–22

1997. Strategic choice in the analysis of action, structure, organizations and environment: retrospect and prospect, *Organization Studies*, 18: 43–76

Child, J. and Smith, C., 1987. The context and process of organizational transformation – Cadbury Limited in its sector, *Journal of Management Studies*, 24: 565–593

Daft, R. L. and Lewin, A. Y., 1990. Can organization studies begin to break out of the normal science straitjacket? An editorial essay, *Organization Science*, 1: 1–9

Giddens, A., 1984. *The Constitution of Society*, Cambridge: Polity

Hambrick, D. C. and Mason, P. A., 1984. Upper echelons: the organization as a reflection of its top managers, *Academy of Management Review*, 9: 193–206

Hamel, G. and Prahalad, C. K., 1994. *Competing for the Future*, Cambridge, MA: Harvard University Press

Hari Das, T., 1983. Qualitative research in organizational behavior, *Journal of Management Studies*, 20: 301–314

Hendry, J., 2000. Strategic decision making, discourse, and strategy as social practice, *Journal of Management Studies*, 37: 955–977

2001. An ethnographic study of culture in the context of organizational change, *The Journal of Applied Behavioral Science*, 37: 426–446

Heracleous, L. and Barrett, M., 2001. Organizational change as discourse: communicative actions and deep structures in the context of IT implementation, *Academy of Management Journal*, 44: 755–778

Heracleous, L. and DeVoge, S., 1998. Bridging the gap of relevance: strategic management and organizational development, *Long Range Planning*, 31: 732–744

Heracleous, L. and Langham, B., 1996. Strategic change and organizational culture at Hay Management Consultants, *Long Range Planning*, 29: 485–494

Jarzabkowski, P. and Wilson, D. C., 2002. Top teams and strategy in a UK university, *Journal of Management Studies*, 39: 355–381

Jemison, D. B., 1981a. The contributions of administrative behavior to strategic management, *Academy of Management Review*, 6: 633–642

1981b. The importance of an integrative approach to strategic management research, *Academy of Management Review*, 6: 601–608

Jick, T. D., 1979. Mixing qualitative and quantitative methods: triangulation in action, *Administrative Science Quarterly*, 24: 601–611

Johnson, G., 1987. *Strategic Change and the Management Process*, Oxford: Blackwell

1988. Rethinking incrementalism, *Strategic Management Journal*, 6: 75–91

Learned, E. P., Christensen, R. C., Andrews, K. R. and Guth, W. D., 1965–9. *Business Policy: Text and Cases* (revised edn.), Homewood, IL: Irwin

Lemke, D. K., Schminke, M., Clark, N. E. and Muir, P., 1999. Whither goest thou? Seeking trends in organization theory into the new millennium, *Academy of Management Proceedings*, OMT: D1–D6

Litterer, J. A. and Young, S., 1984. Organizational paradigm as a tool to analyze organizations and their problems, *Academy of Management Proceedings*, 249–253

March, J. G., 1996. Continuity and change in theories of organizational action, *Administrative Science Quarterly*, 41: 278–287

McGahan, A. M. and Porter, M. E., 1997. How much does industry matter, really?, *Strategic Management Journal*, 18: 15–30

Mintzberg, H., 1978. Patterns in strategy formation, *Management Science*, 24: 934–948

Morgan, G., 1980. Paradigms, metaphors, and puzzle solving in organization theory, *Administrative Science Quarterly*, 25: 605–620

Pettigrew, A. 1992. On studying managerial elites, *Strategic Management Journal*, 13: 163–182

Porter, M. E., 1991. Towards a dynamic theory of strategy, *Strategic Management Journal*, 12: 95–117

   1999. A conversation with Michael E. Porter: a significant extension toward operational improvement and positioning (interviewed by R. M. Hodgetts), *Organizational Dynamics*, 28(1): 24–33

Quinn, J. B., 1978. Strategic change: logical incrementalism, *Sloan Management Review*, 1(2): 7–21

Rumelt, R. P., 1991. How much does industry matter?, *Strategic Management Journal*, 12: 167–185

Rumelt, R. P., Schendel, D. E. and Teece, D. J. (eds.) 1994. *Fundamental Issues in Strategy*, Boston, MA: Harvard Business School Press

Shrivastava, P., Mitroff, I. I. and Alvesson, M., 1987. Nonrationality in organizational actions, *International Studies of Management and Organization*, 17(3): 90–119

Smircich, L., 1983. Concepts of culture and organizational analysis, *Administrative Science Quarterly*, 28: 339–355

Smircich, L. and Stubbart, C., 1985. Strategic management in an enacted world, *Academy of Management Review*, 10: 724–736

Steffy, B. D. and Grimes, A. J. 1986. A critical theory of organization science. *Academy of Management Review*, 11: 322–336

Weber, M., 1991. The nature of social action, in W. G. Runciman (ed.), *Weber: Selections in Translation* (E. Matthews, transl.), Cambridge: Cambridge University Press: 7–32

Weick, K. E., 1977. Enactment processes in organizations, in B. M. Staw and G. R. Salancik (eds.), *New Directions in Organizational Behavior,* Chicago: St. Clair Press: 267–300

Whittington, R., 1996. Strategy as practice, *Long Range Planning,* 29: 731–736

2002. Practice perspectives on strategy: unifying and developing a field, paper presented at the Academy of Management Meeting, Denver, August 9–14

3 | *Strategic thinking or strategic planning?*

In the early 1980s Henry Mintzberg argued that the meaning of the term "strategic planning" was ambiguous, and that there was a need for a clear understanding of that term (Mintzberg 1981). Now not only is "strategic planning" still used in a variety of ways, but the situation is made even more complicated by the introduction of a more recent term, "strategic thinking."

The relationship between strategic planning and strategic thinking is by no means clear in the literature, which has been in a state of confusion over this issue. "Strategic planning" is often used to refer to a programmatic, analytical thought process, and "strategic thinking" to refer to a creative, divergent thought process. The confusion, however, stems from the fact that although there are frequent usages of the terms in the above ways, various authors still use these terms in fundamentally different ways. While for some, such as Mintzberg, strategic thinking and planning are distinct thinking modes which are both useful at different stages of the strategic management process, for others, such as Michael Porter, strategic thinking is not so much creative as analytical. For some strategic planning has remained an analytical activity but the organizational practices surrounding it have been transformed; for others the real purpose of analytical tools of strategic planning is to facilitate creativity and strategic thinking; and for yet others strategic planning is useless in a fast-moving world and should be scrapped in favor of strategic thinking.

An exploration of the literature reveals, therefore, that there is no agreement on what strategic thinking is, what strategic planning is, or what their relationship should be. This chapter has four main aims:

- To disentangle the relationship between the terms "strategic thinking" and "strategic planning," as found in the literature, identifying four main varieties of this relationship

This chapter is a revised and updated version of Heracleous (1998).

- To clarify the nature of strategic thinking and strategic planning by developing the analogy of strategic planning as single-loop learning and strategic thinking as double-loop learning
- To propose a dialectical view of the relationship between strategic thinking and strategic planning which sees them as distinct, but interrelated and complementary thought processes
- To offer real-life examples of strategic thinking and planning and the dialectical process involved.

This discussion illustrates the general orientation of the organizational action (OA) view, the application of organization theory to strategic management issues; in this case using organizational learning concepts to clarify the nature and interrelationship between strategic thinking and strategic planning. In exploring the nature and complementarity of the two concepts it can also potentially contribute to a deeper understanding of strategic choice, a key facet of the OA view.

The relationship between strategic thinking and strategic planning

Four views on the relationship between strategic thinking and strategic planning are found in the literature.

Strategic thinking and strategic planning are two distinct thinking modes, and strategic thinking should precede strategic planning

According to this view, planning cannot produce strategies because it is a programmatic, formalized, and analytical process; it is rather what happens after strategies are decided, discovered, or simply emerge. This is a view associated with Henry Mintzberg, arguably the most trenchant critic of planning. Mintzberg (1994) has sought to limit the theoretical space occupied by the concept of strategic planning by suggesting that it is based on three key fallacies. First, the fallacy of *prediction*, the belief that planners can actually predict what will happen in the marketplace. Secondly the fallacy of *detachment*, the premise that effective strategies can be produced by planners who are detached from the grass roots business operations and the market context. Lastly, the fallacy of *formalization*, the idea that formalized

procedures can in fact produce strategies, whereas their proper function, according to Mintzberg, is to operationalize already existing
strategies.

Critiques of planning in a similar vein have been widespread in the
popular management literature (Albrecht 1994; Kinni 1994). Other
authors within this literature have accepted the conventional critiques
of strategic planning such as those advanced by Mintzberg, but have
gone far beyond them to find no place for planning in organizations,
arguing that strategic planning should be scrapped completely in favor
of strategic thinking (Altier 1991; Harari 1995).

This view, therefore, emphasizes that strategic thinking and strategic
planning involve distinct thought processes, where strategic planning
is analytical and convergent whereas strategic thinking is synthetic and
divergent. It questions strongly the prominence and promise traditionally accorded to strategic planning, seeking to limit planning to the
operationalization of existing strategies rather than seeing it as capable of generating radically new and creative strategies.

Strategic thinking is (and should be) analytical

This is a view associated mainly with Michael Porter, whose analytical
frameworks of five forces analysis, the value chain, the diamond model
of national competitive advantage, and strategy as activity system, are
seminal contributions to the strategic management field. According to
Porter, for example, "strategic thinking involves asking two critical
questions. First, what is the structure of your industry, and how is
it likely to evolve over time? . . . Second, what is your own company's
relative position in the industry?" (Porter 1991a). Others have also
proposed well-defined, analytical approaches as constituting strategic
thinking: Zabriskie and Huellmantel (1991), for example, suggest a
sequential, well-defined six-step process to enable strategic thinking,
and Eden (1990) in a similar vein, describes a strategic thinking process based on cognitive mapping. A similar analytical approach has
also been taken in the popular literature (e.g. Morrisey 1990), where
such formalized approaches are said to constitute strategic thinking.
Porter and others, therefore, use the term "strategic thinking" not as
a synthetic and divergent thought process, but as a convergent and
analytical one, in the same way as other authors would use the term
"strategic planning."

The real purpose of strategic planning is to improve strategic thinking

Related to the above view is the suggestion that *the real purpose of strategic planning is to facilitate strategic thinking,* where structured planning tools are used to aid creative thinking. This is a view stated succinctly in a series of *Harvard Business Review* articles written by former senior managers at Royal Dutch/Shell (De Geus 1988; Wack 1985a, 1985b). The strategic tool associated with this view is "scenario planning," a process of eliciting appropriate responses to reasonably possible futures, designed to question managers' guiding assumptions and sensitize their thinking to potential competitive arenas substantially different from current ones. Wack (1985b) described the scenario planning process at Shell emphasizing that "scenarios serve two main purposes. The first is protective: anticipating and understanding risk. The second is entrepreneurial: discovering strategic options of which you were previously unaware ... Scenarios give managers something very precious: the ability to reperceive reality." De Geus (1988) similarly suggests that the value of the planning process does not reside in the plan itself, but in enriching the mental models of managers involved in this process (for similar arguments see also Nadler 1994).

Strategic planning has over time evolved into strategic thinking

It has been suggested that "strategic planning has changed dramatically since its inception in the early 1970s. Having survived its original design flaws, it has evolved into a viable system of strategic management (or strategic thinking)" (Wilson 1994). The main changes to traditional strategic planning, in this view, include the shift of planning responsibility from staff to line managers, the decentralization of planning to business units, more attention to environmental shifts, more sophisticated selection of planning techniques, and more attention to organization and culture as vital implementation factors (Bonn and Christodoulou 1996). Related to this viewpoint is the literature arguing that strategic planning is useful if it is carried out in an appropriate manner – involving line managers, defining business units correctly, having clear action steps, and integrating the plan with other organizational controls (Gray 1986).

In this view, therefore, strategic planning and strategic thinking are identified more with the organizational practices surrounding them rather than the thought processes involved. Strategic thinking is portrayed as an evolution from strategic planning, which is said to have become less elitist in its origins and more open and sophisticated in its methods.

A learning perspective on strategic thinking and strategic planning

Single-loop and double-loop learning

Having considered the various views found in the literature, there is a need now to clarify the nature of strategic thinking and strategic planning and to place them in an appropriate context. This will be done by suggesting a dual analogy: strategic thinking can be seen as double-loop learning, and strategic planning as single-loop learning. This analogy is helpful in clarifying the nature of strategic thinking and strategic planning, and illustrating why they are different, but ultimately both necessary and complementary.

Bateson (1972), applying Russell's theory of logical types to the concept of learning, differentiated between five types of learning:

- *Zero learning*   Specificity of response not subject to correction
- *Learning I*   Change in specificity of response by correction of errors of choice within a set of alternatives
- *Learning II*   A corrective change in the set of alternatives from which choice is made or a change in the punctuation of experience
- *Learning III*   A corrective change in the system of sets of alternatives from which choice is made
- *Learning IV*   Change in the process of learning III, but probably does not occur in any living organism on earth.

Argyris (1977) concentrates on the distinction between single-loop and double-loop learning, which are analogous to Bateson's learning I and II. Single-loop learning occurs when there is a match between the organization's design for action and the actual outcome, or when such mismatches are corrected by changing actions, but *without critical examination of the governing variables for action*. Figure 3.1 illustrates the process of single-loop learning.

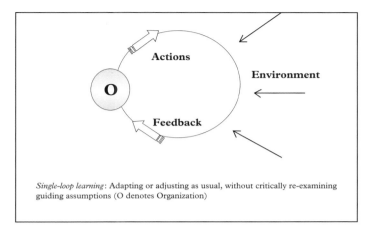

Figure 3.1 Single-loop learning
Note: The figures for single-loop and double-loop learning are adapted from Heracleous (2000).

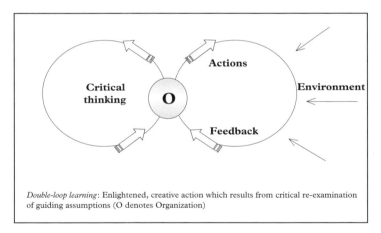

Figure 3.2 Double-loop learning
Note: The figures for single-loop and double-loop learning are adapted from Heracleous (2000).

Double-loop learning, on the other hand, occurs when the correction of mismatches is arrived at by *examining and altering the governing variables for action and then the actions themselves*. Figure 3.2 illustrates the process of double-loop learning.

Fiol and Lyles (1985) similarly differentiate between "lower-level" and "higher-level" learning. Lower-level learning involves the

Table 3.1 *Levels of learning and key authors*

Authors	Levels of learning	
Bateson (1972)	Learning I	Learning II
Argyris (1977)	Single-loop	Double-loop
Fiol and Lyles (1985)	Lower-level	Higher-level
Senge (1990)	Adaptive	Generative

development of cognitive associations which facilitate incremental organizational adaptation but without the questioning of central norms and frames of reference of the organization. Higher-level learning occurs when these norms and frames of reference are challenged and altered, and a more accurate understanding of causal relations exists. These levels of learning are also mirrored in Senge's (1990) distinction between "generative" and "adaptive" learning. Adaptive learning is about coping within existing frames of reference, whereas generative learning is about being creative, and requires new ways of perceiving the world. Table 3.1 portrays the terms used to describe these levels of learning and the key authors who have discussed them.

While there are differences in terminology in all these authors, the central concept common to them all involves on the one hand thinking and acting within a certain set of assumptions and potential action alternatives or on the other hand challenging existing assumptions and action alternatives, potentially leading to new and more appropriate ones.

An example would be an organization faced with deteriorating performance, and which responds by becoming preoccupied with typical actions such as cost-cutting, de-layering or re-engineering which it has also taken in the past (utilizing single-loop learning). This organization responds to hardship in ways that have worked in the past. It takes action from a fixed set of action alternatives and does not consider other, new and potentially more appropriate and creative action alternatives.

The ideal result of a critical reconsideration of governing variables for action (double-loop learning), and existing business systems, however, would be the generation and implementation of a "market-driving" strategy. Market-driving strategies are based on visionary thinking, offer a leap in customer value, are delivered through a unique business system, and re-draw industry boundaries and segmentation structures (Kumar *et al.* 2000). Such ground-breaking strategies are enabled by double-loop learning, since an organization's set of potential action alternatives and mental models expand to include new responses and new ways of thinking about the problems faced, leading to radically different strategic actions from what was done in the past.

Strategic thinking as double-loop learning

Strategic planning in this formulation is seen as an activity carried out within the parameters of what is to be achieved, but does not explicitly question those parameters, and is therefore analogous to single-loop learning. Strategic planning most often takes an already determined strategic direction and helps strategists decide how the organization is to be configured and resources allocated to realize that direction. This situation has given rise to a relatively common thread of the critiques of strategic planning, that it deals with extrapolations of the present and the past that will in all probability turn out to be inaccurate, and that it is overly preoccupied with "fit" between current environmental conditions and organizational arrangements, as opposed to focusing on how to reinvent the future. This urge to influence rather than passively to accept the future has been emphasized in approaches to strategy such as "strategic intent" or "strategy as revolution" (Hamel 1996; Hamel and Prahalad 1989).

The mode of strategy-making which can be associated with such reinventing of the future, and the creation of new competitive space as opposed to struggling over slow growth or even shrinking markets, is identified with strategic thinking. Strategic thinking questions the strategic parameters themselves, and is thus analogous to double-loop learning. Discovering and committing to novel strategies which can re-write the rules of the competitive arena necessitate relaxing or suspending at least part of the conventional wisdom and assumptions about the industry, the industry recipes (Spender 1989), as well as the psychological frames (Bateson 1972) in which these recipes are represented, envisioning a number of potential futures and challenging the existing operating assumptions on which current strategies are built. The desired outcome of the cycle of strategic thinking/planning is not "me-too" strategies but distinct positionings, supported by unique activity systems (Porter 1996). For example, consider the following examples[1]:

- In the early 1900s, cars were built individually and painstakingly by craftsmen, and owning one was a potent status symbol. Going against the prevailing wisdom of the industry, Henry Ford proclaimed "I will build a car for the great multitude...I am going to democratize the automobile...When I'm through, everybody will be able to afford one, and about everybody will have one." This was indeed achieved by continuous productivity improvements in manufacturing, the breakthrough coming with Ford's idea to initiate a moving assembly line. Ford had the idea on a trip to Chicago, where he observed the way the meat packers used the overhead trolley to dress beef, cutting a piece off the carcass as it moved along. Ford reversed this process, having a moving vehicle assembly line where workers added pieces as the vehicle moved along.
- Raymond Kroc, a fifty-two-year-old milk-shake machine salesman in 1954 saw the restaurant of Maurice and Richard McDonald in San Bernardino, operating like a fine-tuned machine in an industry in which such precision and efficiency was unknown. He realized this model would be very successful if implemented elsewhere, but the two brothers were not interested in growing the business. He cut a franchise deal with them, and started expanding what would become the unwitting application of Henry Ford's manufacturing approach to sandwich-making, and a hugely successful business which created new competitive space in the restaurant industry.

While Henry Ford was part of the US vehicle industry, and Ray Kroc at the margins of the US restaurant industry, neither of them accepted conventional industrial wisdom as given, envisioning alternative, plausible futures which would ultimately redefine their industries. More importantly, none of them could have come up with their radical (for the time) conceptions of the future of their industry as a result of formalized planning techniques. Even today, companies which currently add higher value and deliver superior returns to shareholders are those which consistently break the rules of the competitive game (Hamel 1997).

---

[1] These examples are drawn from Gross (1996). For more examples of firms that have re-invented their industry through market-driving strategies, see Kumar *et al.* (2000).

Reconciling the perspectives: a dialectical view of strategic thinking and strategic planning

The two main positions on the proper meaning and interrelationship between the ideas of strategic thinking and strategic planning are those of Henry Mintzberg and Michael Porter. Mintzberg believes that strategic thinking and planning involve distinct thought processes, the former being creative and the latter analytical; whereas Porter believes that strategic thinking is achieved by utilizing analytical tools. The underlying issue with regard to these two views seems to be a focus on different aspects of strategy. Mintzberg, for example, sees strategies as patterns in a stream of decisions and actions, which may be deliberate at times, emergent at other times, or mixed, and mostly based on managerial intuition and creativity (Mintzberg 1978). Porter, on the other hand, being highly analytical, sees strategies as particular configurations of the value chain which are ideally unique and sustainable, providing strategic positions which cannot be easily imitated by competitors (Porter 1996).

Porter (1991b) drew attention to the need to understand both the cross-sectional problem in strategy (the causes of superior performance at a given point in time), and the longitudinal problem (the dynamic process by which strategies are arrived at). Porter's contributions have tended to focus on the cross-sectional rather than the longitudinal problem, however, and Mintzberg's contributions have tended to focus on the longitudinal rather than the cross-sectional problem. Whereas Mintzberg's view of strategy is more process-focused (how strategies are arrived at over time in organizations), Porter's view of strategy is more positioning-focused (what constitutes a sustainable strategic position in terms of particular organizational arrangements). These differential foci lead their proponents to suggest corresponding thinking modes for the aspect of strategy they focus on; Mintzberg emphasizing the creative and synthetic, and Porter emphasizing the convergent and analytical.

Being overly preoccupied with terminology (what each author means by "strategic thinking" or "strategic planning") can make one miss the essential point that to the extent that they constitute distinct thinking modes, strategic thinking and strategic planning are both necessary, and neither is adequate without the other. Creative, ground-breaking strategies emerging from strategic thinking still have to be operationalized through convergent and analytical thought (strategic planning), and planning is vital but cannot produce unique strategies which can challenge industrial boundaries and redefine industries (unless it stimulates the creative mindset in the process, as in the case of using alternative scenarios for the future).

The view proposed here holds that strategic thinking and strategic planning are interrelated in a *dialectical process*, where both are necessary for effective strategic management, and each mode on its own is necessary but not sufficient. This view:

- Suggests a clarification in the meaning of the terms by drawing an analogy with levels of learning; identifying strategic planning with single-loop learning and strategic thinking with double-loop learning
- Complements Mintzberg's view about the usefulness of both strategic thinking and planning, and helps to place the Mintzberg/Porter debate in context by recognizing that focusing on different aspects of strategy (the longitudinal vs the cross-sectional problem) leads these authors to advocate corresponding thinking modes, which in the final analysis are both necessary and complementary.

Mintzberg's view about the differences between strategic thinking and planning and the inability of planning to produce ground-breaking strategies does not necessarily clash with Porter's view that analytical tools are necessary, and that they can also stimulate creativity. The tools one uses at each stage of the strategic management process are not important in themselves but as the means of encouraging the creative and analytical mindset. There ideally needs to be a dialectical thought process of being able to diverge and then converge, being creative and then seeing the real-world implications, and being synthetic but also analytical. It all comes down to the ability to go up and down the ladder of abstraction, and being able to see both the big picture and the operational implications, which are signs of outstanding leaders and strategists. Figure 3.3 portrays this process.

This process will ideally lead to a virtuous circle (Hampden-Turner 1990) of creative thinking and operationalization, without one dominating the other but working in a complementary manner to discover creative strategies, operationalize them, and maintain a critical attitude to avoid "strategic drift" (Johnson 1987), the process where a company's strategy progressively moves away from market realities

Figure 3.3 Strategic thinking and strategic planning as dialectical processes

because of various types of inertia. "Virtuous circles" refer to cycles of self-reinforcing processes with positive outcomes for organizations. For example, the CEO of Akamai explained his company's business model as follows: "[T]hat's the virtuous circle: Better technology attracts more content. More content attracts more networks. More networks means better technology. And around we go" (Carr 2000: 121).

An effective process of strategic thinking and planning is critical, since it was shown that a firm's strategies have a much higher effect on its performance than its industry context or corporate parentage factors (McGahan and Porter 1997; Rumelt 1991); and that strategic planning is associated with higher performance (Miller and Cardinal 1994). It is also necessary for this process to be continually in operation, given that the bases of competitive advantage can shift quickly in fast-moving industries. As Akamai's CEO observed, "[O]ur long term is 90 days. That's it. That's the longest forecast we ever make" (Carr 2000: 122).

After the creative insights of the inventors of the technology on which Akamai is based that enables the delivery of internet content in a faster and more reliable manner to competing technologies, and "push[es] content to the edge of the internet" (2000: 123), a critical attitude is maintained in the midst of meticulous operational planning. This critical attitude is manifested in constant communication and intellectual "ruthlessness":

"The uncertainty is always there, and it always will be. We understand that – in fact, it's built into the way we manage the business. Every Monday the entire management team gathers together, and we argue about the key challenges we face . . . We're intellectually ruthless, and we all cherish that ruthlessness. It's the cornerstone of our culture, really . . . We never let it get personal. It's always constructive – aimed at ripping a question apart so we can be as sure as possible that we come to the best decision . . . I can tell you one thing: everyone here is committed to open communication. The give-and-take is incredibly valuable in ensuring that we do smart things and do them fast. Plus, it's a lot of fun." (2000: 122–123)

At the operational level, successful innovation, arguably the most sustainable element of competitive advantage, can be seen in terms of such virtuous circles. Sparks of genius (creative thinking) require hard work to be accepted, realized, and operationalized (planning). Creating a cultural climate where innovation can flourish is only one side of the coin. Making creative insights tangible through translating them to viable product concepts, developing effective project management processes, and successfully commercializing the new products and services is the other. While the adhesive technology for 3M's "post-it" notes was available in the company from 1968, it took until 1980 for post-it notes to be commercialized, after a new product development manager, Art Fry, took on the idea, designed post-it notes, and convinced all the skeptics and critics within 3M that they could in fact be a viable product in the marketplace. In 1981, one year after their introduction, post-it notes were declared 3M's "Outstanding New Product," and in 1986, Art Fry was named 3M "Corporate Scientist."

The dialectical view of strategic thinking and planning proposed here is not meant to be a description of actual managerial practice, but it is meant to be a suggestion for a normative, but achievable, best practice. Here strategic thinking and planning occur iteratively over time, where there is a continual quest for novel and creative strategies which can be born in the minds of strategists or can emerge from the grass roots; as well as employment of analytical processes to determine such issues as the strategies' desirability and feasibility, and to plan for their realization.

Bibliography

Albrecht, K., 1994. The power of bifocal vision, *Management Review*, April: 42–46

Altier, W. J., 1991. Strategic thinking for today's corporate battles, *Management Review*, November: 20–22

Argyris, C., 1977. Double loop learning in organizations, *Harvard Business Review*, September–October: 15–125

Bateson, G., 1972. *Steps to an Ecology of Mind*, London: Intertext: 293

Bonn, I. and Christodoulou, C., 1996. From strategic planning to strategic management, *Long Range Planning*, 29: 543–551

Carr, N. G., 2000. On the edge: an interview with Akamai's George Conrades, *Harvard Business Review*, May–June: 118–125

De Geus, A., 1988. Planning as learning, *Harvard Business Review*, March–April: 70–74

Eden, C., 1990. Strategic thinking with computers, *Long Range Planning*, 23: 35–43

Fiol, C. M. and Lyles, M. A., 1985. Organizational learning, *Academy of Management Review*, 10: 803–813

Gray, D.H., 1986. Uses and misuses of strategic planning, *Harvard Business Review*, January–February: 89–97

Gross, D., 1996. *Forbes' Greatest Business Stories of All Time*, New York: Wiley

Hamel, G., 1996. Strategy as revolution, *Harvard Business Review*, July–August: 69–82

  1997. Killer strategies that make shareholders rich, *Fortune*, 12, June 23: 30–44

Hamel, G. and Prahalad, C. K., 1989. Strategic intent, *Harvard Business Review*, May–June: 63–76

Hampden-Turner, C., 1990. *Corporate Culture: From Vicious to Virtuous Circles*, London: Economist Books

Harari, O., 1995. Good/bad news about strategy, *Management Review*, July: 29–31

Heracleous, L., 1998. Strategic thinking or strategic planning, *Long Range Planning*, 31: 481–487

  2000. The role of strategy implementation in organization development, *Organization Development Journal*, 18(3): 75–86

Johnson, G., 1987. *Strategic Change and the Management Process*, Oxford: Blackwell

Kinni, T. B., 1994. Find the corporate heartbeat, *Industry Week*, August 15: 43–47

Kumar, N., Scheer, L. and Kotler, P., 2000. From market driven to market driving, *European Management Journal*, 18: 129–142

McGahan, A. M. and Porter, M., 1997. How much does industry matter, really?, *Strategic Management Journal*, 18, Summer Special Issue: 15–30

Miller, C. C. and Cardinal, L. B., 1994. Strategic planning and firm performance: a synthesis of more than two decades of research, *Academy of Management Journal*, 37: 1649–1665

Mintzberg, H., 1978. Patterns in strategy formation, *Management Science*, 24: 934–948

    1981. What is planning anyway?, *Strategic Management Journal*, 2: 319–324

    1994. The fall and rise of strategic planning, *Harvard Business Review*, January–February: 107–114

Morissey, G. L., 1990. Executive guide to strategic thinking, *Executive Excellence*, June: 5–6

Nadler, D. A., 1994. Collaborative strategic thinking, *Planning Review*, September–October: 30–31

Porter, M., 1991a. Know your place, *Inc.*, September: 90–93

    1991b. Towards a dynamic theory of strategy, *Strategic Management Journal*, 12: 95–117

    1996. What is strategy?, *Harvard Business Review*, November–December: 61–78

Rumelt, R. P., 1991. How much does industry matter?, *Strategic Management Journal*, 12: 167–185

Senge, P. M., 1990. The leader's new work: building learning organizations, *Sloan Management Review*, Fall: 7–23

Spender, J. C., 1989. *Industry Recipes*, Oxford: Blackwell

Wack, P., 1985a. Scenarios: uncharted waters ahead, *Harvard Business Review*, September–October: 73–89

    1985b. Scenarios: shooting the rapids, *Harvard Business Review*, November–December: 2–14

Wilson, I., 1994. Strategic planning isn't dead – it changed, *Long Range Planning*, 27: 12–24

Zabriskie, N. B. and Huellmantel, A. B., 1991. Developing strategic thinking in senior management, *Long Range Planning*, 24: 25–32

4 | Leadership research and the board of directors

There is a plethora of research on leadership and on boards of directors from a variety of theoretical perspectives. Unfortunately, research within each of these domains has proceeded independently of each other, which has prevented potentially fruitful cross-fertilization between them. This chapter explores the relevance and applicability of leadership research in enhancing our understanding of boards of directors' functioning and effectiveness. Secondly, it discusses methodological issues with respect to board research and indicates potentially fruitful further approaches.

It is suggested that the leadership research stream focused on traits and competencies is particularly promising for future research on boards, since it has been demonstrated that there are traits that can distinguish leaders from non-leaders or effective leaders from ineffective ones, as well as being relevant competencies to distinguish superior performers from average performers in particular jobs. Consistent with the organizational action view of strategic management, this chapter aims to gain a deeper understanding of the dominant coalition, and shares the methodological perspective of this view. It is proposed that a promising way forward in terms of methodology is to focus on gathering in-depth qualitative longitudinal data of actual board behaviors and processes, based on observation. This in-depth data inform quantitative research so as to enhance the operationalization of theoretical variables, and to help identify the key variables in the first place.

The board as leaders: duties and tasks of the board

In the last few years pressure for reform of boards of directors has been growing. Institutional investors, global organizations such as the OECD and World Bank, governments, and the media have all been calling for improvements in corporate governance. Investors in particular

This chapter is based on Heracleous (1999).

are willing to pay substantial premiums for the shares of what they perceive as well-governed companies (Coombes and Watson 2000) and are becoming more active and vocal with regard to governance issues (Monks 1999; Useem *et al.* 1993). Media reports on reform of corporate governance abound (Boyle 2001; *Economist* 2002).

The normative view on the functions of boards of directors includes monitoring and disciplining top management as well as being actively involved in strategy formation (Finkelstein and Hambrick 1996). Directors do take their strategic responsibilities seriously. They believe that their tasks should involve such issues as setting and influencing the mission, vision, and values of the company, directing the company's strategy and structure, delegating and monitoring the implementation of strategy to management, and fulfilling their responsibilities to shareholders and other parties (Dulewicz *et al.* 1995).

Descriptive studies have long shown, however, that what boards actually do does not fully correspond to this normative view; boards are often not actively involved in strategy formation but at best in its ratification, and usually try to avoid "rocking the boat" (e.g. Patton and Baker 1987; Whistler 1984). Board functioning has been found wanting, particularly in the areas of director and board evaluation which is rarely if ever carried out, and director selection, where there are no systematic processes for identifying and selecting suitable candidates but instead reliance on the personal networks of the chairman, CEO, or other directors (O'Neal and Thomas 1996). CEO pay has risen to exorbitant levels and, most worryingly, often bears no relation to the CEOs' performance (Monks 2001). Several tools and frameworks have been proposed to help close this gap between expectations and actual board performance (e.g. Donaldson 1995; Firstenberg and Malkiel 1994; Garratt 1996; Salmon 1993).

Leadership perspectives and the board of directors

When we plunge into the organizational literature on leadership, we quickly become lost in a labyrinth: there are endless definitions, countless articles and never-ending polemics. As far as leadership studies go, it seems that more and more has been studied about less and less, to end up ironically with a group of researchers studying everything about nothing. (Kets de Vries 1994: 73)

This statement conveys many authors' views about the current state of leadership studies. A diversity of understandings of leadership exists both among academics as well as practitioners (Barker 1997; Rost

1991). Leadership definitions can focus on behavior, on the ability to motivate employees to put in extra effort, on the ability to act as a change agent, on processes of social influence, on creating compelling visions, or on producing favorable performance outcomes. In spite of this diversity, however, there are common elements among definitions, which often involve the concepts of influence, group, and goal. The leader is seen as *influencing others* to act in a certain way; this influence takes place within a *group context*, and the influence is exerted to achieve group *goals* (Bryman 1996). Definitions of leadership can be classified in terms of different categories or perspectives (Bass 1990). Figure 4.1 relates these perspectives to the board of directors.

- *Leadership as personality and its effects*: applied to the board, there are particular competencies and personality traits that effective directors should develop
- *Leadership as the art of inducing compliance*: for example, where the board is using its power to fire the CEO and in general discipline senior management
- *Leadership as the exercise of influence*: board deliberations from a group dynamics perspective are characterized by processes of social influence
- *Leadership as an act of behavior*: for example, the observable behaviors in the group dynamics within the board
- *Leadership as a form of persuasion*: for example persuasive argument within board deliberations
- *Leadership as a power relation*: for example, between the board and senior management or among board roles such as the board Chair, the CEO, Executives and non-Executive directors
- *Leadership as an instrument of goal achievement*: where the board is expected to fulfill certain tasks
- *Leadership as an emerging effect of interaction* between the leader and the group: for example, how the board interacts with top management or how the board Chair interacts with board members
- *Leadership as a differentiated role*: for example, the role expectations placed on the board by virtue of its position at the apex of the organization
- *Leadership as the initiation of structure*: for example, how important decisions by the board can influence the organization structure and actor relations
- *Leadership as the focus of group processes*: for example, how the group dynamics of the board are influenced by the board chair as a leader of the board

---

Figure 4.1 Applying leadership perspectives to the board of directors

If we consider the perspectives on leadership in figure 4.1, we can see that they can all illuminate various aspects of the board such as its functioning, group dynamics, or power relations. Such conceptual links between views of leadership and the board should come as no surprise, given the fundamental role of the board in the organization. In the next section we consider the four main streams of leadership research in order to explore their applicability to the board of directors.

Research streams on leadership

Classifications of the streams of leadership research have been based on several schemes such as the types of variables emphasized in the study, the level of analysis focused on, or the dominant approaches in different chronological periods (Yukl 1998). A useful review of leadership studies by Bryman (1996) describes four stages in theory and research: the *trait approach*, which dominated the area up to the late 1940s; the *leadership style approach* which was the main approach until the late 1960s; the *contingency approach*, coming to prominence from the late 1960s to the early 1980s; and lastly the *"new leadership"* approach, the dominant approach since the early 1980s. The beginning of a new stage does not signal the demise of a previous one, but rather a shift of emphasis.

The trait approach

The trait approach has sought to determine the qualities that can distinguish leaders from non-leaders. Personality traits are stable dispositions to behave in a particular way, and they are determined by inherited factors, as well as by learning (Bouchard *et al.* 1990). The traits examined in early studies can be classified into three main groups: physical traits, abilities, and personality characteristics. Hundreds of studies of traits, however, failed to find any traits that could guarantee leadership success, partly because of design flaws in the research. Such studies searched for correlations between traits and criteria of leadership success, but failed to consider any intervening processes that could account for how the interaction could take place. The correlations were also generally weak and inconsistent.

Early influential reviews of trait research (Gibb 1947; Stogdill 1948) questioned the accumulated usefulness of the findings of the trait approach and led to a considerable dampening of interest. Although fewer

studies were subsequently carried out, they were more robustly designed in terms of methodology. A positive, significant relationship in
these studies meant that: a given trait was significantly correlated with
a certain measure of leadership effectiveness; a sample of leaders was
found to differ significantly from a sample of followers with regard
to a trait; a sample of effective leaders differed from a sample of ineffective leaders on the trait; or a sample of high-status leaders differed
significantly from a sample of low-status leaders on the trait (Bass
1990).

Do traits matter?

A review (Stogdill 1974) of 163 trait studies by the same scholar who
carried out the 1948 review was more positive. This review concluded
that there are indeed traits that can distinguish leaders from non-
leaders: "The leader is characterized by a strong drive for responsibility
and task completion, vigor and persistence in pursuit of goals, venture-
someness and originality in problem solving, drive to exercise initiative in social situations, self-confidence and sense of personal identity,
willingness to accept consequences of decision and action, readiness to
absorb interpersonal stress, willingness to accept frustration and delay,
ability to influence other persons' behavior, and capacity to structure
social interaction systems to the purpose at hand" (Stogdill 1974: 81).
This assessment still held strong in the 1990 edition of the handbook
of leadership (Bass 1990).

Recently there has been new-found interest in the trait approach. A
useful practitioner-oriented review of trait research (Kirkpatrick and
Locke 1991) states that "recent research, using a variety of methods,
has made it clear that successful leaders are not like other people. The
evidence indicates that there are certain core traits which significantly
contribute to business leaders' success. Traits *alone*, however, are not
sufficient for successful business leadership – they are only a precondi-
tion. Leaders who possess the requisite traits must take certain *actions*
to be successful (e.g. formulating a vision, role modeling, setting goals).
Possessing the appropriate traits only makes it more likely that such
actions will be taken and be successful" (Kirkpatrick and Locke 1991:
49, emphasis in the original). Traits that were found to differentiate
leaders from non-leaders include drive, leadership motivation, honesty
and integrity, self-confidence, cognitive ability, and knowledge of the
business.

Within the general domain of the trait approach also fall McClelland's (1965, 1985) research on managerial motivation using Thematic Apperception Tests, Miner's research on managerial motivation using questionnaires (Berman and Miner 1985; Miner 1978, 1986), and Boyatzis' (1982) critical incident research on competencies. Boyatzis' (1982) research, for example, utilized the "behavioral event interview" to discover which competencies differentiated effective from ineffective managers. Incidents from these interviews were coded into competency categories based on the manager's behavior, intentions, and the situation. Effective managers were found to have a strong efficiency orientation, a strong socialized power orientation, high self-confidence, a strong belief in self-efficacy, an internal locus of control, a capacity for good interpersonal skills, and had strong conceptual skills. Methodologies for building competency models for multiple jobs have been described (e.g. Mansfield 1996), and "high performance managerial competencies" have been identified (Cockerill *et al.* 1995).

The evidence therefore shows convincingly that traits do matter. They can distinguish leaders from non-leaders, or effective from ineffective leaders, and the existence of these traits makes it more likely that appropriate actions will be taken by the leader. The related competency approach was also shown to be a useful way to identify behaviors that could distinguish high performers from average performers in a variety of roles.

The leadership style approach

After the late 1940s, the emphasis in leadership research shifted to the leadership styles, or behaviors of leaders. Exemplifying this stream of research were the Ohio State University leadership studies, which consisted of administering behavior description questionnaires to leaders' subordinates to determine leadership styles based on the two dimensions of "consideration" and "initiating structure." "Consideration" denotes the degree to which a leader acts in a friendly and supportive manner, and shows concern for subordinates and their welfare. "Initiating structure" denotes the degree to which a leader defines and structures his or her own role and the roles of subordinates toward attainment of the group's formal goals. Leaders' measures on these two dimensions were then related to outcomes such as morale, job satisfaction, and performance of subordinates.

At around the same time, studies at the University of Michigan identified three types of leadership behaviors that could potentially differentiate between effective and ineffective leaders: *task-oriented behavior*, such as planning and scheduling the work, co-ordinating subordinate activities, or setting high but realistic performance goals; *relations-oriented behavior*, such as being considerate, supportive and helpful to subordinates; and lastly, *participative leadership*, such as using group meetings where the leader guides the discussion in a constructive manner and orients it towards problem-solving.

Does leadership style matter?

The results of the Ohio tradition have been weak and inconsistent for most criteria of leadership effectiveness (Bass 1990; Yukl 1998). In some cases, for example, subordinates were more satisfied and performed better with a *structuring* leader, while in other cases the opposite relationship was found or no significant relationship was found at all. The studies were also inconsistent with regard to correlations between *consideration* and performance criteria. One generally consistent finding, however, was the positive relationship between *consideration* and subordinate satisfaction (but, crucially, not performance).

There were certain methodological problems with the Ohio tradition. Early studies did not consider any situational variables, which would have been useful, since particular leadership styles would be more appropriate in specific situations. Moreover, in general it was not possible to determine the direction of causality between the correlated variables; informal leadership processes were not studied; the aggregation of subordinate responses led to the neglect of intra-group differences; and lastly, there were significant measurement problems, in that responses were influenced by the "implicit leadership theories" that respondents held (their ratings of imaginary leaders were very similar to the ratings for real leaders) (Yukl 1998).

Later researchers developed the idea of the "high-high" leader, who has a concern for both people and production (Blake and Mouton 1964), and proposed that effective leaders have a high concern for both. Again, the results of questionnaire research on these models have been inconclusive; where correlations have been found, they have been weak. One reason that questionnaire research failed to validate leadership style models could be that it generally did not pay attention to the situation in which the styles were used, since different leadership styles could be more appropriate in different situations. On the other hand, however, descriptive research from critical incidents supports the intuitive position that effective leaders must have a concern for both the task and the people.

Thus, while we know that leadership style does matter, as shown by qualitative studies, the quantitative results are inconclusive because of certain methodological and conceptual flaws. In this regard, given the available evidence, leadership style cannot be used to predict effective leadership performance. Contingency theories developed subsequently, attempted to address these conceptual and methodological concerns.

The contingency approach

Contingency approaches seek to discover situational variables which moderate the effectiveness of leadership styles, and in this sense they question universalistic theories of leadership (e.g. that a certain leadership style would be effective in all situations). Contextual characteristics studied include the nature of work performed, the nature of the external environment, and follower characteristics. A related line of research treats managerial behavior as a dependent variable, and explores how this behavior is influenced by aspects of the situation. There are several contingency theories of leadership, such as the path–goal theory, situational leadership theory, leadership substitutes theory, multiple linkage model, LPC contingency theory, cognitive resources theory, and normative decision theory.

Most research on contingency theories led to inconsistent results and problems in measuring key variables. This led to some disillusionment with contingency theories by the early 1980s. Even though leadership and situational context cannot be separated (Fiedler 1993), there is considerable disagreement about what aspects of the situation matter most. The methodological limitations of modeling and quantifying complex situations have meant that contingency theorists have focused on limited aspects of the situation, and of leaders' behavior, with consequent results of limited applicability.

Does the situation matter?

Yukl (1998) notes that the results of research designed to test contingency theories were generally inconclusive for most theories, although weak support was obtained for some. He concluded that "unfortunately, most of the contingency theories are stated so ambiguously that it is difficult to derive specific, testable propositions. Most of the research provides only a partial test of theories. In general, the research suffers from lack of accurate measures and reliance on weak research designs that do not permit strong inferences about direction of causality" (Yukl 1998: 288). For example, reviews of research for path–goal theory (Podsakoff *et al.* 1995; Wofford and Liska 1993) indicated that the results were inconclusive. Similarly, reviews of research for situational leadership theory (Blank *et al.* 1990; Fernandez and Vechio 1997) found little support for it. Some aspects of leadership substitutes theory were supported and some not (Podsakoff *et al.* 1995). The multiple linkage model is still relatively new and little evidence exists to evaluate its validity. The LPC contingency model tends to be supported by empirical research (Peters *et al.* 1985; Strube and Garcia 1981) but not strongly. Cognitive resources theory also receives some support (Fiedler 1992; Vecchio 1990). Normative decision theory tends to receive moderately strong support but deals only with limited aspects of leadership and also suffers from certain conceptual deficiencies (Yukl 1998).

Thus, the situation undoubtedly matters; but the theories developed to account for the interaction between leaders and situation have in general failed to receive strong empirical support, owing to methodological limitations in the research and/or conceptual deficiencies in the theories. Moreover, such theories offer limited guidance for managers beyond common-sense propositions.

The transformational and charismatic leadership approach

New understandings of leadership emerged in the 1980s, such as transformational leadership (Bass 1995; Bass and Avolio 1993; Kuhnert and Lewis 1987) or charismatic leadership (Avolio and Yammarino 1990; Bryman 1993; Klein and House 1995), which are currently receiving considerable attention from leadership theorists. In these approaches leaders are seen as managers of meaning, who define organizational reality by articulating compelling visions, missions, and values. In terms of methodology qualitative case studies are widely used, usually to study very senior leaders.

Charismatic leaders, for example, are described as being change-oriented, and possessing a compelling vision which they can communicate persuasively to others and mobilize their commitment to realize the vision (Conger and Kanungo 1987). Behaviors associated with transformational leadership include giving a high degree of attention and support to individual followers and offering followers intellectual stimulation and engendering a high degree of respect from them (Bycio *et al.* 1995). Research has shown that leaders can be taught how to exhibit more transformational behaviors (Barling *et al.* 1996).

Bass and Avolio (1993) noted that transformational and transactional leadership go beyond the traditional dimensions of initiation of structure and consideration; transformational leaders can be directive or participative, democratic or authoritarian, elitist or leveling. Moreover, transformational leadership does not necessarily equal effective leadership, nor does transactional leadership necessarily equal ineffective leadership. The most effective leaders are both transformational and transactional while the worst leaders are neither, avoiding any display of leadership.

Do charismatic and transformational leadership matter?

Several studies have shown that charismatic and transformational leadership can have significant effects on subordinates' performance and consequently organizational performance. It was found, for example, that subordinates' perceptions of the existence of transformational leadership added to the levels of prediction of their satisfaction and effectiveness ratings. Moreover, the ratings for transformational leadership obtained from subordinates significantly differentiated top-performing managers from ordinary managers (Hater and Bass 1988).

Leaders' actions such as developing and sharing a vision for the organization, modeling the vision, encouraging innovativeness, supporting employee efforts, and allowing employee input into decisions concerning their jobs, were strongly related to outcomes such as higher employee commitment and job satisfaction, and lower role ambiguity (Niehoff *et al.* 1990). Leaders' vision was strongly correlated to participants' attitudes; it led to higher congruence between leaders' and participants' beliefs and values, increased participants' trust in the leader, raised the extent to which participants were intellectually stimulated and inspired by the leader, and increased the extent to which the participants saw the leader as charismatic (Kirkpatrick and Locke 1996). Transformational leadership of school principals led to higher organizational commitment, citizenship behavior, and satisfaction of teachers (Koh *et al.* 1995), while high-performing sales managers exhibited more transformational and transactional leadership than low-performing sales managers; their subordinates also exhibited less role stress, and greater satisfaction and loyalty (Russ *et al.* 1996).

Discussion and implications

Streams of leadership research and the board of directors

The above discussion has shown that leaders' traits and competencies do matter, as they can distinguish effective leaders from ineffective ones. Leadership style and the situation do matter, but the research has been plagued by methodological and conceptual problems so that the results have been inconclusive for most dimensions of the theories tested. Lastly, research shows that charismatic and transformational leadership can have a significant positive impact on organizations.

If we consider the streams of leadership research, the stream on traits appears particularly promising. Since there are traits that can accurately distinguish leaders from non-leaders or effective from ineffective leaders, and competencies which can distinguish effective from ineffective performers in a variety of roles, then further research can aim towards identifying traits and competencies characterizing effective directors. Dulewicz *et al.*'s (1995) research has identified several competencies required by directors, based on directors' views on what they should be doing. An important way forward would be to develop criteria for effective directors, based on complementary data such as actual behaviors within the board. The next step would be to focus on discovering the competencies that can distinguish effective from ineffective directors and constructing developmental programs to instill these competencies.

The research streams of leadership style, situation, and transformational and charismatic leadership are more relevant to the executive directors as leaders who interact with other members of the organization, but may be less applicable to the board as a working group. If there is a need for transformational leadership in the organization, then this is relevant to the executive directors including the CEO as executives of the organization, but perhaps not as members of the board. If there is a need to transform radically the way the board operates, then the transformational leadership perspective can be relevant to the board Chair during the period of achieving the transformation; and the leadership style approach is of relevance to the Chair role, in terms of board leadership. The basic issue with directors as members of a working group, however, is that they have to develop an effective and productive style of interaction (Schein 1988) that is sustainable over the longer term, and relevant competencies, no matter what the contingencies faced by the organization.

Methodological issues on board research

Research on both the domains of leadership and boards of directors has mostly been carried out within the positivist tradition. With regard to board research, for example, board attributes and their interrelations with certain outcomes have been emphasized at the expense of the longitudinal study of processes and group dynamics, which have not received adequate attention. Within the positivist tradition, several potential relationships have not been tested, and mixed results have been obtained with many of the relationships tested, so that there is no solid conclusion on important issues relevant to leadership and to boards. The assumptions underlying research on boards have often been debatable, for example imputing board vigilance by such indicators as outside director representation, CEO non-duality, or level of director compensation. Often there is also theoretical ambiguity, with contrary hypotheses being suggested for testing a theory, for example on the relationship between environmental uncertainty and board involvement in strategic decision-making. Interaction among several potentially influencing factors and multiple directions of causality have not been taken into account in most of the existing research on directors.

Developing criteria of board and director effectiveness based on actual behaviors and group dynamics within the board goes to the heart of addressing a broader shortcoming in existing research. If quantitative designs are not adequately informed by rich, in-depth data, they can potentially ignore vital aspects of the organizational setting, make untenable assumptions about how an attribute should be measured, and end up with mixed and inconsistent results. For example, measuring board vigilance by the structural indicators mentioned above does not get at the real issues of how directors behave, what their thinking is on certain issues, and how they interact with each other. Useful measures of such issues as board vigilance can be developed using qualitative data based on observation of group dynamics. Schein's (1988) work, for example, includes diagnostic instruments for rating group effectiveness and group maturity, which can be utilized and adapted to develop measures for board vigilance. In addition to group processes, the content of group argumentation would also relate to board vigilance, as well as the inputs to meetings (e.g. level of preparation). The concept of board vigilance could fruitfully be viewed from a systems perspective (inputs $\implies$ process and content $\implies$ output). Process would be the critical focus, since group effectiveness largely depends on a productive style of interaction.

In-depth, primary data derived from ethnographic observation of actual board meetings are required for developing such knowledge, which is a touchy issue with boards, given considerations of confidentiality. This is critical, however, in developing further our understanding of what would make for an effective board. Even if standards for good practice at board level sound sensible, we cannot fully rely on them to create effective boards. Research has questioned, for example, whether it really matters whether the CEO and Chair positions are held by the same person or not, or whether there are more non-executive directors on the board (Daily and Dalton, 1997; Heracleous 2001). If such measures which have received substantial public support are shown to *not* make a difference, then board energies could potentially be misdirected in trying to conform to them.

Primary longitudinal data are necessary in clarifying how an effective board should be structured, or how to improve board inputs and interaction processes. Based on such knowledge, trait and competency profiles for effective directors can then be constructed, and development programs created to instill such competencies and stimulate the development of relevant personality traits. In the context of viewing quantitative and qualitative research designs not as mutually exclusive but as synergistic and complementary (e.g. Hari Das 1983; Jick 1979), quantitative research designs could be enhanced through the use of such in-depth qualitative data, with respect to improving the validity of their assumptions, the operationalization of concepts, and the choice of critical variables to be tested.

Bibliography

Avolio, B. J. and Yammarino, F. J., 1990. Operationalizing charismatic leadership using a levels-of-analysis framework, *Leadership Quarterly*, 1:193–208

Barker, R. A., 1997. How can we train leaders if we do not know what leadership is?, *Human Relations*, 50: 343–362

Barling, J., Weber, T. and Kelloway, E. K., 1996. Effects of transformational leadership training on attitudinal and financial outcomes: a field experiment, *Journal of Applied Psychology*, 81: 827–832

Bass, B. M., 1990. *Handbook of Leadership: A Survey of Theory and Research*, Free Press: New York

   1995. Theory of transformational leadership redux, *Leadership Quarterly*, 6: 463–478

Bass, B. M. and Avolio, B. J., 1993. Transformational leadership: a response to critiques, in M. M. Chemers and R. Ayman (eds.), *Leadership and Research: Perspectives and Directions*, San Diego, CA: Academic Press: 49–80

Berman, F. E. and Miner, J. B., 1985. Motivation to manage at the top executive level: a test of the hierarchic role-motivation theory, *Personnel Psychology*, 38: 377–391

Blake, R. R. and Mouton, J. S., 1964. *The Managerial Grid*, Houston: Gulf

Blank, W., Weitzel, J. R. and Green, S. G., 1990. A test of situational leadership theory, *Personnel Psychology*, 43: 579–597

Bouchard, T., Lykken, D. T., McGue, A., Segal, N. L. and Tellegen, A., 1990. Sources of human psychological differences: the Minnesota study of twins reared apart, *Science*, 250: 223–228

Boyatzis, R. E., 1982. *The Competent Manager*, New York: Wiley

Boyle, M., 2001. The dirty half-dozen: America's worst boards, *Fortune*, May 14: 114–118

Bryman, A., 1993. Charismatic leadership in business organizations: some neglected issues, *Leadership Quarterly*, 4: 289–304

   1996. Leadership in organizations, in S. R. Clegg, C. Hardy and W. R. Nord (eds.), *Handbook of Organization Studies*, Beverly Hills: Sage: 276–292

Bycio, P., Allen, J. S. and Hackett, R. D., 1995. Further assessments of Bass's (1985) conceptualization of transactional and transformational leadership, *Journal of Applied Psychology*, 80: 468–478

Cockerill, T., Hunt, J. and Schroder, H., 1995. Managerial competencies: fact or fiction? *Business Strategy Review*, 6(3): 1–12

Conger, J. A. and Kanungo, R. N., 1987. Toward a behavioral theory of charismatic leadership in organizational settings, *Academy of Management Review*, 12: 637–647

Coombes, P. and Watson, M., 2000. Three surveys on corporate governance, *McKinsey Quarterly*, 4: 74–77

Daily, C. M. and Dalton, D. R., 1997. CEO and board chair roles held jointly or separately: much ado about nothing?, *Academy of Management Executive*, 11(3):11–20

Donaldson, G., 1995. A new tool for boards: the strategic audit, *Harvard Business Review*, July–August: 99–107

Dulewicz, V., MacMillan, K. and Herbert, P., 1995. Appraising and developing the effectiveness of boards and their directors, *Journal of General Management*, 20(3): 1–19

Economist, 2002. Corporate governance: designed by committee, June 15: 69–71

Fernandez, C. F. and Vecchio, R. P., 1997. Situational leadership theory revisited: a test of an across-jobs perspective, *Leadership Quarterly*, 8: 67–84

Fiedler, F. E., 1992. Time-based measures of leadership experience and organizational performance: a review of research and a preliminary model, *Leadership Quarterly*, 3: 5–23

1993. The leadership situation and the black box in contingency theories, in M. M. Chemers and R. Ayman (eds.), *Leadership Theory and Research: Perspectives and Directions*, San Diego, CA: Academic Press

Finkelstein, S. and Hambrick, D., 1996. *Strategic Leadership – Top Executives and their Effects on Organizations*, Minneapolis: West

Firstenberg, P. B. and Malkiel, B. G., 1994. The twenty-first century boardroom: who will be in charge?, *Sloan Management Review*, Fall: 27–35

Garratt, B., 1996. *The Fish Rots from the Head*, London: HarperCollins

Gibb, C. A., 1947. The principles and traits of leadership, *Journal of Abnormal and Social Psychology*, 42: 267–284

Hari Das, T., 1983. Qualitative research in organizational behavior, *Journal of Management Studies*, 20: 301–314

Hater, J. J. and Bass, B. M., 1988. Superiors' evaluations and subordinates' perceptions of transformational and transactional leadership, *Journal of Applied Psychology*, 73: 695–702

Heracleous, L., 1999. The board of directors as leaders of the organization, *Corporate Governance: An International Review*, 7: 256–265

2001. What is the impact of corporate governance on organizational performance?, *Corporate Governance: An International Review*, 9: 165–173

Jick, T. D., 1979. Mixing qualitative and quantitative methods: triangulation in action, *Administrative Science Quarterly*, 24: 601–611

Kets de Vries, M. F. R., 1994. The leadership mystique, *Academy of Management Executive*, 8(3): 73–92

Kirkpatrick, S. A., and Locke, E. A., 1991. Leadership: do traits matter?, *Academy of Management Executive*, 5(2): 48–60

1996. Direct and indirect effects of three core charismatic leadership components on performance and attitudes, *Journal of Applied Psychology*, 81: 36–51

Klein, K. J. and House, R. J., 1995. On fire: charismatic leadership and levels of analysis, *Leadership Quarterly*, 6: 183–198

Koh, W. L., Steers, R. M. and Terborg, J. R., 1995. The effects of transformational leadership on teacher attitudes and student performance in Singapore, *Journal of Organizational Behavior*, 16: 319–333

Kuhnert, K. W. and Lewis, P., 1987. Transactional and transformational leadership: a constructive/developmental analysis, *Academy of Management Review*, 12: 648–657

Mansfield, R. S., 1996. Building competency models: approaches for HR professionals, *Human Resource Management*, 35(1): 7–18

McClelland, D. C., 1965. N-achievement and entrepreneurship: a longitudinal study, *Journal of Personality and Social Psychology*, 1: 389–392

1985. *Human Motivation*. Glenview, IL: Scott Foresman

Miller, K. I. and Monge, P. R., 1986. Participation, satisfaction, and productivity: a meta-analytic review, *Academy of Management Journal*, 29: 727–753

Miner, J. B., 1978. Twenty years of research on role motivation theory of managerial effectiveness, *Personnel Psychology*, 31: 739–760

1986. Managerial role motivation training, *Journal of Managerial Psychology*, 1(1): 25–30

Monks, R., 1999. What will be the impact of active shareholders? A practical recipe for constructive change, *Long Range Planning*, 32: 20–27

2001. Redesigning corporate governance structures and systems for the twenty first century, *Corporate Governance: An International Review*, 9: 142–147

Niehoff, B. P., Enz, C. A. and Grover, R. A., 1990. The impact of top-management actions on employee attitudes and perceptions, *Group & Organization Studies*, 15: 337–352

O'Neal, D. and Thomas, H., 1996. Developing the strategic board, *Long Range Planning*, 29: 314–327

Patton, A. and Baker, J. C., 1987. Why won't directors rock the boat?, *Harvard Business Review*, November–December: 10–18

Peters, L. H., Hartke, D. D. and Pohlmann, J. T., 1985. Fiedler's contingency theory of leadership: an application of the meta-analysis procedures of Schmidt and Hunter, *Psychological Bulletin*, 97: 274–285

Podsakoff, P. M., MacKenzie, S. B., Ahearne, M. and Bommer, W. H., 1995. Searching for a needle in a haystack: trying to identify the illusive moderators of leadership behaviors, *Journal of Management*, 21: 423–470

Rost, J. C., 1991. *Leadership for the Twenty-First Century*, New York: Praeger

Russ, F. A., McNeilly, K. M. and Comer, J. M., 1996. Leadership, decision making and performance of sales managers: a multi-level approach, *Journal of Personal Selling & Sales Management*, 16(3): 1–15

Salmon, W. J., 1993. Crisis prevention: how to gear up your board, *Harvard Business Review*, January–February: 68–75

Schein, E. H., 1988. *Process Consultation*, I, Reading, MA: Addison-Wesley

Stogdill, R. M., 1948. Personal factors associated with leadership: a survey of the literature, *Journal of Psychology*, 25: 35–71

    1950. Leadership, membership and organization, *Psychological Bulletin*, 47: 1–14

    1974. *Handbook of Leadership: A Survey of Theory and Research*, New York: Free Press

Strube, M. J. and Garcia, J. E., 1981. A meta-analytic investigation of Fiedler's contingency model of leadership performance, *Psychological Bulletin*, 90: 307–321

Useem, M., Bowman, E. H., Myatt, J. and Irvine, C. W., 1993. US institutional investors look at corporate governance in the 1990s, *European Management Journal*, 11: 175–189

Vecchio, R. P., 1990. Theoretical and empirical examination of cognitive resource theory, *Journal of Applied Psychology*, 75: 141–147

Whistler, T. L., 1984. *Rules of the Game: Inside the Corporate Boardroom*, Homewood, IL: Dow Jones-Irwin

Wofford, J. C. and Liska, L. Z., 1993. Path–goal theories of leadership: a meta-analysis, *Journal of Management*, 19: 858–876

Yukl, G., 1998. *Leadership in Organizations* (4th edn.), London: Prentice-Hall

II Realizing strategy

5 | The complexities of strategy implementation

This chapter highlights the turbulence of the competitive environment, which makes capabilities for strategic thinking and successful realization of strategy even more critical. It addresses the high costs of failed implementation efforts, as well as the reasons for which strategy implementation efforts can fail. Finally, it outlines various concepts and frameworks that can aid successful strategy implementation.

Competencies for success in a turbulent world

Most consultants, management gurus, and academics exhibit a rare instance of agreement on the view that in order to achieve competitive success in the future, existing ways of competing and thinking are not enough; organizations have to learn to compete and think in new ways. Emerging strategic imperatives include goals of not just aiming to optimize within the organization's current industry but trying to generate ground-breaking strategies which will create new niches and markets and re-define whole industries (Porter 1997). In other words, competing not just for market share in existing markets but for "opportunity share" in future markets, in a world of continuous re-definition of industry boundaries and commingling technologies (Prahalad 1997). This means that companies should not merely or exclusively be trying to catch up with the best performers in current competitive games, but be aiming to invent new games, re-write the rules and create new competitive space (Hamel 1997a). Competitive success favors companies that have taken bold approaches and re-written the conventional competitive rules of their industries (Hamel 1997b; Kumar *et al.* 2000).

The end of convention and stability in all business sectors is perhaps inevitable, given global trends such as the spread of market

This chapter draws from Heracleous (2000).

economies, the emergence of a global economy facilitated by technological advances in communications and transport, and the shift from
an era of natural resources-based industries to an era of faster-moving
brainpower-based industries (Thurow 1997).

These trends mean that companies need to develop effective competencies in strategic thinking and planning, as well as realizing strategy, which will help them in a more uncertain and fast-moving world.
Existing bases of competitive advantage and industry structures cannot
be taken for granted. Sustainable competitive advantage in this new environment can come only from continuous innovation and adaptability.
Amazon, for example, has influenced the way books, CDs, and many
other products are traded. Even though profitability has been elusive,
it does not detract from Amazon's success in creating a new retailing
model. Internet telephony, in addition, is slowly but surely eliminating
the traditional profit source of telecoms firms, international calls. Telecoms firms will have to find new ways of competing and develop new
value-added services to make up for the loss of their international calls
"cash cow." Banks, lastly, have to compete with web-based competitors
who have no physical branches at all, and therefore a radically lower
cost structure, but who can offer many banking products at similar
levels of quality and service.

Learning to think and compete in new ways (while simultaneously
keeping in mind unchanging strategic principles, see chapter 12) is
not an incremental alteration, but a fundamental, second-order change
that requires the critical questioning of current operating assumptions,
essentially what Argyris (1977) has referred to as "double-loop learning," and Fiol and Lyles (1985) as "higher-level learning." Double-loop
learning is psychologically uncomfortable because it questions the established values and very identity of the organization, and politically
contentious because it questions established bases of power and influence. To realize second-order change successfully, strategy implementation competencies thus become vital.

The need for radical organizational change

Often piecemeal, incremental change will not be sufficient to ensure
survival, let alone competitive success, if a company is getting more and
more out of touch with what is happening in its environment, creating a
potentially lethal gap known as "strategic drift" (Johnson 1987). When

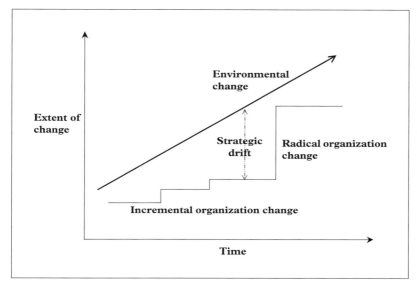

Figure 5.1 Environmental change, organizational change, and strategic drift
Source: Johnson (1987).

the strategic drift widens, unless the company can change radically to get back in touch with its environment, it risks destruction (figure 5.1).

Often companies that get out of touch with their environment have been pursuing effectively a particular strategy which initially leads the company to competitive success (e.g. engineering excellence, shrewd diversifications, focus on innovation or marketing savvy). This strategy, however, can soon dominate the company and blind the executives to other important issues such as cost control, customer focus, or development of new competencies. In these cases the company's greatest asset and source of success can lead to its downfall because it dominates thinking and action at the expense of other important issues, a situation known as the "Icarus paradox" (Miller 1992). The term is derived from Icarus' story from Greek mythology. Icarus and his father were held prisoners on an island. They constructed large wings held together using wax. Icarus was so happy when he managed to fly that he ignored his father's warnings not to fly too close to the sun. The wax melted, and Icarus fell to his death in the Aegean Sea. Relishing too much his success in flying and ignoring warnings brought about his downfall.

Is strategic planning useful?

Is it really important for a company to plan strategically? Despite persistent arguments against the usefulness of strategic planning (for a review see chapter 3), research has shown convincingly that companies which plan strategically generally perform better than those which do not, in terms of such indicators as sales growth, earnings growth, deposit growth, return on assets (RoA), return on equity (ROCE), return on sales, and return on total invested capital. Such benefits are even higher in more turbulent environments (Miller and Cardinal 1994). Moreover, companies which plan for the longer term, as opposed to just undertaking short-term forecasting or annual planning, deliver higher returns to investors both relative to their industry and in absolute terms (Bracker and Pearson 1986; Bracker *et al.* 1988; Pearce *et al.* 1987; Rhyne 1986).

Studies such as these linked strategic planning with company performance, but generally did not examine issues such as whether these companies were also better in implementation, or any side-effects of the planning *process* on such areas as the group dynamics of top management teams and the quality of strategic decisions. There has been a higher focus in the strategy field on strategy formulation and its links with organizational outcomes, with insufficient attention being paid to the intervening process of implementation (Noble 1999; Smith and Kofron, 1996). So while we know that it is important to plan strategically, the process of strategy implementation has not received sufficient attention in academia.

The costs of failed implementation efforts

The costs to the organization of failed implementation efforts are enormous. Apart from wasting significant amounts of time and money, they result in lower employee morale, a diminished trust and faith in senior management, as well as ending up in creating an even more inflexible organization, since an organization that has failed to change will encounter higher levels of employee cynicism in its next attempt. Cynicism is a common enemy of strategy implementation and any type of organizational change. It is worse than skepticism, which still allows for the possibility of successful change, and different from resistance to change, which can result from individuals' self-interest or misunderstanding of the goals of change. Cynicism is a feeling of almost

Table 5.1 *Potential sources and effects of cynicism about organizational change*

Potential causes of cynicism about organizational change
- A history of failed change attempts in the organization
- Feeling uninformed
- Lack of communication and respect from supervisor or boss
- Lack of communication and respect from union representative
- Lack of opportunity for meaningful participation in decision-making
- Negative disposition

Likely effects of cynicism about organizational change
- Lower organizational commitment
- Lower job satisfaction
- Lower motivation to work hard
- Lower willingness to engage in organizational change efforts
- Lower credibility for organization's leaders
- Reduced effectiveness of compensation system as a motivator

Source: Reichers *et al.* (1997).

complete loss of faith in the ability of the change agents to achieve change. Its potential causes and effects are shown in table 5.1.

The paradox is that even "successful" implementation of strategic changes can have high costs for the organization. First, there may be inappropriate criteria for success. A change project can be completed on time, on budget and on specification, but if these are the only criteria for success, without a clear link to strategic outcomes, then there is not likely to be a clear strategic advantage resulting for the organization. Secondly, there may be undesirable consequences of "successfully" achieving the required changes. The vast majority of organizations in most business sectors in the USA and Europe, for example, undertook some form of downsizing from the early 1980s onwards. While they undoubtedly succeeded in downsizing, however, over 60 percent of them cited lower morale among the remaining workforce as the main problem of their downsizing. Other common problems included unexpected increases in the use of temporary workers, overtime, and consultants, losing the wrong people in the downsizing, and incurring higher than expected severance costs (Mirvis 1997). The long-term strategic benefits of short-term operational cost savings of downsizing have been at best elusive and at worst a dream.

Why do strategic plans often remain unrealized?

There are several tools available to help managers analyze the environment, analyze their organization, and generate and evaluate strategic options. But even with the most sophisticated analysis and planning, realizing strategic plans has never been easy. In many cases they remain what they originally were; plans rather than reality. There are several reasons for this, but the most important may be that it is much easier to think of where the organization should be headed than effectively to lead it in that direction; and it is much easier to make a single important mistake in implementation and fail than it is to get most of the things right and succeed.

Sometimes strategic change may not require substantial internal changes in the organization. This happens where there is a radical re-positioning of a brand, or the creation of a new "brand-culture" in the marketplace, which does not necessitate new ways of working internally. In these cases, the complex problems of implementing the internal changes needed for a new external strategy can be avoided. Some examples of such successful repositionings are shown in table 5.2.

In most cases, however, realizing strategy is about *managing change*, in all its complexity. Underestimating this simple fact is a recipe for failure. Organizations are complex social systems with entrenched ways of doing things: systems, behaviors, and cultures. They are inertial, which means that they will tend to go in the direction they are heading already unless potent forces direct them otherwise. Different coalitions in the organization may place higher priority on their own interests than on overall organizational goals. In addition, these coalitions may

Table 5.2 *Successful strategic re-positioning*

Company	Brand positioning – before	Brand positioning – after
Polaroid	Camera for special occasions	Useful tool for everyday life
IBM	Selling computers	Providing solutions for a small planet
Michelin	Durable and high-performance tires	High-tech tires involving feats of engineering
Oil of Olay	Selling youth, beauty is about looking younger	Selling a lifetime of beauty, beauty is about looking beautiful at any age

Source: Dru and Lemberg (1997).

Table 5.3 *Ten reasons for which strategy implementation efforts can fail*

- The so-called "strategic plan" is nothing more than a collection of budgets and vague directions which do not provide clear guidelines for action
- The strategy does not correspond to market realities because it has been developed by strategic planners with no input from the grass roots
- The strategy does not enjoy support from and commitment by the majority of employees and middle management because they do not feel consulted in the development of the strategy
- Middle management does not think the strategy is the right one, or does not feel it has the requisite skills to implement it, so it sabotages the implementation
- Insufficient top management time is spent on communicating about, selling the new strategic direction, and managing the organizational changes involved
- No provision is made for developing the new skills and competencies required by the employees successfully to make the transition and operate within the new strategic direction
- No provision is made for instituting the appropriate organizational systems for the selection, motivation, and reward of people in accordance with the new strategy
- No provision is made for creating a close fit or coherence between the business-level strategy and the various functional-level strategies that can operationalize it
- There are factions in the organization which disagree with the strategy because if implemented it would reduce their power and influence, so they sabotage it by deliberate actions or inactions
- No attempt is made to analyze the culture of the organization and identify aspects which would be barriers and facilitators to change and manage change accordingly

have mutually incompatible perceptions of how their interests will be served. The complexity of organizations, coupled with several potential problems associated with the strategy itself, the way it was developed, or the management of the change process, makes realizing strategy an extremely difficult task (see Heracleous and Barrett 2001 for a discussion of the complexities of implementation at the level of inter-organizational networks). Some potential problems in strategy implementation are shown in table 5.3.

The effects of middle managers on strategy implementation can be crucial. Even if senior management communicates its commitment to a certain course of action, if middle managers feel that their self-interest is being compromised, if they don't think it is the right strategy, or if they don't believe they have the skills to implement it, they can, and do, sabotage strategy implementation both actively and passively:

active intervention can range from persuasive individual verbal arguments against the sponsored strategy in meetings and memos; to seeking other organizational members (coalitions) who will agree to stand in opposition to the strategy; to deliberately taking ineffective action or creating "roadblocks" to implementation; to outright sabotage of the strategy to prove that it was not a good decision in the first place. On the other hand, passive intervention can occur, taking the form of giving low priority to implementation actions, resulting in unnecessary delays and in general "foot-dragging," all of which can seriously compromise the quality of implementation, if not postpone it beyond the time that it is effective. (Guth and Macmillan 1986: 314)

Approaches to strategy implementation

In-depth studies of strategic change that have tracked such processes for years portray their complexity: the political battles, the cultural barriers, the inertia of organization structures and systems, and the bounded rationality of managers (Johnson 1987; Pettigrew 1985). But there are frameworks which can provide managers with useful recommendations in such complexity, for example those which show that different change management styles (intervention, persuasion, participation, or edict for example) are effective in different situations (Nutt 1986, 1987, 1989), and suggest implementation tactics likely to be more effective given the particular context. There has been an evolution of approaches to strategy implementation, from more autocratic to more participative ones (table 5.4).

We know that in more turbulent and fast-moving environments CEOs should act less as commanders or architects and more as

Table 5.4 *CEO roles in strategy implementation*

CEO as a:	The CEO's strategic question:
Commander	How do I formulate the optimum strategy?
Architect	I have a strategy in mind; now how do I implement it?
Co-ordinator	How do I involve top management to get commitment to strategies from the start?
Coach	How do I involve the whole organization in implementation?
Premise-setter	How do I encourage managers to come forward as champions of sound strategies?

Source: Bourgeois and Brodwin (1984).

co-ordinators, coaches, and premise-setters. The reason is that the first two roles separate thinking and acting, strategy formulation and implementation. A strategy or change program formed in the mind of one individual is much more problematic to implement than one which encompasses the input of people who have to live with it, as initially demonstrated by Lewin (1952). Implementation is achieved with much less difficulty if middle managers feel that they have contributed to the strategy's emergence, and if the employees in general feel that their concerns have been heard in its development. In this sense, implementation has already begun from the moment lower-level managers and employees are involved in thinking about the future of the company.

After careful strategic planning using various techniques of industry and internal analysis, senior managers often have a clear strategic direction, but stumble in the implementation process because this strategic direction remains at an abstract level and is not brought down to the day-to-day realities of the organization. "Objective" strategic planning often blinds managers to the "softer" issues that are critical to successful strategy implementation. There may, for example, be insufficient attention to the organizational culture and its implications for strategy implementation. The organization may be highly individualistic and loosely structured for example, but the new strategic plan may call for more teamwork and co-ordination than is the norm. Unless the norm of high individualism is made explicit and addressed, the implementation is likely to stumble on potent cultural barriers (Heracleous 2001; Heracleous and Langham 1996). In addition to culture, there may be issues such as political resistance or insufficient understanding of the human resource competence implications of a new strategic direction.

Both socio-political as well as more technical considerations point to the importance of the concept of "fit" that is critical to strategy implementation efforts. Two types of fit or coherence are needed: first, between the business strategy and the functional strategies, and, secondly, between the business strategy and the specific operational and organizational arrangements (Hamermesh 1988) that will make the strategy real and relate it to employees' daily work. In other words, the business-level strategy must have close correlates in the various functional-level strategies of the organization as well as the detailed functional configurations (Porter 1996). Specifying, for example, that the company will strive for the business strategies of differentiation, cost-leadership, and/or focus on particular product/market segments is only the first step in a complex chain of ideally unique organizational configurations that must be instituted for the organization to realize strategy successfully and achieve the Holy Grail of strategy – sustainable competitive advantage.

There are several frameworks that can help senior managers identify the main areas which must be re-configured to implement strategy successfully. These typically include both the "hard" and "soft" aspects of organizations. McKinsey's 7-S framework is a popular one. The top half contains the "hard" aspects of strategy, structure and systems, and the lower half contains the "softer" aspects of shared values, skills, staff, and style. The "cultural web" (Johnson 1987, 1988), in addition, portrays nine areas including the central "paradigm" of the organization: organizational culture, incentives, control systems, communication, rites and routines, stories and myths, symbols and power structures. The "integrated organizational" model (Heracleous and DeVoge 1998), in addition, portrays the seven "levers" of leadership, management processes and systems, organization, team and job design, work processes and business systems, values and culture, individual and team competence, and reward and recognition. There are also other frameworks such as Weisbord's (1976) "six-box organizational model" and the "Burke–Litwin model of organizational performance and change" (Burke 1994), which contain strategic, leadership, structural, cultural, systemic, and processual variables.

The current popularity of the "balanced scorecard" (Kaplan and Norton 1992) is due to its ability to help an organization not only to exercise monitoring and control of its customer orientation, learning and innovation, internal business processes and financial results (the four perspectives of the scorecard), but also to operationalize its strategy: to express it in terms and metrics that organizational members can relate to and monitor.

All of these frameworks portray the *content* that has to be managed for successful implementation. This should occur, however, within a well-structured *process* of organizational diagnosis, direction-setting, action-planning and implementation, and ongoing monitoring. Hambrick and Cannella (1989), for example, found that successful implementers are action-oriented individuals who first obtain broad-based inputs and participation from others at the strategy formulation stage. They then carefully assess the obstacles to implementation,

Table 5.5 *Ten questions for the reflective practitioner*

- What is your organization's strategic orientation? Is it generally reactive (acts after the event), pro-active (anticipates environmental changes and prepares for them), or pre-active (actively shapes its future and its markets)?
- What, if any, ways does your organization have to monitor its business environment? What use is made of such information?
- Has your organization failed to implement strategic changes in the past? Do you recognize any of the potential reasons given in table 5.3 (p. 79)?
- Has your organization succeeded in implementing strategic changes in the past? What were the criteria for success? Were they clearly linked to long-term strategic goals?
- What were the downsides of past successes in strategy implementation? How do you think these could have been avoided?
- Were you ever cynical about the chances of your organization successfully achieving major changes? Why? What could be done in the future to avoid such feelings?
- How did you or other change agents see their role in implementing strategy in previous implementation efforts (e. g. commander, coach, pace-setter, etc.)?
- With hindsight, was this the best approach? How should future implementation efforts be led?
- What have you learned from past experiences in implementing strategy? Does your company have any ways to codify and share such learning?
- How will you ensure that a close fit and coherence is created between your organization's business-level strategy and its various functional strategies?

before they take co-ordinated actions across a broad array of implementation "levers." They also communicate profusely, persuading other stakeholders about the soundness of the strategy; and in the meantime they continually monitor and fine-tune the implementation process as necessary. The *process* of implementation is a critical aspect, and will be further discussed in chapter 6 on the development of an organizational development approach to strategy implementation.

Table 5.5 presents some key questions that senior executives, as "reflective practitioners" (Schön 1983) might use to reflect on their past experiences of implementing strategy, as well as on current strategically relevant issues, and to gain some insights that can improve the chances of implementation success in the future.

Competitive arenas are fast-moving and more complex and competitive success accrues to those who re-write the rules of the competitive game. The winners of the future will be organizations that manage to develop strategic thinking skills so that they are more future-oriented and think in terms of "opportunity shares" instead of simply market shares, as well as develop sharp implementation skills so that they can avoid the huge costs of implementation failures and their strategic plans can become a reality. This chapter has highlighted the changing competitive environment, which makes strategic thinking and implementation capabilities critical. It has addressed the high cost of failed implementation efforts, as well as the reasons why strategy implementation efforts can fail. Finally, it has discussed key concepts and frameworks that can aid successful strategy implementation.

Bibliography

Argyris, C., 1977. Double loop learning in organizations, *Harvard Business Review*, September–October: 115–125

Bourgeois, L. J., III and Brodwin, D. R., 1984. Strategic implementation: five approaches to an elusive phenomenon, *Strategic Management Journal*, 5: 241–264

Bracker, J. S. and Pearson, J. N., 1986. Planning and financial performance of small, mature firms, *Strategic Management Journal*, 7, 503–522

Bracker, J. S., Keats, B. W. and Pearson, J. N., 1988. Planning and financial performance among small firms in a growth industry, *Strategic Management Journal*, 9, 591–603

Burke, W. W., 1994. *A Process of Learning and Change* (2nd edn.), Reading, MA: Addison-Wesley

Dru, J.-M. and Lemberg, R., 1997. Disrupt your business, *Journal of Business Strategy*, May–June, 24–29

Fiol, C. M. and Lyles, M. A., 1985. Organizational learning, *Academy of Management Review*, 10: 803–813

Guth, W. D. and Macmillan, I. C., 1986. Strategy implementation versus middle management self-interest, *Strategic Management Journal*, 7: 313–327

Hambrick, D. C. and Cannella, A. A., 1989. Strategy implementation as substance and selling, *Academy of Management Executive*, 3: 278–285

Hamel, G., 1997a. Reinventing the basis for competition, in R. Gibson, *Rethinking the Future*, London: Nicholas Brealey: 76–92

1997b. Killer strategies that make shareholders rich, *Fortune*, June 23: 30–34

Hamermesh, R. G., 1988. Note on implementing strategy, *Harvard Business School Note*, 9-383-015

Heracleous, L., 2000. The role of strategic management in organization development, *Organization Development Journal* 18(3): 75–80

2001. An ethnographic study of culture in the context of organizational change, *Journal of Applied Behavioral Science*, 37(4): 426–446

Heracleous, L. and Barrett, M., 2001. Organizational change as discourse: communicative actions and deep structures in the context of information technology implementation, *Academy of Management Journal*, 44: 755–778

Heracleous, L. and DeVoge, S., 1998. Bridging the gap of relevance: strategic management and organizational development, *Long Range Planning*, 31: 732–744

Heracleous, L. and Langham, B., 1996. Strategic change and organizational culture at Hay Management Consultants, *Long Range Planning*, 29: 485–494

Johnson, G., 1987. *Strategic Change and the Management Process*, Oxford: Blackwell

1988. Rethinking incrementalism, *Strategic Management Journal*, 6: 75–91

Kaplan, R. S. and Norton, D. P., 1992. The balanced scorecard: measures that drive performance, *Harvard Business Review*, January–February: 71–79

Kumar, N., Scheer, L. and Kotler, P., 2000, From market driven to market driving, *European Management Journal*, 18, 129–142

Lewin, K., 1952. *Field Theory in Social Science*, London: Tavistock

Miller, C. C. and Cardinal, L. B., 1994, Strategic planning and firm performance: a synthesis of more than two decades of research, *Academy of Management Journal*, 37: 1649–1665

Miller, D., 1992. The Icarus paradox: how exceptional companies bring about their own downfall, *Business Horizons*, 35(1): 24–35

Mirvis, P. H., 1997. Human resource management: leaders, laggards and followers, *Academy of Management Executive*, 11(2): 43–56

Noble, C. H., 1999. The eclectic roots of strategy implementation research, *Journal of Business Research*, 45: 119–134

Nutt, P. C., 1986. Tactics of implementation, *Academy of Management Journal*, 29: 230–261

1987. Identifying and appraising how managers install strategy, *Strategic Management Journal*, 8: 1–14

1989. Selecting tactics to implement strategic plans, *Strategic Management Journal*, 10: 145–161

Pearce, J. A., II, Robbins, K. D. and Robinson, R. B., Jr., 1987. The impact of grand strategy and planning formality on financial performance, *Strategic Management Journal*, 8: 125–134

Pettigrew, A., 1985. *The Awakening Giant: Continuity and Change in ICI*, Oxford: Blackwell

Porter, M. E., 1996. What is strategy?, *Harvard Business Review*, November–December: 61–78

1997. Creating tomorrow's advantages, in R. Gibson, *Rethinking the Future*, London: Nicholas Brealey: 48–61

Prahalad, C. K., 1997. Strategies for growth, in R. Gibson, *Rethinking the Future*, London: Nicholas Brealey: 62–75

Reichers, A. E., Wanous, J. P. and Austin, J. T., 1997. Understanding and managing cynicism about organizational change, *Academy of Management Executive*, 11(1): 48–59

Rhyne, L. C., 1986. The relationship of strategic planning to financial performance, *Strategic Management Journal*, 8: 125–134

Schön, D. A., 1983. *The Reflective Practitioner*, New York: Basic Books

Smith, K. A. and Kofron, E. A., 1996. Toward a research agenda on top management teams and strategy implementation, *Irish Business and Administrative Research*, 17(1): 135–152

Thurow, L., 1997. Changing the nature of capitalism, in R. Gibson, *Rethinking the Future*, London: Nicholas Brealey: 228–249

Weisbord, M. R., 1976. Organizational diagnosis: six places to look for trouble with or without a theory, *Group & Organization Studies*, 1: 430–477

6 | *Organizational culture and strategic change processes*

This chapter considers in depth in one facet of the organizational action view, the organizational paradigm, which provides the context for strategic choices and actions. In chapter 2 it was suggested that at the descriptive level, paradigms include epistemological considerations (knowing what to know), and methodological considerations (knowing how to know). At the normative level, they include values (end purposes) and moral systems justifying these values (Litterer and Young 1984: 249–250). Within strategic management, the concept of organizational paradigm was defined by Johnson (1987, 1988) in terms of organizational culture, as "the set of beliefs and assumptions, held relatively common through the organization, taken for granted, and discernible in the stories and explanations of the managers, which plays a central role in the interpretation of environmental stimuli and configuration of organizationally relevant strategic responses... both intended and realized strategy are likely to be configured within the parameters of the paradigm" (Johnson 1988: 84–85).

This chapter employs a processual approach to examine the nature of organizational culture and its effects, focusing on the close interrelationship between culture and strategic change. The case discussion illustrates how a strategic re-direction involving market repositioning and substantial growth can also entail significant cultural and organizational changes. The discussion suggests that rather than aiming for wholesale cultural change, an organization should recognize what aspects of the culture need to change and what aspects need to be nurtured. The "cultural web" will be employed as a useful framework for understanding the cultural and organizational situation of the firm, and identifying relevant changes. A typified framework for strategic decision-making will also be presented as a useful tool for managing

This chapter is based on Heracleous and Langham (1996) and Heracleous (2001).

the change process, and some important issues of change management arising at each stage will be discussed.

Organizational culture and its effects

The surge of interest by management academics and practitioners since the 1980s in organizational culture and symbolism has been prompted by the publication of books and articles on the importance of culture for organizational effectiveness (Barney 1986; Deal and Kennedy 1982; Peters and Waterman 1982); the academic critique of positivism (Silverman 1970); the increased legitimacy of qualitative methodologies (Jick 1979; Sanday 1979; Sanders 1982); and intensifying global competition with culture seen as a key facilitator of the high economic achievement of countries such as Japan at the time (Turner 1986).

More broadly, organization theory has from early on highlighted the human aspects of organizing (Daft and Weick 1984; Dandridge *et al.* 1980; Pondy and Mitroff 1979). Culture has been studied either as an organizational variable within a functionalist frame of reference, something an organization "has," or as a root metaphor for conceptualizing organization, something an organization "is" (Smircich 1983a). Organizations were seen as shared meanings (Smircich 1983b), or as "distinctive social units possessed of a set of common understandings for organizing action . . . and languages and other symbolic vehicles for expressing common understandings" (Louis 1983: 39). Cultural views of organization emphasize that individuals' actions are based on their subjective definitions of the situation (Thomas and Thomas 1970), and that people "act out and realize their ideas" (Weick 1977: 287), collectively creating their own realities (Berger and Luckmann 1966).

Initial writings on organizational culture portrayed it as an integrating, cohesive mechanism and focused on its potential links with organizational effectiveness, an approach aligned with the structural–functionalist stream in anthropology (Meek 1988). Studies have indeed shown that organizational culture does have potent effects on such issues as employee retention (Sheridan 1992), job satisfaction, and organizational commitment (O'Reilly *et al.* 1991).

There are several challenges, however, to the proposition that organizational culture can provide sustainable competitive advantage. Although culture is a potent force, it cannot fully dominate individuals' thought and action because of the capacity of human agents to comment critically on their situation and to choose to abstain or act otherwise than the dominant cultural norms would dictate (Golden 1992). There is thus the potential for multiple and even competing sub-cultures existing in an organization (Lucas 1987). Culture, moreover, may often vary more across industries than within them, indicating that many cultural elements may not be unique to particular organizations in the same industry (Chatman and Jehn 1994; Gordon 1991). In this sense, cultural values may not always be valuable, rare, and imperfectly imitable (Barney 1986), the criteria for identifying resources and capabilities that can deliver sustainable competitive advantage. Far from the managerialist view of culture as a route to competitive advantage, others argued that culture is in effect a self-disciplining form of employee subjectivity, the last frontier of control of labor by capitalism (Ray 1986; Willmott 1993).

Organizational culture and strategic change

Empirical studies of strategy development over time and in context (Pettigrew 1985; Johnson 1987) have demonstrated the close links between organizational culture and strategy development. Even though strategic planners report that they follow the steps of normative, rationalistic models of strategic management (Ginter *et al.* 1985) this process takes place within a context of taken-for-granted and tacit values, beliefs, and assumptions about the organization and its environment – the organizational paradigm (Johnson 1987, 1988). This set of core values, beliefs, and assumptions develops over time out of the learning experiences of the organization as it copes with its problems of external adaptation and internal integration, and is transmitted to new members through socialization (Schein 1992).

If we want to take organizational culture seriously, we must recognize that normative rationalistic approaches to strategic management are not sufficient in explaining actual processes of strategic development and change in organizations. We need to supplement our explanations with a deep understanding of culture in action; and we can reach this level of understanding only through conducting ethnographic or clinical observation in the field (Schein 1996).

The organizational paradigm, as a set of taken-for-granted values, beliefs and assumptions, is enshrined within a "cultural web" (Johnson 1987, 1988) of artifacts which are both the behavioral manifestations

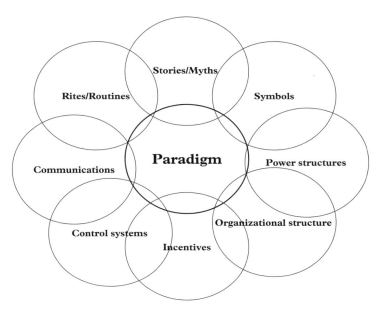

Figure 6.1 The "cultural web"
Source: Johnson (1987).

as well as the contextual legitimations of these values, beliefs, and assumptions. The cultural web (figure 6.1) is a construct which encompasses elements from both ideational views of culture emphasizing shared cognitions and adaptationist views of culture emphasizing behavior (Allaire and Firsirotou 1984). Cognitions are positioned in the center of the cultural web, and behavioral or visible elements are located around the centre, drawing attention to the close links between unobservable cognitions and visible behaviors and artifacts.

The cultural web is therefore potentially consistent with both seeing culture either as a root metaphor for conceptualizing organization within an interpretative frame of reference (something an organization *is*), or as a variable within a functionalist frame of reference (something an organization *has*) (Smircich 1983a). These orientations are not inherent in the cultural web as a construct, but can be manifested in the specific use to which it is put by researchers or managers.

Incrementalism in strategy development has been viewed as an essentially logical and rational process in response to an uncertain environment, where managers are said to proceed cautiously and experimentally in order to try and reduce this uncertainty (Quinn 1978). It has been argued, however, based on the findings of longitudinal qualitative studies of strategic change, that incrementalism can be accounted for not simply by such logical processes, but by the filtering, inertial influences of the organizational paradigm on managerial interpretations and actions (Johnson 1988, 1990). Organizational culture is in this sense a double-edged sword. It can either cause inertia, apathy, and decline, or it can encourage change and innovation, depending on the particular values, beliefs, and assumptions that it enshrines.

From the perspective of the cultural web, transformational change is seen as exceedingly difficult to achieve because of the inertial nature of culture, its taken-for-granted nature which can effectively preclude cultural values from open debate, the close links of culture with the power centers of the organization, and the internal consistency, self-legitimacy, and self-sustenance of the cultural web.

Organizational culture at Hay Management Consultants

Hay has developed a "thick" organizational culture during four decades of operating in the UK. My interviews with past leaders and document analysis indicated that People Associates' early growth was characterized by conditions fostering the development of such cultures, including a long history and stable membership, absence of institutional alternatives, and frequent interaction among members (Wilkins and Ouchi 1983).

Both employees and clients of the organization viewed it as a human resource consulting firm with the core business being job evaluation. Job evaluation had been the firm's core business since its founding and its early consulting projects were based almost exclusively on this methodology. The belief that job evaluation was the core business was manifested in consultants' daily communication using terms related to this methodology, as part of a shared vocabulary which helped to constitute an identity for organizational members (Evered 1983). Although the language of job evaluation was still prevalent in People Associates, the perception that it was the firm's core business had been weakening. Financial analyses had shown that job evaluation sales as a percentage of total sales had been decreasing, while sales from other fields such as organizational change and human resources (HR) planning and development had been on the rise. Senior management had made a conscious effort to develop consultants' expertise in these other fields, through holding consultant training programs and client seminars, and encouraging consultants to inform clients about other consulting services offered by the firm.

Secondly, clients were considered as all important in People Associates, always taking priority over internal systems and commitments. When consultants were asked to explain their actions/inactions, their rationalizations (Giddens 1979) mainly rested on the premise of acting in the best interests of the client. In interviews it was stressed that "if a client says 'jump', you jump!". The organization's high client orientation was reflected in its periodic client satisfaction surveys, in what clients said during these surveys regarding the firm's commitment to them, in the substantial power base of individuals with large client portfolios and strong client relationships, and in the organization's flexible, loose structure allowing it to keep close to, and respond swiftly to, clients.

Thirdly, the organization had been characterized by the strong individualism and high autonomy of its consultants since its inception. This was exemplified by the daily behaviors of its consultants, as well as by the organizational mythology. Many consultants I talked to said that they were attracted to Hay, as opposed to other consulting firms, because of the lack of strict rules and regulations and the high autonomy they enjoyed, provided they met their targets. One consultant joked that "if you meet your targets you can do what you want, even be a double-glazing salesman if you like." In addition, the organizational mythology was replete with figures of "lone rangers," currently senior people who had exhibited highly individualistic behaviors in dealing with clients, and "guidechart jockeys," who would "ride" in an organization with their job evaluation guidecharts to solve client problems.

Fourthly, Hay had been carrying out reorganizations on an annual basis. Over time these changes have become institutionalized as part of its culture, and were referred to as "autumn maneuvers" in the organization's vocabulary. My interviews with senior management indicated that they saw these as fundamental changes (as opposed to incremental ones). The manager of the change steering group said that the group would not have realized on their own that these changes were in fact incremental, focusing solely on structural change without challenging the organization's established assumptions, values, and beliefs.

Fifth, clients often requested advice from consultants in areas in which those particular consultants may not have been the top experts. Because of consultants' high pressures to meet their targets, and the fact that client relationships were a potent power base, consultants were reluctant to relinquish control of those clients to others. They thus offered advice in various HR areas. This situation led to an internal perception of "generalist expertise" in several fields as opposed to deep expertise in selected ones.

Lastly, mainly because of the high autonomy and individualism of consultants who often did not pay much attention to internal procedures, and to the fact that the "autumn maneuvers" did not lead to any fundamental, cultural changes in the organization, the perception developed over time that there were few "real" decisions taken by senior management. On several occasions during the research I observed new internal procedures or rules being "implemented," but not in fact followed. Examples included the requirement that consultants keep detailed written records of how they spent their time during client engagements or any other activity; and new record-keeping procedures for billing clients introduced by the finance department. Both of these were ignored by consultants, who said that they were too time-consuming and cumbersome, and both were subsequently dropped. As one consultant told me, "nobody will be hanged for violating procedures, but they will be hanged for getting it wrong." In other words, at Hay it was more important to get it right with clients than to follow internal procedures.

These values and beliefs represent the predominant, "consulting" sub-culture in Hay UK. Although there are other sub-cultures in this organization (e.g. the sub-cultures of the support staff and of the surveys department) it is the consultants' sub-culture that dominates. Its importance was indicated by the high numbers of its members, its potent influence on organizational decisions and actions, and its strong internal homogeneity. In terms of membership numbers, over two-thirds of the firm's UK employees were consultants, and most of the one-fifth of employees who worked in the survey/IT departments aspired to become consultants or to work closely with them in the longer term. In terms of influence on decisions and actions, leaders of the consulting sub-culture determined the strategic direction and most of the internal organizational arrangements. Lastly, in terms of homogeneity of the dominant consulting sub-culture, my data on the recruitment process, observation of behaviors, and in-depth interviews indicated a highly homogeneous body of consultants. When interviewing new recruits and asking for surprising or puzzling features of Hay, as suggested by Schein (1992), many marveled at how "everybody is so much like me."

This culture was highly coherent. There were strong interconnections among the values and beliefs of Hay. For example, the individualism and high autonomy of consultants were historically related to the nature of the core business (job evaluation), which did not require any teamwork among consultants. The institutionalized incremental changes, which had not led to fundamental organizational change and had not challenged the organization's values and beliefs, in combination with consultants' high autonomy and individualism, led to a further belief that senior management at this organization made few "real" decisions.

Values and beliefs were also highly interconnected with artifacts. With regard to individualism and high autonomy, there were stories and myths about "lone rangers"; the organizational structure accommodated and encouraged individualism by being loosely coupled and chaotic; control systems and incentives focused on and were geared to individual evaluation and performance; communication was informal and largely based on one's own interpersonal networks; and lastly high achievers in terms of billing and sales were individually praised consistently on such occasions as Christmas parties.

Going deeper: governing assumptions of Hay Management Consultants

According to Schein, basic assumptions are "the implicit assumptions that actually guide behavior, that tell group members how to perceive, think about, and feel about things" (1992: 22). These are taken for granted and mutually reinforced and thus are normally not confronted or debated. Challenging basic assumptions leads to high levels of anxiety and initiates defense mechanisms that enable the group to continue functioning in a stable manner. Basic assumptions, according to Schein, are the essence of culture because they represent taken-for-granted beliefs, perceptions, thoughts, and feelings that are the ultimate source of individuals' values and actions. Analysis of qualitative data indicated that five powerful governing assumptions operated in Hay, as portrayed in table 6.1.

Table 6.1 *Governing assumptions at Hay Management Consultants*

Organization's relationship to its environment	The organization should be proactive towards its environment and strive for continuous improvement
Nature of reality and truth	Reality and truth are derived from a combination of that which works (the pragmatic orientation) and that which is scientifically established
Nature of human nature	Individuals should be self-motivated and capable agents and therefore should act entrepreneurially and proactively
Nature of human activity	A "doing" orientation predominates, rather than a "being" or "being-in-becoming" orientation
Nature of time	Time is "polychronic," rather than "monochronic" or "cyclical"

Source: Heracleous (2001).

From a historical perspective, these governing assumptions derive from the vision and actions of the founder and early leaders of the organization, and from the way the organization has approached internal (e.g. recruitment, incentives, and control systems) and external (e.g. market development) issues since its inception (Schein 1983). These governing assumptions are continually manifested in agents' actions and organizational processes and systems, as discussed in detail in Heracleous (2001).

The organization's relationship to its environment

The assumption regarding the proactive and developmental stance of the organization to its environment was embodied in the vision of the founder about the future of the organization. He wrote in 1943: "The human element in industry has not received adequate or sufficiently skillful attention . . . The most successful companies of the future will be the ones to take advantage of improved personnel techniques" (Hay Management Consultants 1993: 2). According to the Chairman and CEO of Hay (Global), "the one common thread through our exhilarating roller-coaster ride between 1943 and today is that [our founder's] original vision has always proved to have flawless clarity" (Hay Management Consultants 1993: 4). The vision was proactive and progressive for its time, as thoughts about the importance of the human side of work were not common in 1943, and indeed academic management thought was very much engaged with the mechanistic approach of "scientific management" (Taylor 1947).

The proactive and developmental nature of People Associates' actions towards its environment could also be seen in its early globalization processes and in its current annual organization change programs. With regard to globalization, "the real enduring impact of this foreign expansion is that once we started, we stayed at it – even if the short-term financials weren't good." This allowed the organization to "stay ahead of the curve... to understand what was – and would be – happening to business in time to develop positions and expertise necessary to help our clients" (Hay Management Consultants 1993: 4–5).

The organization, in addition, has not been complacent about its early monopolistic position in the job evaluation field. It has instead institutionalized annual incremental changes ("autumn maneuvers"), and since the mid-1990s has been proactively pursuing a transformational change program. As senior consultants said, "nobody's holding a gun to our head." In a speech at the start of the change process, the UK Managing Director explicitly recognized that the organization had been successful and that there was no crisis at hand; but also that unless it proactively made significant changes it would, in the near future, be at a competitive disadvantage.

Nature of reality and truth

The assumption regarding truth as a combination of that which works (a pragmatic orientation) and that which is established by scientific method is embodied in the founder's pool of early employees, deriving from his circle of friends in academia (science) and from retired businessmen (pragmatism). Two men who would later prove to be pivotal figures in the development of the organization were hired in 1949. One had twenty-five years' experience in management and manufacturing (pragmatism), and is credited with developing the firm's proprietary job evaluation methodology. The other was a twenty-eight-year-old who had just earned a PhD in industrial psychology and who subsequently developed several psychological assessment tools (science). Bringing together the two elements of pragmatism and science in a combination that provided sustained commercial success for the organization gave rise to a cultural precedent that gradually dropped out of conscious awareness and became a governing assumption.

Nature of human nature

The assumption that individuals are self-motivated, capable, and responsible agents was apparent in Hay's early recruitment policy in the USA. The HR strategy was to develop the geographical markets the firm entered using "the best available local talent." The Canadian office was the first one in what subsequently became an intense drive for market development, leading to Hay's current international presence with ninety offices in thirty countries: "when we went to Canada, we asked who's your best guy in personnel? And then we sought that person out and recruited him" (Hay Management Consultants 1993: 4). The current recruitment policy is a continuation of high standards set historically. Interviews with consultants and the personnel manager have revealed that the recruitment process lasted about three–four months, and commonly consisted of three interviews, three psychometric tests, assessment centers involving debate of real-life organizational problems, and, interestingly, a dinner where the social skills of short-listed applicants were observed by partners. In response to my questions about what organizational features consultants found unexpected or surprising when they entered the firm, several said that the recruitment process was the most extensive they had ever gone through. However, once they had crossed the boundary into the organization, they were equally surprised by their high level of autonomy and the looseness of the organization.

Nature of human activity

A "doing" orientation predominated in Hay, as opposed to "being" or "being in becoming" orientations. A "doing" orientation is one that assumes that "the proper thing for people to do is to take charge and actively control their environment" (Schein 1992: 127). This orientation found expression in the idea that "adding value" to clients and to the organization was of paramount importance, a concept that was implicit in the vision of the organization's founder, as discussed earlier. This concern in turn derived from an industry-wide focus on "adding value" (Chatman and Jehn 1994; Gordon 1991). This "doing" orientation led to the creation of what Harrison (1972) calls a "task" culture, where organization structure and systems, as well as agents' actions, are geared toward and subordinated to achieving the super-ordinate goal of "adding value."

Nature of time

The dominant time orientation in Hay was "polychronic" rather than "monochronic" or "cyclical." Polychronic time is "a kind of medium defined more by what is accomplished than by a clock and within which several things can be done simultaneously" (Schein 1992: 107–108). This was apparent in the complete control consultants historically had over their time/space movements, some not coming into the office for weeks at a time. This was quite acceptable because, as the MD UK said during an informal conversation, if they were in the office this meant that they were not out with clients. Some senior people characterized Hay as a "club" in this sense. Consultants had complete control of what they did and when, and it was normal for them to be engaged in several client projects simultaneously. Secretarial support also operated within a polychronic time orientation, as support staff had to carry out many tasks simultaneously and they partly controlled such issues as their time of arrival to work, their lunch breaks, and their departure from work.

The surveys/IT part of the organization, on the other hand, oper-ated with longer and more defined time horizons. Many surveys were annual, and the "bespoke" ones took a specific amount of time to be completed. Survey production was characterized by highly interde-pendent and sequential tasks, which is consistent with a monochronic time orientation. This dissonance of time orientations may have been a primary reason for the poor interrelationship between these two sub-cultures. Surveys/IT people often complained that they were the poor relation of the consultancy, and consultants for their part complained about the low responsiveness of the surveys/IT function to urgent client and internal issues.

A framework for strategic decision-making

Figure 6.2 is a typified framework of how strategic decision-makers can approach their task, and will be used to structure the discussion of the strategic change program at Hay Management Consultants.

Figure 6.2 A normative strategic decision-making process
Source: Heracleous and Langham (1996).

This process should be repeated continually, for two main reasons. First, strategy is dynamic (Markides 1999). Both market and internal conditions shift over time, so the premises for past, current, and future decisions need to be reconsidered. Secondly, when planning for strategic change, it is implausible to plan for every issue in a single session. The product of the necessarily intuitive, synthetic, and creative act of strategic thinking (Mintzberg 1994) needs to be given initial form by more pragmatic, operational considerations (Heracleous 1998).

The "cultural web" can be a very useful tool in all stages of this strategic decision process:

- *Situation analysis* The cultural web helps to portray and clarify several characteristics of the organization, giving a more robust and holistic understanding of the current internal situation.
- *Policy- and strategy-making* The cultural web foregrounds the beliefs and assumptions which have guided the interpretations, decisions, and actions of the policy- and strategy-making bodies. It can thus encourage the double-loop awareness and critical questioning of assumptions that are so vital in enabling creative views of the organization, its capabilities and its market.
- *Implications* Contrary to what has often been assumed, strategic change does not involve wholesale cultural and organizational change; some values may be vital to continued success, whereas some others need to be un-learned or amended. A valid cultural web can

help to show clearly which values, beliefs, assumptions, and artifacts need to change in accordance with the new strategic direction
and which ones should be maintained and strengthened. The cultural
web can also help change agents predict likely areas of resistance to
change by assessing the nature and salience of existing cultural beliefs and assumptions, and the interconnections between these and
cultural artifacts.

- *Change management* The cultural web portrays the key organizational elements which should be actively managed for a strategic
  change to be successful; for example communication, changes in control systems, incentives, and organizational structure.
- *Monitoring and evaluation* Constructing a cultural web periodically
  (say every six–nine months) and examining any changes in its elements can help the organization track its progress in changing internally to reach its strategic goals.

Where are we now?

The discussion of Hay's culture and organization helps to answer the
question "where are we now?" Based on qualitative data from interviews, observation, and focus groups (see the appendix for details of
the methodology), I constructed the cultural web in Figure 6.3 in the
early stages of the change process, as a representation of Hay's values,
beliefs, and artifacts. The cultural web was then used by senior management as a benchmark on which to articulate the desired strategic
change, as discussed below.

Where do we want to go?

Hay's UK operations had been more profitable relative to other countries in which it had been operating. In the early to mid-1990s, however, there had been a growing awareness among the senior group that
things needed to change. There were several signals that could not be
ignored. Environmental projections by independent research organizations showed that the HR consulting market was expected to grow
at an annual rate of around 12 percent. Internal data showed that
the field in which Hay had traditionally been a leader (job evaluation)
was decreasing in terms of overall returns, and other fields, such as

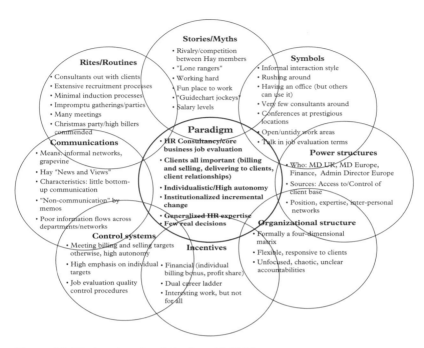

Figure 6.3 Hay's cultural web in the mid-1990s
Source: Heracleous and Langham (1996).

organization change or HR planning and development consulting were growing rapidly. Periodic client satisfaction surveys, indicated certain areas where improvements could be made.

The need for transformational change was based on the fact that because Hay had been operating at near full capacity, and with a robust projected market growth, the strategic options it had were either to remain at its existing size and lose market share to competitors with more spare capacity or who intended to grow, or set and pursue growth targets of about 15 percent compound per annum, which would lead to growth amounting to around doubling its size in five years.

In addition to substantial growth, Hay's strategic redirection included a more focused client relationship management process where consultants would focus their time and energy more effectively on clients within specified size brackets, as opposed to "owning" a portfolio of clients with varying sizes, needs, and demands developed in an unplanned manner. In addition, the strategic change aimed towards an increased breadth and depth of consultants' expertise, within an approach to expertise development and selling which would move away from simply providing tools and methodologies towards an orientation of providing solutions to client problems. This would consequently entail the integration of consulting methodologies in their provision to clients as a package.

This strategic change of aiming for significant growth, focused client relationship management, and increase in the breadth and depth of consultants' expertise, in turn posed the question "what are the implications of this change for our culture and organization?"

What implications does this have for our values, beliefs, structures, and processes?

One important issue that is often ignored is that a strategic change most often has major *cultural repercussions*. Taking Hay as an example, it has been determined that if the strategic change is to succeed, significant changes should take place in the cultural values and beliefs of the organization, as well as in its systems, processes and structure (the artifacts of the cultural web). In particular, it was decided by the change steering group that all beliefs and assumptions portrayed in the inner circle of the cultural web had to change except the belief that clients were all important:

- *Human resources consultancy, with core business job evaluation* Job evaluation had provided Hay with most of its revenues for decades. The perception that job evaluation was Hay's core business was still potent in the mid-1990s in both Hay's market as well as internally, although this specific activity accounted for less than a quarter of Hay's consulting revenues, and less than 60 percent of reward as a whole. If perceptions that "Hay is Pay" were to be broken, Hay needed to broaden its consultants' understanding of the integrated human resource offering, and to position job evaluation as just one of its main areas of expertise. The core business was to become, instead, "change through people."
- *Client focus* This is clearly of strategic importance to any organization as a driver and the *raison d'être* of organizational synergies,

capabilities, and competencies which can produce a sustainable competitive advantage. Hay's client-oriented vision for the future provided a common thread between its past and the desired future state. This common thread legitimized the vision and helped to ensure employees' commitment to achieving it.

- *Individualistic/high autonomy* Consulting in the job evaluation area had frequently been done by individual consultants, the "lone rangers" of Hay's mythology. They had high autonomy and were rarely in the office. If the organization was to grow significantly and offer its services to a demanding market, however, this individualistic climate had to change to one of teamwork and more co-ordinated resource allocation and consultant development, which had previously been based almost exclusively on the operation of an internal market.

- *Institutionalized incremental change* Hay had made sure that its early almost monopolistic power in the job evaluation area did not lead to a complacent approach to its development. Hay had institutionalized internal change on an annual basis, the "autumn maneuvers" of the organizational vocabulary. This, however, had an "anesthetizing" effect on the organization with regard to change and led to a difficulty in convincing employees that the planned strategic change was not simply an "autumn maneuver" but a transformational one. This belief had to change to one that the organization could indeed achieve transformational change.

- *Generalist expertise* The individualism of Hay and the perceived high emphasis of financial performance for consultants' appraisal led to their tendency to consult on a variety of areas within the HR field. If, however, Hay wished to offer deep integrated expertise to the market on a broad range of fields through teamwork of its consultants, then this had to change. The aim was to have experts on particular areas (with a broader understanding of other areas) as members of teams which as a whole could offer leading edge advice on a variety of fields.

- *Few "real" decisions* This belief had emerged from the employees' perceptions that although decisions were taken, Hay's values, beliefs, and assumptions did not change. The "autumn maneuvers" have been incremental changes, not having challenged any cultural values. The individualism and high autonomy of consultants also

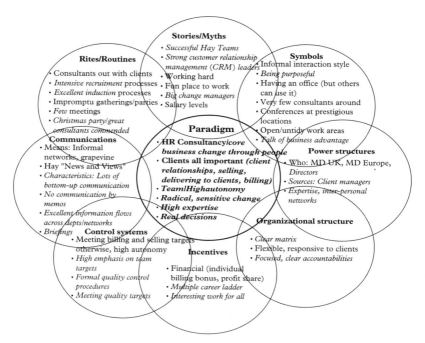

Figure 6.4 The cultural web aimed for
Source: Heracleous and Langham (1996).

meant that certain changes in systems had been "implemented" but not followed by them, again reinforcing the belief that there were no real decisions. This also had to change, with decisive leadership and decisions directly supported by control systems.

Figure 6.4 portrays the cultural web aimed for, with the desired changes in italics.

How should we manage the transition?

There are different ways to manage change, depending on the extent of potential change, the time and information available, and the power distribution in the organization (Kotter and Schlesinger 1979). In Hay, a participative approach was used, combined with extensive communication. It was shown long ago (Coch and French 1948; Lewin 1947) that involving people who will be affected by changes in the planning process decreases resistance to change because it builds ownership of the process through participation. At Hay there had been several internal projects under way which resulted in detailed suggestions for operational changes in processes and systems. Attention was being paid to integrating the various smaller-scale initiatives towards reaching the strategic aims.

In addition, there is an insatiable need for information at times of change. It is important to communicate a clear rationale for the change and identify the end state with outcomes which are important for stakeholders, as well as to build their confidence that the organization can reach this end state with the right efforts (Armenakis *et al.* 1993). Especially in the context of large-scale change, it is important to use richer, personal means of communication as often as possible and to seek employees' views and concerns. The rationale for change was clearly articulated in Hay, and it became clear to most employees why it had to undergo a transformational change although it did not face any crisis. What was also apparent was the importance of communication not only in informing, motivating, and co-ordinating, but also in managing employee expectations. Since changes were expected to occur over a long period and were likely to involve significant ambiguity at some points, then this was clearly communicated in advance in order to avoid potential loss of momentum, disappointment, and cynicism. Lastly, it was important that if communication was going to be more effective in motivating employees, it should address their actual concerns. In this context, I conducted individual and group interviews and surveys to gauge employees' concerns and attitudes towards the change process over time, and gave relevant feedback to senior management.

In addition, in strategic change, there should be visible, active, and credible leadership of the process. Leaders' actions are highly symbolic (Johnson 1990) and they should show by their own actions what is going to be valued in the organization. At Hay, senior management had consciously taken some visible steps towards demonstrating its commitment to carrying the change through, such as frequent and clear communication, in both written form as well as organization-wide meetings. It also encouraged senior consultants to role model the new behaviors that the organization wanted to institutionalize.

Proper investment should be made for the development of any new skills which will be required by the changed organization, especially if the change involves new technology and new roles. At Hay one of the most important new roles was that of the regional "team managers" who would have greater responsibility for work allocation, consultant development, and coaching. The skills needed to fulfill these roles were identified and training programs planned.

How will we know how we are doing?

Any change needs to be actively managed throughout its duration and monitored through both "soft" and "hard" data. Ideally there should be periodic feedback from individuals elicited in a non-threatening but in-depth way. Assessing changes in the elements of the cultural web (as well as in their relative strength) is one important internal indication of the progress of the organization in reaching its strategic goals. At Hay, the cultural web framework was used periodically to assess the shifts towards the desired end state.

This chapter has examined the nature of organizational culture and its effects, and specifically the close interrelationship between organizational culture and strategic change. Hay's case has illustrated how a new strategic direction involving market repositioning and substantial growth also involved significant cultural and organizational changes. It was suggested that an organization should not aim for wholesale cultural change, however, but should rather recognize what needs to change and what needs to be nurtured. In this context, the cultural web can be a very useful framework for understanding the cultural and organizational situation of the firm, and identifying relevant changes. A typified framework for strategic decision-making was also presented, as a useful general tool for managing the change process, and some important issues of change management arising at each stage were discussed. The case analysis has also exemplified the significance of the organizational paradigm in providing a context for strategic decisions and actions.

Appendix: research methodology

In early 1994 I set out to study the role of organizational culture in the context of organizational change. I collected the empirical data reported here between June 1994 and March 1996. I also conducted retrospective data gathering that focused on the organization's history and critical incidents, going back to the organization's founding in the UK in 1963. In mid-1999 I collected further interview data to gauge the extent to which Hay's organizational culture was shifting towards the desired direction.

The philosophical commitments guiding the research program centered on interpretivism, the conviction that accounts of social life must consider the actors' frame of reference and be adequate at this level of first-order meaning (Weber 1978). "Reality," in this view, is not seen as a hard and objective entity to be broken down and measured through positivist methods, but as an inter-subjective and socially constructed reality to be explored and interpreted inductively (Berger and Luckmann 1966; Schein 1996). I thus aimed to observe and make sense of agents' actions in their real-life context so as to gradually gain "access to the conceptual world in which our subjects live so that we can, in some extended sense of the term, converse with them" (Geertz 1973: 24). This viewpoint presupposes knowledgeable agents whose actions are not structurally determined and who could always choose to act otherwise (Giddens 1979).

I employed the methodological paradigm of ethnography with an action research or "clinical" element. My role approximated to what Schein (1987) calls "the ethnographer as clinician." I partly acted as a clinician because I was allowed access to the organization on the assumption that my involvement would "add value" to the organization change program under way. Gradually I was expected to take initiative and be self-sufficient in terms of gaining access to employees and building my own networks in the organization as sources of data. I was soon asked to provide not only data describing what I found, but also recommendations for action based on the data.

The commitment to understanding the "natives'" frames of meaning (Geertz 1973) means that qualitative methodologies have to be employed. I employed the research strategy of a longitudinal case study (Eisenhardt 1989). Within this strategy, I used the methods of in-depth interviewing, participant and non-participant observation, cultural audits through focus group sessions, informants, periodic descriptive surveys, and document analysis. I conducted a total of 104 interviews involving consultants, surveys and IT staff, support staff, and past leaders of the organization. I triangulated the data within and across methods, in order to increase the internal validity of the findings and to discover within- or between-method divergences or convergences that could lead to new lines of inquiry (Jick 1979). After I discerned the main cultural values and beliefs of the organization, my findings were circulated to all employees, who widely judged them to be representative of their organization. This process is an important validating criterion for ethnographic research (Hammersley and Atkinson 1995).

My initial analytical task was to detect patterns and processes which could help to "make sense of what is going on in the scenes documented by the data" (Hammersley and Atkinson 1995: 209–210). I was conscious throughout the research program, in this regard, that "what we call our data are really our own constructions of other people's constructions of what they and their compatriots are up to" (Geertz 1973: 9). This, in effect, is what Giddens (1993) calls the "double hermeneutic" in social science, and Van Maanen (1979) "first and second-order concepts" in ethnography. Within this process I continually sought to differentiate between "presentational" and "operational" data (Van Maanen 1979) and to reflect on what these data revealed about the agents involved and the research setting.

I did not take individual fragments of data as indicative of cultural features, but interpreted them as part of a wider corpus of data. The data analysis was characterized by a hermeneutic, iterative process of going back and forth from critical reflection to the data, and from part to whole, searching for key themes and patterns, and questioning, redefining, or buttressing the key themes and patterns identified with further evidence (Kets de Vries and Miller 1987; Thachenkery 1992).

Bibliography

Allaire, Y. and Firsirotu, M. E., 1984. Theories of organizational culture, *Organization Studies*, 5: 193–226

Armenakis, A. A., Harris, S. G. and Mossholder, K. W., 1993. Creating readiness for organizational change, *Human Relations*, 46: 681–703

Barney, J. B., 1986. Organizational culture: can it be a source of sustained competitive advantage?, *Academy of Management Review*, 11: 656–665

Berger, P. and Luckmann, T., 1966. *The Social Construction of Reality*, London: Penguin

Chatman, J. A. and Jehn, K. A., 1994. Assessing the relationship between industry characteristics and organizational culture: how different can you be?, *Academy of Management Journal*, 37: 522–553

Coch, L. and French, R., 1948. Overcoming resistance to change, *Human Relations*, 46(6): 681–703

Daft, R. L. and Weick, K. E., 1984. Toward a model of organizations as interpretation systems, *Academy of Management Review*, 9: 284–295

Dandridge, T. C., Mitroff, I. and Joyce, W. F., 1980. Organizational symbolism: a topic to expand organizational analysis, *Academy of Management Review*, 5: 77–82

Deal, T. and Kennedy, A., 1982. *Corporate Cultures: The Rites and Rituals of Corporate Life*, Reading, MA: Addison-Wesley

Eisenhardt, K. M., 1989. Building theories from case study research, *Academy of Management Review*, 14: 532–550

Evered, R., 1983. The language of organizations: the case of the navy, in L. R. Pondy, P. J. Frost, G. Morgan and T. C. Dandridge (eds.), *Organizational Symbolism*, Greenwich, CT: JAI Press: 125–143

Geertz, C., 1973. *The Interpretation of Cultures*, New York: Basic Books

Giddens, A., 1979. *Central Problems in Social Theory*, London: Macmillan 1993. *New Rules of Sociological Method* (2nd edn.), Stanford, CA: Stanford University Press

Ginter, P. M., Rucks, A. C. and Duncan, W. J., 1985. Planners' perceptions of the strategic management process, *Journal of Management Studies*, 22(6): 581–596

Golden, K., 1992. The individual and organizational culture: strategies for action in highly-ordered contexts, *Journal of Management Studies*, 29: 1–21

Gordon, G. G., 1991. Industry determinants of organizational culture, *Academy of Management Review*, 16: 396–415

Hammersley, M. and Atkinson, P., 1995. *Ethnography: Principles in practice* (2nd edn.), London: Routledge

Harrison, R., 1972. Understanding your organization's culture, *Harvard Business Review*, May–June: 119–128

Hay Management Consultants, 1993. *The Edge*, May 2–7: Entering a sixth decade of high quality consulting, Philadelphia: Hay Management Consultants

Heracleous, L., 1998. Strategic thinking or strategic planning?, *Long Range Planning*, 31: 481–487
2001. An ethnographic study of culture in the context of organizational change, *Journal of Applied Behavioral Science*, 37: 426–446

Heracleous, L. and Langham, B., 1996. Strategic change and organizational culture at Hay Management Consultants, *Long Range Planning*, 29: 485–494

Jick, T., 1979. Mixing qualitative and quantitative methods: triangulation in action, *Administrative Science Quarterly*, 24: 602–611

Johnson, G., 1987. *Strategic Change and the Management Process*, Oxford: Blackwell
1988. Rethinking incrementalism, *Strategic Management Journal*, 9: 75–91

1990. Managing strategic change: the role of symbolic action, *British Journal of Management*, 1: 183–200

Kets De Vries, M. F. R. and Miller, D., 1987. Interpreting organizational texts, *Journal of Management Studies*, 24: 233–247

Kotter, J. P. and Schlesinger, L. A., 1979. Choosing strategies for change, *Harvard Business Review*, March–April: 106–114

Lewin, K., 1947. Frontiers in group dynamics I, *Human Relations*, 1: 5–41

Litterer, J. A. and Young, S., 1984. Organizational paradigm as a tool to analyze organizations and their problems, *Academy of Management Proceedings*: 249–253

Louis, M. R., 1983. Organizations as culture-bearing milieux, in L. R. Pondy, P. J. Frost, G. Morgan and T. C. Dandridge (eds.), *Organizational Symbolism*, Greenwich, CT: JAI Press: 39–54

Lucas, R., 1987. Political–cultural analysis of organizations, *Academy of Management Review*, 12: 144–156

Markides, C., 1999. A dynamic view of strategy, *Sloan Management Review*, Spring: 55–58

Meek, V. L., 1988. Organizational culture: origins and weaknesses, *Organization Studies*, 9: 453–473

Mintzberg, H., 1994. The fall and rise of strategic planning, *Harvard Business Review*, January–February: 107–114

O'Reilly, C. A., Chatman, J. and Caldwell, D. F., 1991. People and organizational culture: a profile comparison approach to assessing person–organization fit, *Academy of Management Journal*, 34: 487–516

Peters, T. J. and Waterman, R. H., Jr., 1982. *In Search of Excellence: Lessons from America's Best-Run Companies*, New York: Harper & Row

Pettigrew, A. M., 1985. *The Awakening Giant: Continuity and Change in ICI*, Oxford: Blackwell

Pondy, L. R. and Mitroff, I. I., 1979. Beyond open systems models of organization, *Research in Organizational Behavior*, 1: 3–39

Quinn, J. B., 1978. Logical incrementalism, *Sloan Management Review*, 1(20): 7–21

Ray, C. A., 1986. Corporate culture: the last frontier of control?, *Journal of Management Studies*, 23: 287–297

Sanday, P. R., 1979. The ethnographic paradigm(s), *Administrative Science Quarterly*, 24: 527–538

Sanders, P., 1982. Phenomenology: a new way of viewing organizational research, *Academy of Management Review*, 7: 353–360

Schein, E., 1983. The role of the founder in creating organizational culture, *Organizational Dynamics*, Summer: 13–28

1987. *Process Consultation: Lessons for Managers and Consultants*, II, Reading, MA: Addison-Wesley

1992. *Organizational Culture and Leadership* (2nd edn.), San Francisco: Jossey-Bass

1996. Culture: the missing concept in organization studies, *Administrative Science Quarterly*, 41: 229–240

Sheridan, J. E., 1992. Organizational culture and employee retention, *Academy of Management Journal*, 35: 1036–1056

Silverman, D., 1970. *The Theory of Organizations*, London: Heinemann

Smircich, L., 1983a. Concepts of culture and organizational analysis, *Administrative Science Quarterly*, 28: 339–359

1983b. Organizations as shared meanings, in L. R. Pondy, P. J. Frost, G. Morgan and T. C. Dandridge (eds.), *Organizational Symbolism*, Greenwich, CT: JAI Press: 55–65

Taylor, F. W., 1947. *Scientific Management*, London: Harper

Thachenkery, T., 1992. Organizations as "texts": hermeneutics as a model for understanding organizational change, *Research in Organization Change and Development*, 6: 197–233

Thomas, W. I. and Thomas, D. S., 1970. Situations defined as real are real in their consequences, in G. P. Stone and H. A. Faberman (eds.), *Social Psychology through Symbolic Interaction*, Toronto: Xerox College Publishing: 154–156

Turner, B., 1986. Sociological aspects of organizational symbolism, *Organization Studies*, 7: 101–115

Van Maanen, J., 1979. The fact of fiction in organizational ethnography, *Administrative Science Quarterly*, 24: 539–550

Weber, M., 1978. The nature of social action, in W. G. Runciman (ed.), *Weber: Selections in Translation* (E. Matthews, transl.), Cambridge: Cambridge University Press: 7–32

Weick, K., 1977. Enactment processes in organizations, in B. M. Staw and G. R. Salancik (eds.), *New Directions in Organizational Behavior*, Chicago: St. Clair Press: 267–300

Wilkins, A. and Ouchi, W., 1983. Efficient cultures: exploring the relationship between culture and organizational performance, *Administrative Science Quarterly*, 28: 468–481

Willmott, H., 1993. Strength is ignorance; slavery is freedom: managing culture in modern organizations, *Journal of Management Studies*, 30: 515–552

7 | *The role of organizational discourse in understanding and managing strategic change*

Continuing chapter 6's focus on the ideational aspects of the organization and a change perspective, this chapter emphasizes that effective change management is not just about the "hard" structural aspects of organizations; it requires an in-depth appreciation of the cultural, human aspects of organizations, and taking actions based on this understanding. The chapter suggests that organizational discourse can provide access to this conceptual world of organizations and can also be used as an avenue for influencing it. Use of metaphor by change agents is discussed as a prime example of how discourse can help to achieve effective organizational change.

How can change be effectively managed?

Organizations are characterized by both stability and change. While forces such as inertia, uncertainty reduction, minimization of transaction costs, and the nurturing of social capital foster stability, other forces such as the need to adapt to the environment, to control costs, to gain or sustain competitive advantage, and to satisfy impatient capital markets demand continuous change (Leana and Barry 2000).

Even though some organizations are adept at managing change, sustained competitive success for most is fleeting. A study by McKinsey Consultants, for example, found that over a ten-year period, only three out of 208 firms managed to sustain their superior profitability and rate of growth (Ghemawat 2000: 20). This difficulty in sustaining a firm's competitive advantage over the longer term has been termed the "Red Queen" effect, after Lewis Carroll's story of *Alice's Adventures in Wonderland*, where the Red Queen said to Alice "here, you see, it takes all the running you can do, to keep in the same place. If you want to get somewhere else, you must run at least twice as fast."

This chapter is based on Heracleous (2002a).

There is an immense amount of practitioner-oriented literature on how effectively to manage change (e.g. Champy and Nohria 1996; Kotter 1996). Common prescriptions for effectively managing change include encouraging participation from as many employees as possible, addressing their concerns in the change program, tapping the energy and commitment of change champions, demonstrating the commitment of senior management by allocating time and resources to change programs, or ensuring that leaders act as role models for the changes. Even with ample advice, however, the vast majority of change-related programs fail to meet their objectives (Nohria 1993). Many, such as downsizing or re-engineering, can lead to undesirable long-term consequences such as a weakening of the organization's knowledge base and low employee morale (Eliezer 1996; Mabert and Schmenner 1997).

Why is there such a high rate of failure? One important reason is that the "soft" cultural and social aspects of organizations often receive insufficient attention in organization change programs (Heracleous 2001; Pascale *et al.* 1997). Change-management approaches oriented to "hard" understandings of organizations, such as "business process re-engineering," are unlikely to be able to identify relevant cultural, political, and social issues, understand their impact on proposed changes, or manage them accordingly. Organizational discourse is a useful way both to understand the conceptual world of organizations, as well as to influence this world in the context of organizational change programs.

The need to gain a deeper understanding of change processes

There is often an assumed dichotomy between "understanding," associated with the interpretive paradigm, and "managing," associated with the functionalist paradigm. Even though the theoretical constructs and motivations of researchers in these paradigms may indeed be different (Heracleous and Barrett 2001), effective *management* of change also requires deep *understanding* of the subtle issues involved. In order to be able to improve the effectiveness of change management, therefore, we need a more refined understanding of not only the content of change but also its context and process (Pettigrew 1987).

The organization change literature contains analytical distinctions such as anticipatory/reactive change, or incremental/organizational change (Nadler and Tushman 1989), and describes several change management styles that can potentially be adopted based on contingency considerations (Kotter and Schlesinger 1979). Such understandings, however, may need to be complemented by rich data deriving from in-depth, longitudinal methodologies, that can adequately shed light on some of the complex issues involved in organizational change (Johnson 1987; Pettigrew 1987).

Tan and Heracleous (2001), for example, explored the implementation of organizational learning in an Asian National Police Force in the context of a longitudinal action research program. The aim was to acquire an interpretive, in-depth understanding of the related processes of transformational change, and the barriers to change, in a machine bureaucracy with entrenched structure and culture not ordinarily conducive to learning and adaptation; and, secondly, to explore the applicability of universalist change management prescriptions in this context.

This research found several structural and cultural barriers to transformational change. The structural barriers included inter-unit rivalry and turf battles, and consequently lower inter-unit co-ordination and co-operation, a rigid hierarchical organizational structure, and poor information flows inhibited by rivalry and secrecy. The cultural barriers included little participative decision-making, vision directed from the top and not collectively owned, discipline motivated more by fear rather than by respect, a sanctioning rather than a learning attitude to mistakes, and unproductive internal status distinctions enshrined in the culture, that favored plain clothes officers more than uniformed ones. These structural and cultural barriers were in the medium term successfully contested through a consciously designed bottom-up participative change process, the existence of change champions, tangible experiences that challenged the prevailing culture, and change actions that were congruent with the organization's broader, political authorizing environment.

The usefulness of change management approaches such as interpretively oriented action research are that they help to uncover such barriers, in co-operation with the organization that is attempting to change. In the case of this National Police Force, unless such barriers were clearly identified, and raised to conscious awareness by candid discussion, then they could not be productively addressed. This process requires not only having appropriate expertise as a change agent or change facilitator, but also the courage and determination on behalf of the senior levels of the organization to go ahead with what often becomes a long and uncomfortable process. Traditional "hard" change management approaches, or universalist change management approaches more broadly, may not be able to detect subtle cultural values and their behavioral consequences, and may therefore be unproductive in achieving effective organizational change.

Diagnosing and dealing with organizational culture is one of the key factors for achieving effective organizational change (Heracleous and Langham 1996; Pascale *et al.* 1997). In this context, Heracleous (2001) employed an ethnographic research approach, combined with a clinical element, to explore the nature and role of culture in the context of organizational change at the UK operations of a global HR consulting firm, Hay Management Consultants. Using Schein's (1992) levels of culture model, the author identified cultural assumptions and values, and explored how these related to employee behaviors, using his ethnographic/clinical relationship with the organization as a rich data source.

This study illustrated how an organizational culture develops historically, is internally coherent, and has potent effects on behaviors that should be studied and understood by managers and clinicians undertaking organizational change programs. For example, in Hay Management Consultants, there were deep cultural assumptions relating to the organization's relationship to its environment, the nature of reality and truth, the nature of human nature, the nature of human activity, and the nature of time. These assumptions were deeply ingrained in the culture, and were continually manifested in specific classes of behaviors. Understanding such cultural assumptions helps change agents assess the extent to which organization change is compatible with them, the expected levels of cultural resistance, and to identify cultural and behavioral areas where they should focus their efforts so that they can effectively manage change.

These studies illustrate the need for gaining in-depth, grounded understanding of the social and cultural issues involved in organizational change, and that gaining such an understanding is an important part of effective change management. Change management approaches that downplay such "soft" aspects of organizations are unlikely to be able to identify them, or understand their impact on agents' thought and action.

What is discourse anyway?

At a broad level, "discourses" are collections of communicative actions, both verbal and textual, that are patterned and underlain by certain structural features, and that are constructive of social and organizational reality (Heracleous and Barrett 2001). These discourses create, embody, and sustain conditioned local rationalities (Gergen and Thatchenkery 1996), as opposed to universal rationalities that would apply to closed systems such as mathematics or geometry. In other words, discourses are intimately and causally related to ways of thinking and acting of members of particular social systems or cultures (Sherzer 1987).

The interrelation between discourse, thought, and action of organizational actors is a dynamic one. As Barrett *et al.* (1995) have put it, "it is through patterns of discourse that relational bonds are formed; that action and structure are created, transformed, and maintained; and that values and beliefs are reinforced or challenged. The process is recursive: Interpretive repertoires are extended to include various practices. At the same time, these practices augment and alter the interpretive code" (1995: 367). This interpretive perspective emphasizes that meaning is constructed, sustained, and potentially challenged through discursive social interaction, and that discourse is not merely informational, but constructive of social and organizational reality (Heracleous 2002b).

In the same way that different genres of movies can be identified (i.e. drama, action, comedy), discourses can be described as groups of texts that share certain common features. They can operate at the transnational level (for example, the discourses of pro-globalization as well as anti-globalization); at the national level (for example, discourses of race and gender equality, immigration policy, or national security in different countries); at the industry level (for example, discourses embodying the "industry recipes," to use Spender's 1989 term, the conventional wisdom of how business should be conducted in particular industries); or at the organizational level, where researchers employ in-depth qualitative methodologies to identify specific discourses within particular social and organizational contexts (e.g. Heracleous 2002c; Heracleous and Barrett 2001).

There are different streams of discourse research, which employ different views of discourse and its relation to organizational change. The *functional* approach views discourse as language-based communication, used instrumentally by social actors to achieve their ends. It employs teleology as a dominant theory of change, where the key metaphor is purposeful co-operation and the orientation is prescriptive.

The *interpretive* approach views discourse as communicative action, which is constructive of social and organizational reality; it has no strong connections with an ideal-type theory of change, and has a descriptive orientation. The *critical* approach views discourse as power/knowledge relations that are embedded in social practice; it has a revolutionary orientation and is linked to a dialectic theory of change, where the key metaphor is opposition or conflict. The *structurational* approach, lastly, views discourse as a duality of deep discursive structures and surface communicative actions. It aims to bridge dualisms of structure and action in social analysis and suggest that understanding of social change should focus, *inter alia*, on structural principles as manifested in discrete episodes; it has a descriptive orientation (Heracleous and Barrett 2001: 756).

How can discourse contribute to effective organizational change?

How is discourse related to organizational change? If we accept Pondy and Mitroff's (1979) suggestions that we should view the nature of organizations as going beyond the orthodoxy of open systems theory, as composed of "self-conscious language users" who possess "a sense of social order, a shared culture, a history and a future, a value system" (1979: 9), then it becomes apparent that any significant organizational change will affect and be affected by these "softer" aspects of organizations. Therefore, change agents need both to understand and shape these "softer" aspects towards the desired directions. Organizational discourses (with their own vocabularies, root metaphors, or rhetorical strategies) are the mirror of the conceptual world of the organization, as well as a central avenue by which it can be influenced.

There is a significant amount of research on how change agents can use communication[1] to achieve more effective organizational change. Armenakis *et al.* (1993), for example, have argued that the change message is the primary means of creating readiness for change in an

---

[1] Communicative actions are the building blocks of discourse. They occur at specific points in time, are functional, situational, and explicit. Discourses are constituted of collections of communicative actions; they are longitudinal, constructive, transcend situations, and their features are implicit (Heracleous and Hendry 2000).

organization. Lengel and Daft (1988) stressed the importance of employing rich media (e.g. face-to-face communication) by change agents if the issue addressed is non-routine and complex, such as organization change. Chesley and Wenger (1999) suggested that strategic conversations can foster organizational transformation by helping organizational members foreground their assumptions through dialogue, create shared understandings, and learn how to learn.

Conger (1991) argued that great leaders will not only need to be effective strategists, but also rhetoricians who can inspire, persuade, and energize their audience. They must be able to articulate and communicate a compelling organizational mission, explain convincingly its rationale, sketch an image of the "enemy" that compels people to expend discretionary effort, and build up the organization's confidence so that it can succeed in spite of all the obstacles. The use of stories, analogies, and metaphors is a key feature of effective rhetorical discourse.

Research by Heracleous and Barrett (2001) illustrates the unique capability of organizational discourse to contribute to in-depth understanding of organizational change, and to help in its effective management. This research explored the role of discourse in shaping organizational change processes through its influence on actors' interpretations and actions, using a longitudinal field study of electronic trading implementation in the London Insurance Market. Through a focus on both discourse and its context the researchers were able to make sense of the multiple perspectives of different stakeholder groups and their interrelations. They were able to explore actors' own arguments, interpretations, and actions with regard to the proposed implementation of electronic trading in order to gain an in-depth hermeneutic understanding of change processes. These interpretations and actions shaped the trajectory and ultimate failure of the process of electronic trading implementation.

This study sought to address the research challenge of exploring multiple discourses, their interrelations, and their impact on practice (Boje 1995; Grant *et al.* 1998). It found that the discourses of each stakeholder group were pervaded and patterned by relatively stable deep structures which functioned as organizing mechanisms that guided myriads of surface communicative actions which might otherwise appear unconnected and disparate. There were discursive clashes among stakeholder groups over contested terrain, illustrating both conflict and discursive interpenetration and influence among their discourses. There was fragile agreement and co-operation at the surface communicative level, which was based on potentially conflicting deep structures that could assert themselves in different ways under different contextual conditions. There was discursive fragmentation, leading to conflicting actions, even within the same stakeholder group sharing the same deep structures, arising because one actor could deem that their key goals could better be served by actions that were in conflict with the actions of their own stakeholder group. Lastly, stakeholder groups talked past each other, rather than to each other, because of their almost diametrically opposed discourses, at both the deep structure levels and communicative action levels, with little common ground on which to base a dialogue.

Discourse in this perspective is far from "just talk." It is central to individuals' interpretation and action, and it can help change agents both to understand the intricacies of the organizational setting as well as manage the change process. Discourse itself becomes action that can either aid or hinder change processes, and paying insufficient attention to organizational discourse also means forgoing the richness that this lens can provide.

How can metaphor foster effective organizational change?

There has been a significant amount of research in organization theory on the role of metaphors in facilitating organizational change. Metaphors can offer new ways of looking at existing situations (Heracleous 2003; Lakoff 1990; Morgan 1980, 1983), while simultaneously acting as a bridge from a familiar to a new state (Pondy 1983). The high latitude of interpretation afforded by metaphorical statements can help to accommodate the interpretations of organizational groups perceiving their interests to be mutually incompatible (Crider and Cirillo 1991), and unstructured situations can be made more concrete and comprehensible through the use of metaphor (Sackmann 1989). Researchers have shown that the metaphors used by organizational actors are empirically related to such areas as the extent and speed of organizational change (Oswick and Montgomery 1999) or to aspects of organizational and national culture (Gibson and Zellmer-Bruhn 2001). Change agents can employ an organization's prevalent metaphors as a diagnostic tool that reflects actors' ways of thinking about their organization and the need for change, as well as a facilitating mechanism for change by introducing metaphors that can align organizational participants' interpretations and actions towards a desired direction (Marshak 1993).

Constructionist views of metaphor suggest that metaphor shapes agents' thoughts by projecting "associated implications" of a secondary subject on a primary subject. Agents creatively select, emphasize, suppress, and organize features of the primary subject by applying to it statements isomorphic with the secondary subject's implicative complex (Lakoff and Johnson 1980). If a change program is portrayed as a journey, for example, actors can see it as a long-term effort which has a desired destination and which will involve interesting learning experiences along the way. If a competitor's actions are interpreted as "war," then employees may perceive the situation as one that demands immediate, co-ordinated response and full commitment to staving off the threat.[2]

Metaphors have been typologized according to their potential for affording creative insights. Schön (1979), for example, distinguished generative metaphors from non-generative ones by the former's ability to generate new perceptions, explanations, and inventions (1979: 259) and Black (1979) distinguished strong from weak metaphors by the former's possessing a high degree of "implicative elaboration" (1979: 27). Metaphors' creative potential is derived from sufficient differences between the source and target domains for a creative tension to exist (Morgan 1983). As Aristotle has put it, "metaphors should be transferred from things that are related but not obviously so" (Aristotle 1991: 3: 11: 5). Metaphors and stories are more memorable and impactful than literal language because they appeal simultaneously "to the emotions, to the intellect, to imagination, and to values" (Conger 1991: 39). In terms of research on persuasive communication, organizational actors are more likely to both understand the message, take it

---

[2] Constructionist views of metaphor are aligned to the interpretive stream of discourse research in their assumptions about the potency of metaphor to redefine social reality. Metaphors *per se* are paradigm neutral, however, transcending individual discourse streams. Metaphors, for example, can be functionally utilized in organization change programs, they can be employed as tools of critical analysis, or their deep features can be identified and analyzed in research programs following the structurational paradigm.

as having personal relevance, and spend more time thinking about it (Petty and Cacioppo 1986).

Metaphors can move agents to action because of their evaluative loading which points implicitly towards what "ought" to be done under situations framed metaphorically, the "normative leap" resulting from metaphors' naming and framing processes (Schön 1979: 264–265). As Hirsch and Andrews (1983) have noted in the context of their analysis of the language of corporate takeovers, "once the roles and relations are assigned, proper procedures and/or proper outcomes can be readily deduced. Sleeping Beauty must be liberated and wed; the shark must be annihilated; the black-hat brought to justice; the honorable soldier must fight doggedly, and so on" (1983: 149).

Metaphors can thus facilitate organizational change by creatively re-defining reality for organizational actors and enabling them to see familiar situations or actions in a new light; metaphors can help to mediate political conflict by providing mutually acceptable visions of the future; they can make otherwise abstract organizational futures appear more clear and desirable; and they can spur agents to action through their evaluative loading, and their memorable images.

Conclusion

This chapter has highlighted that effective change management is not just about the "hard" structural aspects of organizations; it requires, rather, an in-depth appreciation of the cultural, human aspects of organizations, and taking actions based on this understanding. Organizational discourse was discussed as a useful way to gain access to the conceptual world of organizations and also as a central avenue that can be used by change agents for influencing it. This suggestion was based on an interpretive perspective which emphasizes that meaning is constructed, sustained, and potentially challenged through discursive social interaction, and that discourse is not merely informational but constructive of social and organizational reality. Recent examples of empirical research were drawn on to clarify the importance of understanding the "soft" aspects of organizations in the context of organizational change, and the role that discourse can play in this process. Lastly, the use of metaphor by change agents was discussed as a prime example of how discourse can help to achieve effective organizational change.

Bibliography

Aristotle, 1991. *On Rhetoric* (Kennedy, G. A., Transl.), New York: Oxford University Press

Armenakis, A. A., Harris, S. G. and Mossholder, K. W., 1993. Creating readiness for organizational change, *Human Relations*, 46: 681–703

Barrett, F. J., Thomas, G. G. and Hocevar, S. P. 1995. The central role of discourse in large-scale change: a social construction perspective, *Journal of Applied Behavioral Science*, 31: 352–372

Black, M., 1979. More about metaphor, in A. Ortony (ed.), *Metaphor and thought*, Cambridge: Cambridge University Press: 19–43

Boje, D. M., 1995. Stories of the storytelling organization: a postmodern analysis of Disney as "Tamara-Land," *Academy of Management Journal*, 38: 997–1035

Champy, J. and Nohria, N., 1996. *Fast Forward: The Best Ideas on Managing Business Change*, Boston, MA: Harvard Business School Press

Chesley, J. A. and Wenger, M. S., 1999. Transforming an organization: using models to foster a strategic conversation, *California Management Review*, 41(3): 54–73

Conger, J. A., 1991. Inspiring others: the language of leadership, *Academy of Management Executive*, 5(1): 31–45

Crider, C. and Cirillo, L., 1991. Systems of interpretation and the function of metaphor, *Journal for the Theory of Social Behavior*, 21: 171–195

Eliezer, G., 1996. Cleaning up after reengineering, *Business Horizons*, 39(5): 71–78

Gergen, K. J. and Thatchenkery, T. J., 1996. Organization science as social construction: postmodern potentials, *Journal of Applied Behavioral Science*, 32: 356–377

Ghemawat, P., 2000. Competition and business strategy in historical perspective, *Harvard Business School Teaching Note*, 9-798-010

Gibson, C. B. and Zellmer-Bruhn, M. E., 2001. Metaphors and meaning: an intercultural analysis of the concept of teamwork, *Administrative Science Quarterly*, 46: 274–303

Grant, D., Keenoy, T. and Oswick, C., 1998. Organizational discourse: of diversity, dichotomy and multi-disciplinarity, in D. Grant, T. Keenoy and C. Oswick, *Discourse and Organization*, London: Sage: 1–13

Heracleous, L., 2001. An ethnographic study of culture in the context of organizational change, *Journal of Applied Behavioral Science*, 37: 426–446

2002a. The contribution of discourse in understanding and managing organizational change, *Strategic Change*, 11: 253–261

2002b. Four propositions toward a theory of the process of discursive reality construction, *Working Paper*, Faculty of Business Administration, National University of Singapore

2002c. A tale of three discourses: the dominant, the strategic and the marginalized, *Working Paper*, Faculty of Business Administration, National University of Singapore

2003. A comment on the role of metaphor in knowledge generation, *Academy of Management Review*, 28: 190–191

Heracleous, L. and Barrett, M., 2001. Organizational change as discourse: communicative actions and deep structures in the context of IT implementation, *Academy of Management Journal*, 44: 755–778

Heracleous, L. and Hendry, J., 2000. Discourse and the study of organization: toward a structurational perspective, *Human Relations*, 53: 1251–1286

Heracleous, L. and Langham, B., 1996. Strategic change and organizational culture at Hay Management Consultants, *Long Range Planning*, 29: 485–494

Hirsch, P. M. and Andrews, J. A., 1983. Ambushes, shootouts and knights of the roundtable: the language of corporate takeovers, in L. R. Pondy, P. J. Frost, G. Morgan and T. C. Dandridge (eds.), *Organizational Symbolism*, Greenwich, CT: JAI Press: 145–155

Johnson, G., 1987. *Organizational Change and the Management Process*, Oxford: Blackwell

Kotter, J. P., 1996. *Leading Change*, Boston, MA: Harvard Business School Press

Kotter, J. P. and Schlesinger, L. A., 1979. Choosing strategies for change, *Harvard Business Review*, March–April: 4–11

Lakoff, G., 1990. The invariance hypothesis: is abstract reason based on image-schemas?, *Cognitive Linguistics*, 1: 39–74

Lakoff, G. and Johnson, M., 1980. *Metaphors we Live By*, Chicago: Chicago University Press

Leana, C. R. and Barry, B., 2000. Stability and change as simultaneous experiences in organizational life, *Academy of Management Review*, 25: 753–759

Lengel, R. H. and Daft, R. L., 1988. The selection of communication media as an executive skill, *Academy of Management Executive*, 2: 225–232

Mabert, V. A. and Schmenner, R. W., 1997. Assessing the roller coaster of downsizing, *Business Horizons*, 40(4): 45–53

Marshak, R. J., 1993. Managing the metaphors of change, *Organizational Dynamics*, 22(1): 44–56

Morgan, G., 1980. Paradigms, metaphors and puzzle solving in organization theory, *Administrative Science Quarterly*, 25: 660–671

1983. More on metaphor: why we cannot control tropes in administrative science, *Administrative Science Quarterly*, 28: 601–607

Nadler, D. A. and Tushman, M. L., 1989. Organizational frame bending: principles for managing reorientation, *Academy of Management Executive*, 3(3): 194–204

Nohria, N., 1993. Managing change: course overview, *Harvard Business School Teaching Note*, 9-494-042

Oswick, C. and Montgomery, J., 1999. Images of an organization: the use of metaphor in a multinational company, *Journal of Organizational Change Management*, 12: 501–523

Pascale, R., Milleman, M. and Gioja, L., 1997. Changing the way we change, *Harvard Business Review*, November–December, 127–139

Pettigrew, A., 1987. Context and action in the transformation of the firm, *Journal of Management Studies*, 24: 649–670

Petty, R. E. and Cacioppo, J. T., 1986. The elaboration likelihood model of persuasion, in L. Berkowitz (ed.), *Advances in Experimental Social Psychology*, *19*, Orlando, FL: Academic Press: 123–205

Pondy, L. R., 1983. The role of metaphors and myths in organization and the facilitation of change, in L. R. Pondy, P. J. Frost, G. Morgan and T. C. Dandridge (eds.), *Organizational Symbolism*, Greenwich, CT: JAI Press: 157–166

Pondy, L. R. and Mitroff, I. I., 1979. Beyond open systems of organization, *Research in Organizational Behavior*, 1: 3–39

Sackmann, S., 1989. The role of metaphors in organizational transformation, *Human Relations*, 42: 463–485

Schein, E., 1992. *Organizational Culture and Leadership* (2nd edn.), San Francisco: Jossey-Bass

Schön, D. A., 1979. Generative metaphor: a perspective on problem-setting in social policy, in A. Ortony (ed.), *Metaphor and Thought*, Cambridge: Cambridge University Press: 254–283

Sherzer, J., 1987. A discourse-centered approach to language and culture, *American Anthropologist*, 89: 295–309

Spender, J. C., 1989. *Industry Recipes*, Oxford: Blackwell

Tan, T. K. and Heracleous, L., 2001. Teaching old dogs new tricks: implementing organizational learning in an Asian National Police Force, *Journal of Applied Behavioral Science*, 37: 361–380

8 | *Strategic change processes: an organization development approach*

This chapter describes an organization development (OD) approach to managing strategic change processes, based on an "integrated organizational model" developed for this purpose, and illustrates its use through an empirical example. The process of applying the model and learning from this and other OD interventions shows how closer integration between the fields of OD and strategic management can help to bridge the gap of relevance between academic and practitioner concerns. The findings also highlight useful lessons which merit careful consideration by top management teams when developing strategy, and planning and leading strategic change. In terms of the organizational action (OA) view, this chapter exemplifies a processual approach to strategic choice and implementation that takes into account key organizational factors in planning for and implementing change. In addition, it presents an OD-oriented decision process that can support strategic choices by the dominant coalition; in doing so, it emphasizes the value of integrating OD with strategic management, in terms of enhanced practitioner relevance and more effective strategy implementation.

The need for relevance of the strategic management field

Strategic management is an applied field and as such its survival and growth depends not only on its theoretical sophistication and methodological rigor, but also on its relevance to practitioners (Bower 1982; Seth and Zinkhan 1991). In spite of that, practitioners often do not perceive such relevance (Bennett 1988; *Business Week* 1990). Bettis (1991) has argued that strategy research is prematurely stuck in a normal science straightjacket, is based on out-dated concepts, relies too much on statistical methodologies which often compromise relevance for

This chapter is based on Heracleous and DeVoge (1998).

scientific rigor, and is characterized by a lack of prescriptive guidelines for practitioners based on research findings. Research aiming to develop a research agenda for strategic management has acknowledged the importance of practitioner viewpoints for the development of this agenda (Lyles 1990). Research which elicited practitioners' viewpoints and compared them with academics' agendas has confirmed, however, that the interests of academics and practitioners are indeed substantially different (Gopinath and Hoffman 1995). This chapter thus proposes that OD is uniquely positioned to fulfill the criteria of research relevance, as outlined by Thomas and Tymon (1982) and that closer interaction between OD and strategic management is a potent way to bridge the gap of relevance between academic and practitioner interests in the strategic management field.

These propositions are illustrated by presenting an "integrated organizational model" based on the action research paradigm, and discussing its utilization in an OD intervention. This model was developed on the basis of extensive research, a sub-set of which is discussed in the appendix. Experience of using the model in several OD interventions has shown that it is a powerful tool for diagnosis, action planning, and implementation of strategic change. This and other OD interventions, moreover, have revealed several important issues related to change management and the perceptions of top management teams which merit further investigation, as discussed in the "implications for management" section.

Linking strategic management and organization development

The barriers inhibiting closer interaction between strategic management and OD have been breaking down. It has been suggested, for example, that strategic management has a primarily external focus whereas OD has an internal focus (Buller 1988), but this is inaccurate. It has been recognized within the strategy field that unless broad strategic directions become translated into internal operational systems, processes, structures, competencies, and cultural norms then the desired strategic direction cannot be pursued effectively (Johnson and Scholes 1993). The OD field, in addition, has from its early days been concerned with "long-range efforts to improve an organization's problem-solving capabilities and its ability to cope with changes in its external environment" (French 1969). OD has also developed a number of approaches relevant to system-wide, strategic change (Argyris and Schon 1996; Beckhard and Harris 1987). Strategic change has in fact been an important influence on the development of the theory and practice of OD (Cummings and Worley 1993).

It has been argued, in addition, that strategic management is mainly concerned with financial performance and survival, whereas OD mainly with interpersonal processes within the organization (Buller 1988). Meta-analyses of OD interventions, however, have shown that OD can lead to long-term improvements in worker productivity (Beekun 1989; Guzzo *et al.* 1985) and worker satisfaction and attitudes (Neuman *et al.* 1989) thus pointing to the strategic value of OD in improving organizational effectiveness. Strategic management and OD have differed in their emphases on "hard" elements (structures, systems) and "soft" elements (processes, culture, interpersonal relationships). It has increasingly been recognized as critical, however, that both "hard" and "soft" organizational features should be congruent and in support of a particular strategic direction, if this direction is to be successfully implemented (Heracleous and Langham 1996; Johnson and Scholes 1993).

Lastly, while the knowledge and skills of agents within strategic management and OD have differed (Buller 1988) strategic management has increasingly incorporated concerns traditionally within the domain of OD, and vice versa. For example, strategic management researchers have focused on the human aspects of strategy; the social, cultural, and political issues (Johnson 1987; Pettigrew 1985). Effective human resource management (HRM), moreover (traditionally enjoying more emphasis in the OD than the strategic management field), has increasingly been recognized as an invaluable strategic resource (Devanna *et al.* 1981; Schuler 1992) and particular human resource (HR) practices have been shown to lead to improved long-term organizational performance (Huselid 1995; Koch and McGrath 1996). It has also been recognized in both the strategy and OD fields that issues of power and politics are central to organizational life and should therefore be given due consideration both in strategic management processes (Hickson *et al.* 1973; Mintzberg 1985) and OD interventions (Cobb 1986; Cobb and Margulies 1981).

Organizational development and the relevance of strategic management

OD is an application of behavioral science knowledge related to system-wide planned change. It aims to increase organizational effectiveness and foster employee development (French 1969; French and Bell 1995). The primary methodological model for OD is action research (Burke 1994). Kurt Lewin, the founder of action research, was concerned with the application of social science to the pressing social problems of his time. He suggested that research capable of aiding the improvement of social conditions was "a type of action-research, comparative research on the conditions and effects of various forms of social action, and research leading to social action. Research that produces nothing but books will not suffice" (Lewin 1947). Rapoport (1970: 499) further elaborated that "action research aims to contribute both to the practical concerns of people in an immediate problematic

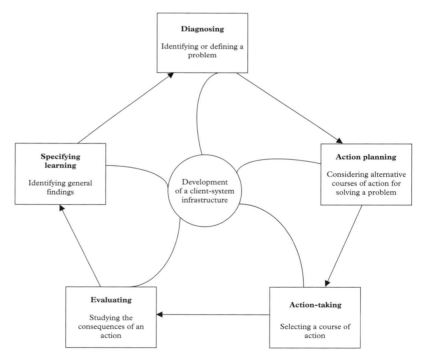

Figure 8.1 The process of action research
Source: Susman and Evered (1978).

Table 8.1 *Practitioners' need for relevance*

Practitioners' need	Definition
Descriptive relevance	The accuracy of research findings in capturing phenomena encountered by practitioners in their organizational setting
Goal relevance	The correspondence of outcome variables in a theory to the things practitioners want to influence
Operational validity	The ability of practitioners to implement the action implications of a theory by manipulating its causal variables
Non-obviousness	The degree to which a theory meets or exceeds the complexity of common sense theory already used by practitioners
Timeliness	The requirement that a theory be available to practitioners in time to use it to deal with organizational problems

situation and to the goals of science by joint collaboration within a mutually acceptable ethical framework." Figure 8.1 portrays the action research process (Susman and Evered 1978).

Thomas and Tymon (1982) suggested five criteria of research relevance based on a practitioner perspective, as outlined in Table 8.1.

Action research, as the primary methodological model of OD, is uniquely positioned to fulfill these criteria. First, it is carried out by definition in organizations rather than the laboratory or based solely on conceptual research. Secondly, it upholds such guiding principles as the commitment to *joint* diagnosis, action planning, and implementation with the practitioners concerned, and aims to impart diagnostic and process management skills to them for future use. More specifically, it has:

- *Descriptive relevance* Action research takes place by definition in the practitioners' organizational setting. The action researcher aims to help practitioners with respect to particular issues they encounter, but more importantly by passing on diagnostic skills and knowledge to them so that they can recognize and act on similar issues in the future (Schein 1988, 1990). Involving practitioners in the whole process of action research, and especially in the diagnostic stage in order to arrive at a definition of the issues faced, ensures that the knowledge generated by action research interventions is highly relevant to issues encountered by practitioners in their organizational settings.

- *Goal relevance*   Goal relevance arises as a corollary to the high descriptive relevance arising from both the location of action research in the field, and practitioner involvement in the action research process. The outcome variables in theories developed or elaborated in this manner are more likely to correspond to the issues that practitioners wish to influence. Such issues include, for example, how to improve leadership, communication processes, group and intergroup effectiveness, and performance management (Schein 1988), how to intervene and manage change (Beckhard and Harris 1987; Schein 1987), or how to create a learning organization (Argyris and Schön 1996).

- *Operational validity*   Knowledge derived from action research interventions has high operational validity, for two main reasons. First, because it has emerged from the field and not from the laboratory or purely conceptually. Secondly, because the action researcher and practitioners jointly conduct action planning and implementation and therefore take into account the particular contingency conditions of the social system under consideration (Schein 1990). The actors' commitment to achieving change is also increased through involvement in the whole process (Coch and French 1948). The ability of practitioners to implement the action implications of a theory is increased, therefore, through the content of the theories which exhibit high descriptive and goal relevance, as well as through the *process* of implementation which can draw from the knowledge and skills of the action researcher as well as the local knowledge of the practitioners.

- *Non-obviousness*   Common sense theories of practitioners are themselves not obvious and require particular methodologies to be determined (Huff 1990). Action research interventions often involve a comprehensive diagnosis of the social and cultural aspects of organizations which are subconscious and taken for granted and therefore not immediately obvious to the actors concerned. They can act, however, as very potent barriers or facilitators to change and thus foregrounding these socio-cultural aspects, and considering their implications for the particular strategic direction an organization wishes to pursue is necessary for the success of system-wide strategic interventions (Heracleous and Langham 1996). OD theories contain a wealth of non-obvious insights, as even a cursory consideration of important OD works can reveal (Beckhard and Harris 1987; Burke 1994; Schein 1987, 1988).

- *Timeliness* The timeliness of OD theories derives first from the fact that the action researcher intervenes in a social system when its members determine the need for change themselves. Secondly, it derives from the fundamental OD aim of passing on to practitioners diagnostic and process management skills so that they can avoid or resolve future issues themselves in a timely fashion (Rapoport 1970; Schein 1990).

An integrated organizational model

One example of an OD model which is relevant to practitioner concerns and which has been used in several action research interventions is the "integrated organizational model" portrayed in figure 8.2.

The OD process shown in figure 8.2 draws from the action research paradigm, which includes the stages of diagnosis, action planning, implementation, and monitoring and evaluation. Because this model was developed with the main aim of being utilized in strategic, system-wide interventions, its *content* includes categories that are empirically highly relevant to organizations (e.g. the specification of external direction and internal characteristics supporting this direction, the seven organizational "levers" included in the model, and the end goal of increasing organizational effectiveness).

The "integrated organizational model" bears similarities in content to other models such as Weisbord's (1976) "six-box organizational model" and the "Burke–Litwin model of organizational performance and change" (Burke 1994), which contain strategic, leadership, structural, cultural, systemic, and processual variables. The integrated organizational model differs from them, however, in three main ways:

- It incorporates relevant content variables *within a process of application of the model*, drawn from action research (French and Bell 1995; Susman and Evered 1978)
- It is designed to strike a balance between comprehensiveness of relevant content variables and simplicity of portrayal of these variables in order to *facilitate and encourage practitioner involvement* in the whole process of intervention

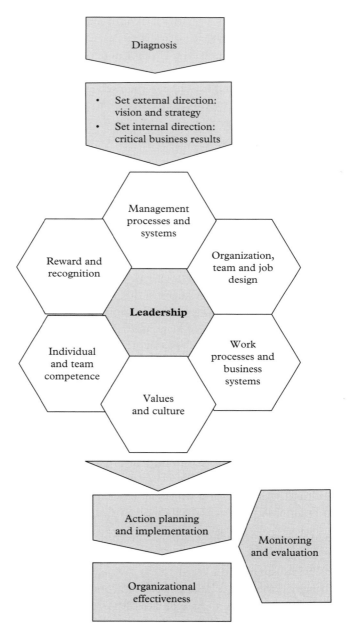

Figure 8.2 The integrated organizational model

- It is based on extensive research which links each of the content variables to definable measures of organizational effectiveness. Substantiating the linkages to organizational effectiveness was seen as critical by the developers of the model, since a common primary aim of both OD and of practitioners is actually to improve organizational effectiveness. A sub-set of the research on which the model is based is discussed in the appendix.

Applying the "integrated organizational model" in a UK commercial bank

Hay Management Consultants was approached by the asset finance division of a UK commercial bank, at a time when more than thirty internal change projects were under way. The internal change initiative was characterized by ambiguity and confusion which had prompted top management to seek external help. In order to begin addressing this issue, there was initially a diagnostic phase. This phase aimed to gather information on such issues as the internal state of the organization and the views of the top management team, and to introduce the integrated organizational model through which a deeper joint diagnosis, action planning, implementation, and monitoring of the strategic change program could be conducted.

The diagnostic phase utilized several data sources; interviews with the managing director and with each of the seven members of the top management team, observation of behavior of the top management team and other employees, internal documents related to the existing change programs, and published annual reports of the company. All these were interpreted in the context of the organization developers' in-depth knowledge based on extensive experience of conducting OD interventions in that sector.

Three workshops were held with the managing director and the top management team, with the themes of setting internal and external direction; integrated change planning, and training on leading change. Table 8.2 gives an overview of the main phases of the OD intervention, the questions that were used to guide joint diagnoses, direction-setting and action planning, the main activities, and lastly the outputs of the first two workshops.

Although it is the primary task of top management to think strategically, top management often get caught in fire-fighting and operational

Table 8.2 *Applying the integrated organizational model*

Phases	Guiding questions	Activities	Outputs
• Set external direction (strategic objectives)	• What is our vision for the future? • What do we want to achieve externally? • How do we define our strategic objectives? What are the measures?	A Agree vision B Agree strategic objectives C Define strategic objectives D Agree measures	• Vision statement • Four–six statements of strategic objectives • Elaboration and measures of strategic objectives
• Set internal direction (CSFs)	• What internal results are critical to achieving strategic objectives? • What are the measures of success?	A Brainstorm CSFs B Agree priority CSFs C Agree merged list of CSFs D Prepare a CSF matrix linking strategic objectives to CSFs	• A list of CSFs per strategic objective • Three–four prioritized CSFs per strategic objective • Merged list of CSFs • CSF matrix
• Integrated change planning	• What organization levers will get us the internal business results we want? • How do these relate to each other for an integrated change plan? • What are the priorities? • What change programs do we stop, add, keep?	A Clarify and describe CSFs B Plenary review C Re-cap D Input: organization levers and integration E Brainstorm impact of levers to CSFs F Plenary review and consolidation of lever outcomes required to achieve CSFs	• Description statements for each CSF • Agreed description of CSFs • List outcomes required to achieve each CSF • Merged list of outcomes required for CSFs
• Action planning and implementation	• Change management • Change leadership • Integrated monitoring		

issues and do not devote enough time to developing a competitive strategy and the internal arrangements to support this strategy, or to learn how they might go about performing this task more effectively (Garratt 1996). The need for strategic change was reactively sensed by top management in this case, for example, when external data revealed that market share was declining and internal data showed that the organization's cost base was too high compared to competitors.

The first workshop was essentially a team-building intervention aimed at helping the top management team clarify its vision for the future, its strategic objectives, and the measures for these objectives. The output from this workshop included the vision statement in box 8.1.

Box 8.1 Commercial bank vision statement

The Vision:

- We aim to be the dominant provider of asset finance in our chosen markets
- We want to be feared and admired by our competitors, and we want our competitors to benchmark us
- We wish to remain a desirable place to work, characterized by honesty and integrity
- We aim to achieve sustained, long-term profitability and customer satisfaction.

Four strategic objectives were developed and each connected to two–three critical success factors (CSFs) (table 8.3).

CSF "owners" were then assigned for each CSF. They had the responsibility for fulfilling the CSF, which would in turn achieve the strategic objectives. This and other OD interventions have shown that individuals should not be responsible for change projects *per se*, but for CSFs, as will be discussed below.

The "integrated change planning" phase involved use of the "integrated organizational model" to stimulate thinking first about what *actions* should be taken, by thinking through the change levers portrayed and how they related to the CSFs – that is, what actions should be taken to fulfill the CSFs. Secondly, to remind the top management team that the elements of social systems are interdependent, so that changes in one sub-system (e.g work processes and business systems)

Table 8.3 *Identifying strategic objectives and critical success factors*

Strategic objectives	Critical success factors
1 *Vendor finance* Minimize leakage points in primary bank channels and seek to dominate the provision of asset finance to the customers of our chosen vendors	A Able to identify material leakage points through dealerships B Have tailored relationship (package services) offerings to capture dealer distribution business (bank and non-bank) C Include the most innovative product
2 *Bank personal car finance* Dominate the provision of personal car finance to the bank's personal customers	D The most effective and efficient processing system in the world E The most efficient way to identify, retain, and capture our personal customers for car finance (integrated with the bank sales process)
3 *Bank commercial agri customers* Dominate the provision of asset finance to the bank's commercial customers	F Most efficient and effective customer sensitive (world-class) sales process G The best sales support training (integrated with branch) H The smartest and most suitable credit policy and assessment processes/criteria for our markets
4 *Franchise* Perceived (and in fact) by the bank as adding customer value to the bank's franchise: – Bring something to the party – Consistent with the bank's vision and values	I Must have good "PR" with the bank – world-class communication – sell/market our crucial position with the bank J Have a climate which reinforces the bank's values

necessitate changes in other sub-systems (e.g individual and team competencies, reward and appraisal systems).

Essentially, as was shown in table 8.2, the main questions asked at this phase were:

- What organizational levers will get us the internal business results we want?
- How do these relate to each other in an integrated change plan?
- What are our priorities? What change projects do we terminate or initiate based on the above?

Because of the clarity provided by asking the right questions, the number of internal change programs already under way was reduced by around 50 percent. The change programs which remained were then redefined according to the focus provided by the diagnosis processes, setting of internal/external direction, and integrated change planning.

As a result of integrating OD in this strategic change process, top management developed a clear, relevant, and useful way of thinking about how to clarify their strategic direction and how effectively to manage the transition. This decision process, characterized by clear guiding questions, group activities, and production of desired outputs, provided crucial clarity to management on the strategic objectives, CSFs linked with each objective, and actions required to achieve each CSF. This clarity meant that unrelated and wasteful change projects were eliminated and energy focused on the ones clearly related to the CSFs and strategic objectives, leading to more focused, effective, and efficient change management. Lastly, group activities involved in the whole decision process were in themselves productive team-building interventions, increasing the integration and effectiveness of the top management team as a whole.

Implications for management

OD processes such as the integrated organizational model, as applied to empirical OD interventions, have revealed several important characteristics of situations relevant to top management teams, change management, and OD processes:

- Often top management teams do not share a common vision and strategic objectives. This is often assumed by top managers, but when debate starts, differences, often very stark, become apparent. It is important to foreground such differences and debate them, so that a common vision and goals can then be developed.
- Top management teams often confuse strategic objectives with measures. When asked to develop strategic objectives they most often come up with measures instead. For example, instead of posing "vendor finance" as a strategic objective, the top management team referred to achieving "higher volume" or "market share," which are measures for this objective.
- Top management also often confuses CSFs with actions. For example, instead of posing "able to identify material leakage points through

dealerships" as a CSF, the top management team referred to the need
to install an IT system, which is an action needed to achieve the CSF.

- Top management teams tend to try to link strategic objectives directly
  with actions without developing CSFs. Trying to establish required
  actions from strategic objectives leads to numerous unrelated change
  projects, whereas change projects based on CSFs focus on what needs
  to be achieved to reach the full array of strategic objectives.

- Top management teams tend to assign loose "stated" accountabilities of change. For example, the only point of real accountability
  for change in this case had been with project managers (accountable
  for time, cost and, delivery to specification). By establishing accountabilities directly based on the CSFs developed, however, individuals
  were clear about what needed to be achieved to reach the strategic
  objectives.

- The theoretical content/process distinction is practically debatable.
  It is certainly more productive to be a process consultant than just a
  content expert without much knowledge of organizational processes.
  Experience of several OD interventions has shown, however, that
  being knowledgeable about both content and process while carrying
  out OD interventions is very useful. Content knowledge enables the
  organizational developer to challenge practitioners' assumptions and
  proposed actions if it is appropriate to do so.

The lessons from this and other OD interventions have important
implications for senior managers:

- Do not assume or take for granted that your top management team
  as a whole has a shared vision and a clear strategic direction for the
  future, because the odds are that it does not.

- Set aside enough time to discuss and debate strategic, long-term issues looking at the big picture, instead of focusing exclusively on
  operational issues.

- When having such debates, use frameworks which can direct them
  and make them more productive and focused on relevant issues.
  Make sure that there is open, constructive interaction – as opposed
  to, for example, having predetermined ideas of what the result of the
  debates should be and directing them to that end.

- Beware of the common errors of confusing strategic objectives with
  measures for these objectives, or CSFs factors with actions needed to
  fulfill them.

- Ensure that your change projects are clearly focused on the actions required to achieve CSFs and eliminate any projects that are unrelated. Unrelated projects arise when trying to establish required actions directly from strategic objectives instead of establishing CSFs for each objective.
- Assign clear accountabilities to project managers, not so much for delivering change projects on time, cost, and specification, but for achieving the CSFs linked to each project, since this makes individuals clear about what needs to be achieved to reach the strategic objectives.

The need for closer integration

This chapter has suggested that closer integration between the OD and strategy fields can help to bridge the gap of research relevance by providing insights into issues emerging from practice rather than the laboratory or purely conceptually, within a process whose guiding principles render it uniquely positioned to claim practitioner relevance. The "integrated organizational model" portrays the process and the organizational levers used to stimulate thinking, so as to determine appropriate actions to be taken to fulfill CSFs and thus ultimately reach the strategic objectives set.

Application of this model at the asset finance division of a UK commercial bank has illustrated generic processes of strategic change planning and implementation which would be relevant in any strategic change program (setting external direction, setting internal direction, integrated change planning, and action planning and implementation). Secondly, it has clarified how strategic objectives are linked with CSFs, and the critical focus this can provide in any change program, with less time, money and energy being wasted on ill-defined change projects which are not connected with particular CSFs. Thirdly, it illustrated how in this and most other strategic OD interventions in the author's experience, there are common detrimental features in the thinking of top management teams as well as their management of strategic change programs, which can severely jeopardize such programs.

These features merit further investigation, not only because of their intrinsic importance but most importantly because substantial experience of carrying out OD interventions suggests that similar features are present in the majority of organizations in which interventions are conducted, irrespective of industry or sector. This means that they are highly relevant to the needs and concerns of practitioners who have to develop and implement strategy. Some of the above findings are vital to understanding managers' strategic thought. If further research supports the findings, for example, that top managers routinely confuse strategic objectives with measures and CSFs with actions, what are the implications of this critical fact for both the strategic management field and management education and development?

These findings also illustrate how closer integration between the OD and strategy fields can lead to more fruitful interdisciplinary linkages for both the academic and practitioner communities. Strategic management can address new problem areas emerging from practice, thus helping to bridge the gap of relevance between practitioner and academic concerns.

Appendix: the integrated organization model

- **Strategic planning**   The presence of strategic planning positively influences firm performance, irrespective of firm size and capital intensity. The more turbulent a firm's environment, moreover, the more it can benefit from strategic planning (Miller and Cardinal 1994). Firms higher on a planning continuum of: Short-term forecasting Budgeting Annual planning Long-range planning Strategic planning, were shown to achieve higher ten-year total returns to investors both relative to their industry and in absolute terms (Rhyne 1986). The degree of formality of strategic planning was also positively correlated with higher financial performance (Armstrong 1982; Pearce *et al.* 1987).
- **Leadership**   Leadership is included as the core of the model because of its critical role in organizations. Leadership actions were shown strongly to influence employee commitment, job satisfaction, and reduce role ambiguity (Niehoff *et al.* 1990). Leadership is central to managing change, and effective leadership in the context of change varies with respect to situational contingencies (Dunphy and Stace 1988, 1993; Nutt 1989).
- **Management processes and systems**   Investment in high-performance HRM practices is associated with lower employee turnover and greater productivity and corporate financial performance (Huselid 1995; Schuler 1992). The higher the employees' perceptions

of a company's commitment to its human resources, the more their attitudes towards company values are improved and their job satisfaction increased (Kinicki *et al.* 1992). Use of more sophisticated staffing practices is associated with higher levels of annual profit and profit growth (Terpstra and Rozzell 1993).

- **Organization, team, and job design**   Job redesign was shown to increase functional behaviors and decrease dysfunctional behaviors by employees (Luthans *et al.* 1987) and job enrichment interventions were shown to be effective at reducing employee turnover (McEnvoy and Cascio 1985). The relevance of several criteria of team effectiveness derived from the literature was confirmed empirically (Campion *et al.* 1993; Cohen *et al.* 1996). Lastly, organization performance is higher, when organization/environment alignment is higher, and vice versa (Ghoshal and Nohria 1993).

- **Work processes and business systems**   Organizational variables (emphasis on human resources and goal accomplishments) were shown to be twice as important as economic factors (industry profitability and firm size) as determinants of performance (Hansen and Wernerfelt 1989). Spending on information systems and on IS labor was shown to produce a net marginal product of 67 percent assuming a service life of three years (Brynjolfsson and Hitt 1996). Re-engineering which defines processes to be redesigned broadly and which utilizes several "depth levers" can lead to dramatic cost reductions (Hall, Rosenthal and Wade 1993).

- **Values and culture**   Several studies have shown that certain cultural characteristics lead to higher organizational performance. For example, "constructive" cultures which encourage interaction and ways of approaching tasks that will help employees meet their higher-order satisfaction needs, and which are characterized by achievement, self-actualising, humanistic-encouraging and affiliative norms (Klein *et al.* 1995) as well as more homogeneous cultures which value adaptability (Gordon and DiTomaso 1993). In addition, the higher the employees' commitment to the organization and overall job satisfaction, the lower their intent to leave the organization (O'Reilly *et al.* 1991). The higher the individual/organization fit, the higher the organization's effectiveness (Ostroff 1993).

- **Individual and team competence**   Employee competencies are critical for improved organizational performance. Eleven high-performance managerial competencies were identified and validated

(Cockerill *et al.* 1995). Employee training to enhance individual and team competencies was shown to lead to higher productivity (Bartel 1994) and performance (Russell *et al.* 1985).

- **Reward and recognition**   It is vital that performance appraisal systems reward desired behaviors and are congruent with the organization's HR and competitive strategies, among other things (Sashkin 1981; Stonich 1981, 1984). There is as much as a 127 percent potential variability in employee performance in high-complexity jobs (Williams and Livingstone 1994), which the reward systems can capitalize on by enhancing employee satisfaction and commitment. Reward systems featuring pay-for-performance were shown to lead to higher employee satisfaction (Heneman *et al.* 1988) and profit sharing was shown to lead to higher productivity (Shepard 1994).

Bibliography

Argyris, C. and Schön, D. A., 1996. *Organizational Learning II: Theory, Method and Practice*, Reading, MA: Addison-Wesley

Armstrong, J. S., 1982. The value of formal planning for strategic decisions: review of empirical research, *Strategic Management Journal*, 3: 197–211

Bartel, A. P., 1994. Productivity gains from the implementation of employee training programs, *Industrial Relations*, 33: 411–425

Bartunek, J., 1983. How organization development can develop organizational theory, *Group & Organization Studies*, 8: 303–314

Beckhard, R. and Harris, R. T., 1987. *Organizational Transitions: Managing Complex Change*, Reading, MA: Addison-Wesley

Beekun, R. I., 1989. Assessing the effectiveness of sociotechnical interventions: antidote or fad?, *Human Relations*, 42: 877–897

Bennett, A., 1988. When management professors gather, relevance sometimes rears its ugly head, *Wall Street Journal*, August 15

Bettis, R. A., 1991. Strategic management and the straightjacket: an editorial essay, *Organization Science*, 2: 315–319

Bower, J. L., 1982. Business policy in the 1980s, *Academy of Management Review*, 74: 630–638

Brynjolfsson, E. and Hitt, L., 1996. Paradox lost? Firm-level evidence on the returns to information systems spending, *Management Science*, 42: 541–558

Buchanan, D. and Boddy, D., 1992. *The Expertise of the Change Agent*, Englewood Cliffs, NJ: Prentice-Hall

Buller, P. F., 1988. For successful strategic change: blend OD practices with strategic management, *Organizational Dynamics*, Winter: 42–55

Burke, W. W., 1994. *A Process of Learning and Change* (2nd edn.), Reading, MA: Addison-Wesley

Business Week, 1990. Is research in the ivory tower "fuzzy, irrelevant, pretentious"?, October 29: 62–66

Campion, M. A., Medsker, G. J. and Higgs, A. C., 1993. Relations between work group characteristics and effectiveness: implications for designing effective work groups, *Personnel Psychology*, 46: 823–850

Cobb, A., 1986. Political diagnosis: applications in organization development, *Academy of Management Review*, 11: 482–496

Cobb, A. and Margulies, N., 1981. Organization development: a political perspective, *Academy of Management Review*, 6: 49–59

Coch, L. and French, R., 1948. Overcoming resistance to change, *Human Relations*, 2: 512–532

Cockerill, T., Hunt, J. and Schroder, H., 1995. Managerial competencies: fact or fiction?, *Business Strategy Review*, 6(3): 1–12

Cohen, S. G., Ledford, G. E., Jr. and Spreitzer, G. M., 1996. A predictive model of self-managing work team effectiveness, *Human Relations*, 49: 643–676

Cummings, T. G. and Worley, C. G., 1993. *Organization Development and Change* (5th edn.), New York: West

Devanna, M. A., Fombrum, C. and Tichy, N., 1981. Human resources management: a strategic perspective, *Organizational Dynamics*, Winter: 51–67

Dunphy, D. C., and Stace, D. A., 1988. Transformational and coercive studies for planned organizational change: beyond the O.D. model, *Organization Studies*, 9: 317–334

　1993. The strategic management of corporate change, *Human Relations*, 46: 905–920

French, W., 1969. Organization development: objectives, assumptions and strategies, *California Management Review*, 12: 23–24

French, W. L. and Bell, C. H., 1985. *Organization Development: Behavioral Science Interventions for Organization Improvement*, Englewood Cliffs, NJ: Prentice-Hall

Garratt, B., 1996. Helicopters and rotting fish: developing strategic thinking and new roles for direction-givers, in B. Garratt (ed.), *Developing Strategic Thought*, London: McGraw-Hill: 242–256

Ghoshal, S. and Nohria, N., 1993. Horses for courses: organizational forms for multinational corporations, *Sloan Management Review*, Winter: 23–35

Gopinath, C. and Hoffman, R. C., 1995. The relevance of strategy research: practitioner and academic viewpoints, *Journal of Management Studies*, 32: 575–594

Gordon, G. G. and DiTomaso, N., 1992. Predicting corporate performance from organizational culture, *Journal of Management Studies*, 29: 783–798

Guzzo, R. A., Jette, R. D. and Katzell, R. A., 1985. The effects of psychologically based intervention programs on worker productivity: a meta-analysis, *Personnel Psychology*, 38: 275–291

Hall, G., Rosenthal, J. and Wade, J., 1993. How to make reengineering really work, *Harvard Business Review*, November–December: 119–131

Hall, J. L., Posner, B. Z. and Harder, J. W., 1989. Performance appraisal systems: matching practice with theory, *Group and Organization Studies*, 14: 51–69

Hansen, G. S. and Wernerfelt, B., 1989. Determinants of firm performance: the relative importance of economic and organizational factors, *Strategic Management Journal*, 10: 399–411

Heneman, R. L., Greenberger, D. B. and Strasser, S., 1988. The relationship between pay-for-performance perceptions and pay satisfaction, *Personnel Psychology*, 41: 745–759

Heracleous, L. and DeVoge, S., 1998. Bridging the gap of relevance: strategic management and organizational development, *Long Range Planning*, 31: 732–744

Heracleous, L. and Langham, B., 1996. Strategic change and organizational culture at Hay Management Consultants, *Long Range Planning*, 29: 485–494

Hickson, D. J., Hinings, C. R., Lee, C. A. and Pennings, J. M., 1973. A strategic contingencies' theory of intra organizational power, in G. Salaman and K. Thompson (eds.), *People and Organizations*, Milton Keynes: Open University Press: 174–189

Huff, A. S., 1990. *Mapping Strategic Thought*, Chichester: Wiley

Huselid, M. A., 1995. The impact of human resource management practices on turnover, productivity, and corporate financial performance, *Academy of Management Journal*, 38: 635–672

Johnson, G., 1987. *Strategic Change and the Management Process*, Oxford: Blackwell

Johnson, G. and Scholes, K., 1993. *Exploring Corporate Strategy: Text and Cases* (3rd edn.), Englewood Cliffs, NJ: Prentice-Hall

Kinicki, A. J., Carson, K. P. and Bohlander, G. W., 1992. Relationships between an organization's actual human resource efforts and employee attitudes, *Group and Organization Management*, 17: 135–152

Klein, A. S., Masi, R. J. and Weidner, C. K., II, 1995. Organization culture, distribution and amount of control and perceptions of quality: an empirical study of linkages, *Group and Organization Management*, 20: 122–148

Koch, M. J. and McGrath, R. G., 1996. Improving labour productivity: human resource management policies do matter, *Strategic Management Journal*, 17: 335–354

Lewin, K., 1947. Frontiers in group dynamics II. Channels of group life: social planning and action research, *Human Relations*, 1: 143–153

Luthans, F., Kemmerer, B., Paul, R. and Taylor, L., 1987. The impact of a job redesign intervention on salespersons' observed performance behaviors: a field experiment, *Group and Organization Studies*, 12: 55–72

Lyles, M. A., 1990. A research agenda for strategic management in the 1990s, *Journal of Management Studies*, 27: 363–375

McEvoy, G. M. and Cascio, W. F., 1985. Strategies for reducing employee turnover: a meta-analysis, *Journal of Applied Psychology*, 70: 342–353

Miller, C. C. and Cardinal, L. B., 1994. Strategic planning and firm performance: a synthesis of more than two decades of research, *Academy of Management Journal*, 37: 1649–1665

Mintzberg, H., 1985. The organization as political arena, *Journal of Management Studies*, 22: 133–154

Neuman, G. A., Edwards, J. E. and Raju, N. S., 1989. Organizational development interventions: a meta-analysis of their effects on satisfaction and other attitudes, *Personnel Psychology*, 42: 461–489

Niehoff, N. P., Enz, C. A. and Grover, R. A., 1990. The impact of top-management actions on employee attitudes and perceptions, *Group and Organization Studies*, 15: 337–352

Nutt, P. C., 1989. Selecting tactics to implement strategic plans, *Strategic Management Journal*, 10: 145–161

O'Reilly, C. A., Chatman, J. and Caldwell, D. F., 1991. People and organizational culture: a profile comparison approach to assessing person–organization fit, *Academy of Management Journal*, 34: 487–516

Ostroff, C., 1993. Relationships between person–environmental congruence and organizational effectiveness, *Group and Organization Management*, 18: 103–122

Pearce, J. A., II, Robbins, K. D. and Robinson, R. B., Jr., 1987. The impact of grand strategy and planning formality on financial performance, *Strategic Management Journal*, 8: 125–134

Pettigrew, A. M., 1985. *The Awakening Giant: Continuity and Change in ICI*, Oxford: Blackwell

Rapoport, R. N., 1970. Three dilemmas in action research, *Human Relations*, 23: 499-513

Rhyne, L. C., 1986. The relationship of strategic planning to financial performance, *Strategic Management Journal*, 7: 423–436

Russell, J. S., Terborg, J. R. and Powers, M. L., 1985. Organizational performance and organizational level training and support, *Personnel Psychology*, 38: 849–863

Sashkin, M., 1981. Appraising appraisal: ten lessons from research for practice, *Organizational Dynamics*, Winter: 37–50

Schein, E., 1987. *Process Consultation II, Lessons for Managers and Consultants*, Reading, MA: Addison-Wesley

    1988. *Process Consultation: Its Role in Organization Development*, Reading, MA: Addison-Wesley

    1990. Back to the future: recapturing the OD vision, in F. Massarik (ed.), *Advances in Organization Development*, *1*, Norwood, NJ: Ablex: 13–26

Schuler, R. S., 1992. Strategic human resources management: linking the people with the strategic needs of the business, *Organizational Dynamics*, Summer: 18–32

Seth, A. and Zinkhan, G., 1991. Strategy and the research process: a comment, *Strategic Management Journal*, 12: 75–82

Shepard, E. M., 1994. Profit sharing and productivity: further evidence from the chemicals industry, *Industrial Relations*, 33: 452–466

Stonich, P. J., 1981. Using rewards in implementing strategy, *Strategic Management Journal*, 2: 345–352

    1984. The performance measurement and reward system: critical to strategic management, *Organizational Dynamics*, Winter: 45–57

Susman, G. and Evered, R., 1978. An assessment of the scientific merits of action research, *Administrative Science Quarterly*, 23: 582–603

Terpstra, D. E. and Rozzell, E. J., 1993. The relationship of staffing practices to organizational level measures of performances, *Personnel Psychology*, 46: 27–48

Thomas, K. W. and Tymon, W. G., 1982. Necessary properties of relevant research: lessons from recent criticisms of the organizational sciences, *Academy of Management Review*, 7: 345–352

Weisbord, M. R., 1976. Organizational diagnosis: six places to look for trouble with or without a theory, *Group & Organization Studies*, 1: 430–477

Williams, C. R. and Livingstone, L. P., 1994. Another look at the relationship between performance and voluntary turnover, *Academy of Management Journal*, 37: 269–298

III

Current themes and applications

9 | *State ownership, privatization, and performance*

While the traditional belief, supported by empirical work, has been that private ownership is generally associated with superior performance, the experience of Singapore is an example to the contrary. This chapter outlines global privatization trends and the impact of privatization programs. Using a variant of the organizational action (OA) view as a theoretical framework, Singapore Telecom is analyzed as a case where state ownership combined with several contextual and firm-related factors, especially firm strategy, has led to sustained world-class performance relative to its peers. This analysis challenges the widely held position that public ownership is associated with inferior performance and points to the importance of strategy as a key factor in aiding superior performance even under public ownership. Some theoretical and practical implications of the analysis are then outlined.

Global trends and the impact of privatization

The push to expand state ownership in the 1960s and 1970s met with a radical reversal in the 1980s, when governments progressively reduced their involvement in service provision by increasing private sector involvement, especially in the areas of power generation, telecommunications, water provision, and transport services, with significantly higher private sector involvement in the first two (Price Waterhouse 1996). Privatization in broad terms involves the transfer of ownership and/or control of state-owned organizations to private investors. More specifically, privatization can take several forms: it can be complete or partial, in terms of the amount of equity sold to private investors; it can be full or selective in terms of which parts of the state enterprise are sold; it can involve liberalization, where a competitive climate and

This chapter is based on Heracleous (1999, 2001).

market forces are promoted in place of the previous monopolistic or oligopolistic climate; it can involve higher regulation to ensure a level playing field for privatized entities and new entrants; and, lastly, it may or may not involve transfer of ownership, where the latter can be achieved through methods such as leasing of state facilities for a fee, bringing in external management, or contracting out the provision of a particular service.

The particular motivations for privatization vary from country to country (Miller 1997). A primary factor, however, is the generally disappointing performance state-owned enterprises (SOEs) in terms of efficiency and profitability. Developing countries have relied more on SOEs than developed ones, and in many cases SOEs became a heavy fiscal burden on the state. The growth of the private sector in many developing countries has been slowed down through government regulation of industries and the directing of scarce credit to inefficient SOEs (Kikeri *et al.* 1994). In addition to poor SOE performance, privatization activity has been spurred on by several other drivers, as described in table 9.1.

Some authors are critical of the unreflective application of management principles and techniques to the public sector (*Economist*, 1996; Mintzberg 1996). There is now a considerable body of theoretical (Cantor 1996) and empirical evidence, however, attesting to the effectiveness of privatization and deregulation in improving the performance of SOEs. This includes evidence from the USA, for example, showing that deregulation in four industries resulted in higher productivity through more competitive pay scales and changes in work rules, and lower consumer prices (Bailey 1986). A report by the US General Accounting Office (1997) indicates that the reported benefits of such programs include substantial cost savings, higher revenues, and improved service to citizens. Research from Canada, moreover, based on a sample of 370 private companies, mixed enterprises, SOEs and co-operatives, has shown that private companies generally have higher performance than the rest in terms of profitability and efficiency (Vining and Boardman 1992).

An extensive study by the World Bank on the effects of twelve privatization programs in four countries, found that productivity rose in nine cases and remained constant in three cases; high capital investments took place; workers as a whole were not worse off, and in three cases were even better off through equity participation in the

Table 9.1 *Drivers of privatization*

Ideological shifts	Collapse of Marxist ideologies and the movement towards free-market economies
Donor pressure	Donor agencies and nations have been exerting increasing pressure on governments to encourage private participation in infrastructure development
Regional bandwagoning	States which do not embark on privatization programs risk becoming technologically obsolete compared to neighboring states/regions which have done so
Fiscal imperatives	High subsidies to inefficient SOEs become a burden on scarce government resources and intensify the risk of economic stagnation
Globalization of commerce	Global competition further exposes the inefficiencies of SOEs and increases the pressure for improvement
Globalization of finance	The easier availability of global funds as well as the growth of local capital markets facilitates the finance of large privatization projects
Institutional capacity	The appointment of state boards to assist privatization and international agencies' encouragement of private investment has aided the privatization process
Growing middle class	A growing middle class has increased the demand for premium goods and services in such areas as communications and transportation, thus encouraging private sector involvement in their provision
Technological advancement	The private sector now has the knowledge to design and manage infrastructure efficiently, as well as the capacity to operate beyond the boundaries of national networks, e.g. as in the case of telecommunications

Source: Adapted from Price Waterhouse (1996).

privatized firms; and that consumers mostly received better service and lower prices, except in five cases where prices rose to reflect cost structures more realistically (Galal *et al.* 1994). Lastly, a study of the outcomes of sixty-one privatized enterprises in thirty-two industries in eighteen countries found that the profitability, sales, operating efficiency, and capital investment of privatized enterprises increased significantly after privatization, and there was even a slight increase in employment (Megginson *et al.* 1994). It is thus now widely recognized that

Table 9.2 *Benefits of privatization programs*

Direct benefits
• Swift delivery of vital infrastructure
• Generation of funds to support debt reduction or redeployment of investment into other social programs
• Improvement in the efficiency of public sector construction, operation, and maintenance
• Upgrading of infrastructure quality through the use of world-class equipment and new technologies
• Rationalization of complex and restrictive regulators
• Improved economic efficiency via transparent prices and well-quantified cross-subsidies

• **Indirect benefits**
• Attraction of industrial and capital investment caused by improvements in transport capacity and cost
• Enabling of other competitiveness initiatives (e.g. regional finance centre, export promotion, software)
• Accelerated development of capital markets
• Improved public policy through targeting of cross-subsidies and development of mechanisms to monitor their effectiveness
• Potent signaling of the seriousness of the liberalization program
• Redistribution of wealth if special equity allocations provided to designated groups

Source: Adapted from Durchslag *et al.* (1994).

privatization, if implemented well, can have several direct and indirect benefits, both for the enterprises themselves and also for the state as a whole, as outlined in table 9.2.

The ownership debate: does ownership matter?

According to neoclassical economic theory, efficiency is mainly a function of market and incentive structures rather than ownership. In other words, in theory it does not matter who owns the enterprise, as long as it operates in a competitive market without barriers to entry or exit; the owner gives autonomy to management and instructs management to follow the signals of the market; and lastly management is rewarded and sanctioned on the basis of performance (Nellis 1994). States can, in theory, still own enterprises and ensure that the above conditions hold. In practice, however, there are two main problems. First, the full set of the above conditions is rarely met, and secondly even when it is met, it is not usually sustained in the longer term. Politicians can (and do) impose social objectives as well as commercial ones on SOEs, which can lead to the inefficient use of resources (Boycko *et al.* 1996). Often in times of fiscal crisis governments may focus on commercial objectives and grant managerial autonomy, but as soon as the crisis fades, commitment to managerial autonomy and primacy of commercial goals can fade as well (Kikeri *et al.* 1994).

While the existence of social goals is morally desirable, one has to ask: under what conditions would such goals be better achieved – under public or private ownership? It would appear paradoxical that in most cases private ownership of previously SOEs, without an explicit focus on social objectives, does result in services of higher quality and more competitive prices for the public than public ownership. Privatization originates a process of change in the organization's goals, incentives, controls, strategy, structure, and culture (Cuervo and Villalonga 2000; Cunha and Cooper 1998, Zahra *et al.* 2000), which bring about such improvements. Privatization gradually de-institutionalizes actors' "public sector" norms, and institutionalizes new, competitive "private sector" norms (Johnson *et al.* 2000).

Advocates of the position that ownership matters point to the fact that private firms usually outperform public firms. The World Bank has found, for example, that rates of return on equity invested in public enterprises are about one-third of those invested in the country's private sector (Nellis 1994). There is a significant body of empirical work which shows convincingly that privatization involving ownership transfer substantially improves various indicators of performance (e.g. Galal *et al.* 1994; Megginson *et al.* 1994; Vining and Boardman 1992). There is thus a strong case that ownership matters; in other words, private ownership will in general lead to superior performance in both financial and service quality aspects compared to public ownership.

On the other hand, others (e.g. Bradbury 1999) suggest that ownership *per se* does not matter. In early assessments of privatization, a key issue was whether superior performance could be attributed to the different market environment that SOEs and private companies faced, as opposed to their ownership, the implication being that a more competitive market climate was responsible for superior performance of private companies, rather than the fact that they were privately owned (Kay and Thompson 1986). Others have questioned the chain of causality, asking whether firms are more likely to be privatized if they are more efficient and profitable, or whether privatization brings about higher efficiency and profitability. There is evidence that the output, profits, and margins of early privatized enterprises in the UK increased, and their employment fell, but trends in this direction were occurring before privatization, so that the direction of causality was unclear (Bishop and Kay 1989).

It has been suggested that SOEs are relatively inefficient not because of their ownership, but rather owing to the absence of explicit goals and objectives focusing on efficiency and competitiveness, as well as organizational cultures and control systems to support these goals and objectives (Wortzel and Wortzel 1989). Others point to concerns that with transfer of ownership from the state to private hands, government accountability and legal responsibility to citizens may be lost (Gilmour and Jensen 1998).

Evidence from Hungary indicates that ownership transfer in itself did not generate radical alterations in firm structure and behavior; rather, if the firm faced a financial crisis, or if it was owned by foreign firms, then radical changes were under way (Whitley and Czaban 1998). Evidence from Russia, moreover, shows that the survival potential of firms was not related to their ownership, firm size, industry, or monopoly position; it was rather related to whether the firms had a sound financial basis, were linked to financial institutions, and whether they had strategies for the future, especially relating to financing and production arrangements (Linz 1997; see also Jones 1998).

While SOE inefficiency and lower profitability than private enterprises have been the general pattern, in some cases SOEs have been highly efficient and have continually delivered operational surpluses, as for example in Singapore (Singh and Ang 1999). These cases constitute a potent challenge to the widely held view that private ownership is an indispensable prerequisite to superior performance. The rest of this chapter utilizes Singapore Telecom as a case example of this challenge, and discusses certain implications for the theory and practice of privatization.

Singapore Telecom's strategy and performance

Lewin (1981: 1324) stated in the early 1980s that "research on SOEs is still in its infancy." While several studies have been conducted since,

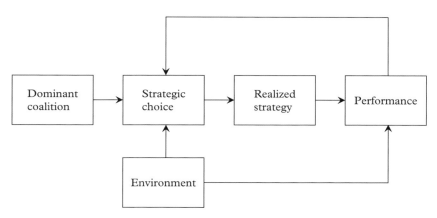

Figure 9.1 Strategic choice, realized strategy, and performance

primarily from an economics perspective, SOEs have still "received almost no attention in mainstream strategy research" (Singh and Ang 1999: 5). This is unfortunate, as studies from a strategic management perspective can improve researchers' understanding of the sources of efficient and profitable performance of SOEs. The search for the sources of superior performance has characterized the strategy field from its early days. This is apparent, for example, in Chandler's classic historical studies of how firms progressively adapted their structures to respond to new strategic imperatives (Chandler 1962); in Andrews' (1971) discussion of the need to identify core competencies and match these to environmental success factors; and in Ansoff's (1965) view of the role of strategy in providing a common thread between such elements as product/market scope, firm growth vector, and internal synergies.

This chapter adopts a variant of the conceptual framework outlined in chapter 2, the organizational action (OA) view of strategic management, to structure the analysis of the Singapore Telecom case (see chapter 2 for a detailed discussion). This framework draws from the strategic choice perspective (Child 1972, 1997), Mintzberg's (1978) distinctions between intended, realized, unrealized, and emergent strategies, and the strategic management field's concern with firm performance (Rumelt *et al.* 1994) (figure 9.1).

The discussion of the Singapore Telecom case is based on research of published documents from various sources, including *Annual Reports* of Singapore Telecom (Sing Tel), Government statistics, and press reports. Data collection was concerned with gathering current data as well as retrospective data that could shed light on Singapore Telecom's context, strategy, and performance. Extensive data on these areas are discussed in Heracleous and Singh (2000).

Singapore's broad strategic actions with regard to national development have aimed to leverage its natural advantage of strategic location by establishing world-class transportation and materials handling facilities; extending this concept to the manufacturing, financial, and service domains by developing a sophisticated telecommunications and IT infrastructure; continuously improving workforce skills; and monitoring and absorbing global technological developments (Sisodia 1992).

National infrastructure, and information infrastructure in particular, has played a key part in Singapore's development (Knoop *et al.* 1996). The Singapore government has viewed the telecommunications infrastructure as a national asset, aiding its early development by providing financial support, protection from market forces and managerial talent, while simultaneously urging the adoption of competitive rates. At a later stage, the state ceased providing public funds to Singapore Telecom, in order to enforce market discipline on it. In addition, there has been gradual privatization in order to provide Singapore Telecom with greater flexibility in dealing with technological challenges and global competition, and gradual liberalization in order to provide it with controlled competition (Singh 1995).

Privatization can have several goals: raising private capital for infrastructural development, easing the fiscal burden of the state, or improving the quality of service and reducing prices for consumers. These traditional objectives of privatization were not the primary motivating factors in the case of Singapore Telecom, however, as it had achieved high performance under state ownership. Given this fact, as well as the unique context of a small country which lacks natural resources and which has a strategic interest in ensuring the development and control of its telecommunications sector, together with the perceived potential of negative social implications resulting from the uncontrolled flow of information from other countries to Singapore, only limited privatization has been pursued, which would ensure the continuing control of telecommunications infrastructure by Singapore Telecom (Kuo *et al.* 1989).

The privatization of Singapore Telecom occurred in the context of a wider effort intended to reduce the state's involvement in business (Low 1995; Tan 1992), and its main aims were to increase Singapore

Telecom's flexibility, and prepare it for the challenges of global competition and technological advancements (Singh 1995), as well as to stimulate the development of the Singapore stock market which at that time lacked both depth and scope (Kuo *et al.* 1989; Low 1995; Toh and Low 1990a, 1990b). The government remains the largest shareholder, holding about 80 percent of issued capital (Center for Business Research and Development 1999; Singh 1998).

The telecommunications equipment market was liberalized in 1989, while a new entrant to the mobile-phone market started competing in April 1997, capturing significant market share. In January 2000, the Singapore Government announced that it would fully deregulate the telecoms market from April 1, 2000, bringing full deregulation forward by two years as compared with the original plans. In April 2000 another telecommunications company entered the Singapore market, offering the whole spectrum of telecoms services.

Singapore Telecom's strategy includes focusing on short- and medium-term profitability, pursuit of globally competitive service and efficiency standards, and high investment in proven technologies. The company has also undertaken related diversification in IT and value-added services in order to sustain its growth and profitability levels, has initiated foreign investments in several countries, and has engaged in strategic alliances in order to gain market entry and acquire technological skills (Singh 1995).

In terms of geographical diversification, the company made initial investments in Asia in the 1980s, and subsequently expanded into Europe. Given that European investments, with few exceptions were not profitable, however (Singh 1999), most were disposed of and the focus has returned to investing in Asia. According to the Chairman's letter to shareholders in the company's 2001–2 *Annual Report*, "from being a Singapore-based telco with a small home market, SingTel is today a leading player in Asian telecommunications."

In 1999, Singapore Telecom re-organized "to increase our focus on the people that matter most to us – our customers," according to its Chairman (*Annual Report*, 1998–9). Entering the area of electronic commerce, which it has identified as a growth platform, Singapore Telecom "intends to exploit synergies and capabilities to offer total solutions" (*Business Times* 1999), utilizing its subsidiaries Singapore Telecom Mobile, SingNet (an internet provider), and Singapore Post in implementing this strategy of related diversification.

The *World Competitiveness Report* issued by the Institute of Management Development and the World Economic Forum in Switzerland ranked the quality of Singapore's telecommunications infrastructure as the world's best every year between 1991 and 1994 (Sisodia 1992; www.Singtel.com). Singapore's infrastructure ranked first in a survey of ten South-East Asian countries in 1997 (*Straits Times* 1997). It ranked third in the Asia-Pacific Telecommunications Index 1998 issued by the National University of Singapore's Center for Telemedia Studies, closely following Japan and Australia (*Straits Times* 1998b), and rose to first place in the 1999 ranking (*Straits Times* 1999).

Singapore Telecom's share price has generally outperformed the market, which is in line with research showing that the share price of privatized government-linked companies in Singapore significantly outperforms non-government-linked companies after privatization (Tan *et al.* 1993). After partial privatization, Singapore Telecom has continued to deliver high returns despite majority ownership by the government. Table 9.3 contains selected performance figures for the period 1994–2002. For comparison purposes, the median performance figures of telecommunications firms included in *Fortune's* Global 500 annual surveys for the same period are also cited. Singapore Telecom's relatively high performance is consistent with recent findings that SOEs in Singapore perform on a par with privately owned corporations (Singh and Ang 1999).

Trends of deregulation, technological advancement, and privatization are causing turmoil in a once stable and highly profitable industry. The advent of competition is exerting continuous pressure on prices, with margins falling as a result, and necessitates the introduction of value-added services to sustain volume and profitability. Even though the future looks uncertain, however, this does not detract from the fact that Singapore Telecom has sustained exceptional financial performance under both full and majority state ownership.

Discussion and implications

The Singapore Telecom case demonstrates that the dominant view that state ownership is associated with inefficiency should be re-considered. Singapore Telecom's strategies, aided by a supportive institutional context, have led it to exceptional performance even as an SOE. In

Table 9.3 *Singapore Telecom, comparative financial performance 1994–2002*

	2002		2001		2000		1999		1998		1997		1996		1995		1994	
	Sing Tel	Fort. 500	Sing Tel	Fort. 500	Sing Tel	Fort. 500	Sing Tel	Fort. 500	Sing Tel	Fort. 500	Sing Tel	Fort. 500	Sing Tel	Fort. 500	Sing Tel	Fort. 500	Sing Tel	Fort. 500
Change in revenues	49	7.5	1.2	18.5	(0.4)	16.4	(1.2)	12.8	16.5	4.5	6.0	8.5	13.7	6.9	10.2	8.2	15.6	10.1
Change in profits	(18.7)	(52.9)	(21.0)	36.2	25.0	9.6	3.7	(2.2)	11.8	34.4	12.4	(9.9)	12.6	3.8	10.5	(16.3)	19.9	26.4
Return on assets	4.7	0.8	12.4	4.2	18.4	4.4	16.1	5.4	17.5	5.3	20.3	4.8	22.3	6.9	22.5	2.6	23.2	4.9
Return on revenues	22.2	2.4	40.7	10.6	38.2	11.7	40.4	10.2	44.6	10.2	47.1	7.3	49.2	9.1	49.1	4.5	47.4	7.0

Sources: Singapore Telecom performance figures: Heracleous and Singh (2000: 74), and Singapore Telecom Annual Reports. Global telecommunications industry median performance figures: Fortune magazine, Global 500 Surveys: April 15, 2002; April 16, 2001; April 17, 2000; August 2, 1999; April 27, 1998; April 28, 1997; August 5, 1996; August 7, 1995.

this case, the state did not impose demands on Singapore Telecom that could compromise its efficiency and profitability, as for example in the (often implicit) requirement to maintain a high level of employment irrespective of the adverse efficiency implications. On the contrary, the dominant coalition, Singapore Telecom's senior management, was positively influenced by state demands for efficiency, profitability, and the achievement of world-class quality standards. Singapore Telecom's intended and realized strategies, as set out above, were commercially oriented, without the shackles of state demands that can often be inconsistent with the pursuit of profitability.

Of course, some of Singapore Telecom's strategies remain unrealized. For example its corporate-level strategy in the 1980s of becoming a successful global competitor (as opposed to a regional competitor), which was implemented through significant investments in Europe, was not achieved when most of these investments proved unprofitable. The strategy then shifted to a regional focus, illustrating an example of managerial learning, albeit an expensive one. In terms of the framework in figure 9.1, this indicates a feedback loop from performance to strategic choice.

The influence of the environment on performance can be seen in terms of the trends towards reduced performance after 1998, when the effects of the Asian crisis of 1997 began taking their toll. The influence of the environment on strategic choice can be illustrated by the strategy of engaging in related diversification in electronic commerce and the aim of exploiting synergies between Singapore Telecom's subsidiaries, given environmental conditions such as the prevalence of technologically aware consumers in Singapore and the higher acceptability of electronic transactions. This related diversification strategy is expected to be a positive influence on performance in future, given research findings that related diversification is more beneficial in terms of performance than unrelated diversification or focus on single-line businesses (Lubatkin and Rogers 1989; Palich *et al.* 2000).

Environmental factors that have aided Singapore Telecom's success by influencing the dominant coalition's strategic choices include clear state policies relating to the pursuit of globally competitive standards of quality and service, a well-educated and motivated workforce, a civil service recognized for its efficiency, meritocracy, and pragmatism (Guan 1997; *Straits Times* 1998a), a robust institutional and regulatory environment, and clear long-term development strategies at the national level.

From an economic perspective, this case supports the proposition that efficiency is mainly a function of market and incentive structures rather than of ownership *per se*. It also lends credence to suggestions that the SOEs in many countries are relatively inefficient not because they are owned by the state, but because of the lack of explicit goals and objectives, state demands that can compromise the pursuit of efficiency and profitability, as well as the lack of commercially oriented organizational cultures and systems (Wortzel and Wortzel 1989).

In this light, private ownership is neither a necessary nor a sufficient condition for world-class performance. It can rather be usefully seen as a member of a class of conditions that support and engender such performance. These conditions include a competitive market, a robust institutional and regulatory environment, appropriate incentive mechanisms for managers, and, most importantly, clear goals and objectives at the enterprise level, manifested in appropriate strategic choices and realized strategies.

The Singapore Telecom case also has some wider policy-related implications concerning the implementation of privatization programs. It suggests that privatization is more successful if it is carried out within a well-developed institutional and regulatory context, supporting suggestions by World Bank researchers that "privatization of both competitive and noncompetitive SOEs is easier to launch and more likely to yield financial and economic benefits in countries that encourage entry and free trade, offer a stable climate for investment, and have a relatively well-developed regulatory and institutional capacity" (Kikeri *et al.* 1994: 256–257; see also Durchslag *et al.* 1994).

In addition, it suggests that there should be clear policy objectives concerning what privatization is expected to achieve. Privatization has often been carried out for fiscal and efficiency considerations (Pouder 1996), that are often the primary goal of privatization (Kikeri *et al.* 1994). Singapore has been untypical in this regard. Liberalization and privatization were implemented to prepare Singapore Telecom for global competition and technological challenges, and to stimulate the stock market, rather than to improve efficiency. These considerations are consistent with Ramamurti's (2000) multi-level privatization model that relates firm-, industry-, and country-level factors to privatization strategy and outcomes.

This case illustrates that the approach to privatization, in addition, should reflect the policy objectives of the state. In Singapore Telecom's case, there was a well-planned, phased approach which involved gradual liberalization (the telecoms equipment market in 1989, the mobiles' market in 1997, and full liberalization in 2000), as well as increased regulation to ensure high levels of quality and service, within an approach described as "managed competition" (Singh 1998). This "liberalization lag" (Doh 2000) has allowed the incumbent, Singapore Telecom, more time and less pressure in learning to compete in a liberalized market. In other contexts, "shock-treatment" and further deregulation may be desirable, but in the Singapore context there was no compelling reason to adopt it since Singapore Telecom was not a drain on public funds, and there was a high-quality infrastructure and tele-density rate and globally competitive standards of quality and service. Lastly, the Singapore Telecom case confirms that SOEs should receive appropriate prior preparation for privatization depending on the industry context and the state of the enterprise. In Singapore, for example, the gradual introduction of "managed competition" was deemed necessary, while in other contexts swift efficiency-improvement measures may be warranted prior to privatization, such as employing private managers who are given autonomy as well as held closely accountable for performance (Beardsley and Patsalos-Fox 1995; Kikeri *et al.* 1994).

Using a variant of the organizational action view (OA) as a theoretical framework, Singapore Telecom was analyzed in this chapter as a case where state ownership combined with several contextual and firm-related factors, especially firm strategy, led to sustained world-class performance relative to its peers. Some theoretical and practical implications of the analysis were then outlined. This analysis challenges the widely held position that public ownership is associated with inferior performance and points to the importance of strategy as a key factor in aiding superior performance even under public ownership.

Bibliography

Andrews, K. R., 1971. *The Concept of Corporate Strategy*, Homewood, IL: Irwin

Ansoff, H. I., 1965. *Corporate Strategy*, New York: McGraw-Hill

Bailey, E. E., 1986. Price and productivity change following deregulation: the US experience, *The Economic Journal*, 96: 1–17

Bank of America, 1996. *Guide to Telecommunications in Asia,* Hong Kong: Euromoney Publications: 1–6

Beardsley, S. and Patsalos-Fox, M. P., 1995. Getting telecoms privatization right, *The McKinsey Quarterly*, 1: 3–26

Bishop, M. R. and Kay, J. A., 1989. Privatization in the United Kingdom: lessons from experience, *World Development*, 17(5): 643–657

Boycko, M., Shleifer, A. and Vishny, R. W., 1996. A theory of privatization, *The Economic Journal*, 106: 309–319

Bradbury, M. E., 1999. Government ownership and financial performance in a competitive environment: evidence from the corporatization of the New Zealand government computing services, *Asia Pacific Journal of Management*, 16: 157–172

Business Times, 1999. Group wants bigger role in e-commerce, June 5

Cantor, P., 1996. To privatize or not to privatize?: That is the question; what is the answer?, *Review of Radical Political Economics*, 28(1): 96–111

Center for Business Research and Development, 1999. *Financial Highlights of Companies on the Stock Exchange of Singapore 1994–1998*, Singapore: National University of Singapore

Chandler, A. D., 1962. *Strategy and Structure: Chapters in the History of Industrial Enterprise*, Cambridge, MA: MIT Press

Child, J., 1972. Organizational structure, environment and performance: the role of strategic choice, *Sociology*, 6: 1–22

    1997. Strategic choice in the analysis of action, structure, organizations and environment: retrospect and prospect, *Organization Studies*, 18(1): 43–76

Cuervo, A. and Villalonga, B., 2000. Explaining the variance in the performance effects of privatization, *Academy of Management Review*, 25(3): 581–590

Cunha, R. C. and Cooper, C. L., 1998. Privatization and the human factor, *Journal of Applied Management Studies*, 7(2): 201–210

Doh, J. P., 2000. Entrepreneurial privatization strategies: order of entry and local partner collaboration as sources of competitive advantage, *Academy of Management Review*, 25(3): 551–571

Durchslag, S., Puri, T. and Rao, A., 1994. The promise of infrastructure privatization, *The McKinsey Quarterly*, 1: 3–19

Economist, 1996. Leviathan re-engineered, October 19

    1998, *Pocket World in Figures*, London: Profile Books

Galal, A., Jones, L., Tandon, P. and Vogelsang, I., 1994. *Welfare Consequences of Selling Public Enterprises,* New York: Oxford University Press

Gilmour, R. S., 1998. Reinventing government accountability: public functions, privatization, and the meaning of "state action," *Public Administration Review,* 58(3): 247–257

Guan, L. S., 1997. Sustaining excellence in government: the Singapore experience, *Public Administration and Development,* 17: 167–174

Heracleous, L., 1999. Privatization: global trends and implications of the Singapore experience, *International Journal of Public Sector Management,* 12: 432–444

2001. State ownership, privatization and performance: an exploratory study from a strategic management perspective, *Asia Pacific Journal of Management,* 18: 69–81

Heracleous, L. and Singh, K., 2000. Singapore Telecom: strategic challenges in a turbulent environment, *Asian Case Research Journal,* 4(1): 49–77

Johnson, G., Smith, S. and Codling, B., 2000. Microprocesses of institutional change in the context of privatisation, *Academy of Management Review,* 25(3): 572–580

Jones, D. C., 1998. The economic effects of privatization: evidence from a Russian panel, *Comparative Economic Studies,* 40(2): 75–102

Kay, J. A. and Thompson, D. J., 1986. Privatization: a policy in search of a rationale, *The Economic Journal,* 96: 18–32

Kent, J. D., 1998. Elisabeth I and the limits of privatization, *Public Administration Review,* 58(2): 99–100

Kikeri, S., Nellis, J. and Shirley, M., 1994. Privatization: lessons from market economies, *World Bank Research Observer,* 9(2): 241–272

Knoop, C. I., Applegate, L. M., Neo, B. S. and King, J. L., 1996. Singapore unlimited: building the national information infrastructure, *Harvard Business School Case,* 9-196-012

Kuo, E. C. Y., Low, L. and Toh, M. H., 1989. The Singapore telecommunications sector and issues affecting its competitive position in the Pacific region, *Colombia Journal of World Business,* Spring: 59–71

Lemke, D. K., Schminke, M., Clark, N. E. and Muir, P., 1999. Whither goest thou? Seeking trends in organization theory into the new millennium, *Academy of Management Proceedings,* OMT: D1–D6

Lewin, A. Y., 1981. Research on state-owned enterprises – introduction, *Management Science,* 27(11): 1324–1325

Linz, S. J., 1997. Russian firms in transition: champions, challengers and chaff, *Comparative Economic Studies,* 39(2): 1–36

Low, L., 1995. Privatization in Singapore: the big push, paper for Symposium on Privatization, organized by the Asian Productivity Organization, Bangkok, July 4–6

Lubatkin, M. and Rogers, R. C., 1989. Diversification, systematic risk, and shareholder return: a capital market extension of Rumelt's 1974 study, *Academy of Management Journal*, 32(2): 454–465

McDonald, K. R., 1993. Why privatization is not enough, *Harvard Business Review*, May–June: 2–7

McGahan, A. M. and Porter, M., 1997. How much does industry matter, really?, *Strategic Management Journal*, 18, Summer Special Issue: 15–30

Megginson, W. L., Nash, R. C. and Randenborgh, M. van, 1994. The financial and operating performance of newly privatized firms: an international empirical analysis, *Journal of Finance*, 49, 403–452

Miller, A. N., 1997. Ideological motivations of privatization in Great Britain versus developing countries, *Journal of International Affairs*, 50(2): 391–407

Ministry of Trade and Industry, 1999. *Economic Survey of Singapore, 1998*, Singapore: SNP Publishers

Mintzberg, H., 1978. Patterns in strategy formation, *Management Science*, 24(9): 934, 948

  1996. Managing government, governing management, *Harvard Business Review*, May–June: 75–83

Nellis, J., 1994. Is privatization necessary?, *Public Policy for the Private Sector*, Washington, DC: World Bank, May

Palich, L. E., Cardinal, L. B. and Miller, C. C., 2000. Curvilinearity in the diversification-performance linkage: an examination of over three decades of research, *Strategic Management Journal*, 21: 155–174

Porter, M. E., 1980. *Competitive Strategy: Techniques for Analyzing Industries and Competitors*, New York: Free Press

  1985. *Competitive Advantage: Creating and Sustaining Superior Performance*, New York: Free Press

Pouder, R. W., 1996. Privatizing services in local government: an empirical assessment of efficiency and institutional explanations, *Public Administration Quarterly*, Spring: 103–126

Price Waterhouse, 1996. Infrastructure privatization, paper prepared for USAID

Quinn, J. B., 1978. Strategic change: logical incrementalism, *Sloan Management Review*, Fall: 7–21

Ramamurti, R., 2000. A multilevel model of privatization in emerging economies, *Academy of Management Review*, 25(3): 525–550

Rumelt, R. P., 1991. How much does industry matter?, *Strategic Management Journal*, 12: 167–185

Rumelt, R. P., Schendel, D. E. and Teece, D. J. (eds.), 1994. *Fundamental Issues in Strategy*, Boston, MA: Harvard Business School Press

Sikorski, D., 1993. A general critique of the theory on public enterprise: part II, *International Journal of Public Sector Management*, 6(5): 56–67

Singh, K., 1995. Corporate strategy in the intelligent island: the case of Singapore Telecom, *Industrial and Corporate Change*, 4: 691–702

    1998. Guided competition in Singapore's telecommunications industry, Presented at the 4th Annual Conference of the Consortium for Research on Telecommunications Policy and Strategy, University of Michigan, Ann Arbor, June

    1999. Singapore Telecom in Europe, *Asean–EU Management Center Cases Series*

Singh, K. and Ang, S. H., 1999. Governments in business: an empirical analysis of the strategies and success of government linked corporations in Singapore, *Academy of Management Proceedings*, PNS: C1–C6

Sisodia, R. S., 1992. Singapore invests in the nation-corporation, *Harvard Business Review*, May–June: 4–11

So, J. and Shin, B., 1995. The private infrastructure industry – A global market of US$60 billion a year, *Public Policy for the Private Sector*, Washington, DC: World Bank

Straits Times, 1997. Singapore is tops for business...August 22

    1998a. PS21 turns three: Service best in Asia, May 25

    1998b. S'pore ranks third on Asia-Pac telecom index, January 13

    1999. S'pore is tops again in telecoms ranking, January 19

Tan, C. H., 1992. Singapore Telecom: from public to private sector, *International Journal of Public Sector Management*, 5(4): 4–14

Tan, R. S. K., Yeo, G. H. H. and Kwok, B., 1993. Aftermarket share price performance of government-linked companies upon privatization, *Securities Industry Review*, 19(2): 25–31

Toh, M. H. and Low, L., 1990a. Towards greater competition in Singapore's telecommunications, *Telecommunications Policy*, August: 303–314

    1990b. Privatization of telecommunications services in Singapore, in J. Pelkmans and N. Wagner (eds.), *Privatization and Deregulation in ASEAN and EC: Making Markets More Effective*, Singapore: Institute of South East Asian Studies, National University of Singapore: 82–93

United States General Accounting Office, 1997. *Privatization: Lessons Learned by State and Local Governments*, March

Vining, A. R. and Boardman, A. E., 1992. Ownership versus competition: efficiency in public enterprise, *Public Choice*, 73: 205–239

Whitley, R. and Czaban, L., 1998. Institutional transformation and enterprise change in an emergent capitalist economy: the case of Hungary, *Organization Studies*, 19(2): 259–280

Wortzel, H. V. and Wortzel, L. H., 1989. Privatization: not the only answer, *World Development*, 17(5): 633–641

Zahra, S. A., Ireland, R. D., Gutierrez, I. and Hitt, M. A., 2000. Privatization and entrepreneurial transformation: emerging issues and a future research agenda, *Academy of Management Review*, 25: 509–524

10 | *Does corporate governance make a difference to organizational performance?*

Research on the importance of generally accepted "best practices" in corporate governance has generally failed to find convincing connections between these practices and organizational performance. This chapter discusses research outcomes on the relationship between two such "best practices" (CEO/Chair duality and insider/outsider composition) and organizational performance, that find this relationship to be insignificant. We propose four possibilities for this tenuous relationship, that are not mutually exclusive: first, the possibility that "best practices" in governance are indeed irrelevant to organizational performance; secondly, that the operationalization of theoretical concepts has low face validity; thirdly, that studies are too narrow, aiming to relate board attributes directly to organizational performance and ignoring other systemic factors; and fourthly, the possibility that different types of organizations require different practices in corporate governance. The methodological and substantive implications of each of these possibilities are then addressed.

This chapter suggests, *inter alia*, that in order to gain an understanding of the strategic role and impact of boards, studies of structural board factors are insufficient; we must rather use in-depth qualitative methodologies to explore actual board functioning, and track the board's role in specific strategic decisions and actions. This shares the methodological perspective of the organizational action (OA) view, its focus on strategic choices by the dominant coalition, and the importance of following through the decisions' impact on realized strategy and performance.

The legal formation of limited liability companies has separated ownership from control of corporations (Fama and Jensen 1983), where salaried managers are hired to safeguard and grow the investment of the shareholders, who are the legal owners of the business. The

This chapter is based on Heracleous (2001).

well-documented tendency of managers to engage in excessive "on-the-job consumption" and wasteful empire-building, however, at the expense of the owners' assets and often of the viability of the business itself, has necessitated the institution of monitoring mechanisms, of which the Board of Directors is an important one.

The effectiveness of boards of directors (or lack thereof) has become a global concern. Corporate collapses, fraud cases, shareholder suits, or questionable strategic decisions are attracting attention to the top decision-making body of the corporation. In an attempt to raise the standards of corporate governance, "codes of best practice" have been drawn up by several countries, global institutions, and institutional investor organizations, and companies with ineffective corporate governance face adverse publicity in the media.

One premise for such activism is that good governance means higher returns for shareholders, and vice versa. The problem, however, is that research findings have generally failed to support the purported linkage between such best practices and organizational performance. We suggest four possibilities for this tenuous relationship, and discuss their implications. We then draw attention to the need for an explicit focus on the strategic role of the board of directors, by scholars, practitioners, and regulators, if meaningful relationships between corporate governance and organizational performance are to be established.

"Best practices" in corporate governance

Best practices and organizational performance: the research evidence

Best practices suggested by the various codes include separating the roles of CEO and Chairman; having a balanced board in terms of both skills and competencies, as well as in terms of inside/outside representation; having defined criteria for director independence; establishing audit and other committees, such as the remuneration, nomination, and strategy committees; having robust and transparent processes for director appointment; carrying out effective performance evaluations; linking rewards to performance; and communicating adequately and openly with investors. All of these are essentially aimed at improving board independence, transparency, and accountability to the company's shareholders and other stakeholders, and board effectiveness in fulfilling both its conformance *and* performance functions (Garratt 1996). Does the institution of best practices make a difference to company performance? The weight of the evidence, is that certain best practices that have been researched are not strongly associated with higher firm performance.

Studies by McKinsey Consultants explored whether a monetary value could be placed on "good governance" (Coombes and Watson 2000). The definition of "good governance" in these studies drew from conventional perceptions of best practice. It was defined as having a majority of outsiders on the board; having independent directors with no management ties and who own a significant amount of the stock of the company; who are remunerated to a large extent by stock and who are formally evaluated; and, lastly, who are responsive to investor requests. These studies found that institutional investors are willing to pay premiums of 18 percent–28 percent, depending on the country, for companies they perceive as having good corporate governance. The premiums are higher in countries with higher levels of investment risk. It is important to note, however, that the results of this study do not demonstrate the effects of best practices on firm performance as such. The results demonstrate the effects of investors' *perceptions* of the existence of best practices, on a specific measure of performance, stock price; they are also based on what investors *say* they would do, not what they actually do, which can considerably diverge.

Business Week (e.g. 2000b, 2002), *Fortune* (2001) and other business periodicals regularly carry out surveys and features on corporate governance. These have been influential in drawing public attention to organizations whose boards either excel or are cited as the worst ones. Criteria used in *Business Week*'s (2000b) survey included board independence, board accountability to shareholders, and board quality. Rather unsurprisingly, the survey concluded that "good governance, however, is no guarantee of superior performance, as clearly demonstrated by the recent results at Campbell Soup and Compaq. In the past 18 months, the performances of both companies have badly trailed their industry peers and Standard and Poor's 500-stock index." Campbell Soup was third and Compaq was fourth on the then current list of best boards.

Business periodicals have regularly used individual examples of corporations in their features to illustrate either effective or undesirable practices in governance. Such features are useful in exerting pressure on boards seen as ineffective to shape up. Even though these examples are interesting to note, they are far from representative of the general population of firms, having low external validity.

More rigorous academic research on directors' effects on performance has been extensive, focusing on such aspects as board size, outside director representation, director equity, director background and experiences, CEO duality (where the CEO also occupies the board chair role), board involvement in strategy-making, board power, and other board attributes (Finkelstein and Hambrick 1996). This research has produced mixed results, however, not lending clear support to any board attributes as being important determinants of organizational performance. Reasons for the mixed results include methodological and conceptual issues such as ignoring contextual factors and their effects on boards and company performance, insufficient attention to group dynamics at board level, the high complexity of the processes involved which cannot be captured adequately by statistical models, variations in how board attributes are measured across studies, and the use of different measures of performance.

Research on CEO/Chair duality

A key recommendation in codes of best practice is that a separation between the chair and CEO position leads to more independent boards. The Cadbury Code of Best Practice (*Cadbury Report* 1992), for example, recommended that "there should be a clearly accepted division of responsibilities at the head of the company, which will ensure a balance of power and authority, such that no individual has unfettered powers of decision." The suggestion of separating the CEO/Chairman roles is consistent with agency theory (Eisenhardt 1989), which assumes that the separation of ownership and control of corporations can lead to self-interested actions of the managers and conflicts of interest in their role as agents of the owners. Agency theory therefore suggests that CEO duality (the situation where the CEO is also the chairman of the board) reduces the monitoring effectiveness of the board over management, and supports separation of the CEO/Chairman roles. Stewardship theory (Davis *et al.* 1997), on the other hand, regards managers as inherently trustworthy and unlikely to appropriate organizational resources for their own ends. It thus views CEO duality as fostering strong and unified leadership, rather than as weakening the board's independence from management and its monitoring role.

Empirical evidence, while sometimes supporting this CEO/Chair separation (e.g. Rechner and Dalton 1991), at other times calls it into serious question. Daily and Dalton (1997), for example, found that CEOs who are also chairs of the board are not necessarily more independent from board influence than CEOs who are not. Baliga *et al.* (1996), in addition, found no significant relationship between duality status and organizational performance, and suggested that a change in this status from duality to non-duality might be a symbolic move by the board to signal that they are exercising their governance role, rather than a substantive move that can affect performance. Brickley *et al.* (1997) also found no systematic link between duality status and organizational performance or market value, suggesting that "if anything, the evidence suggests that dual leadership is associated with systematically lower cash flows and value – not higher cash flows and value, as reformers claim" (1997: 218).

Research on board insider/outsider composition
Similarly, agency theory supports the idea that boards should be dominated by outside directors, to increase the board's independence from management. The Cadbury Code suggests that "the board should include non-executive directors of sufficient calibre and number for their views to carry significant weight in the board's decisions." Stewardship theory, on the other hand, would suggest that control should accrue to firm managers rather than to outsiders, since there is no need to monitor management which is regarded as able and trustworthy.

The common assumption that the existence of social or business ties between CEOs and other board members is detrimental to board effectiveness, because it reduces the board's independence from management, was shown to be debatable. Such ties can potentially promote more collaborative strategic decision-making without necessarily reducing effective board control or vigilance (Dalton and Daily 1999b; Westphal 1999).

A study from the late 1990s found no evidence that increasing outsider board representation can improve firm performance; that firms with a supermajority of outside directors perform worse than other firms; and that firms with a higher proportion of inside directors perform as well as firms with a higher proportion of outside directors (Bhagat and Black 1999). Wagner *et al.* (1998) reviewed the empirical research related to board composition and concluded that the results were inconsistent. They then carried out a meta-analysis of twenty-nine empirical studies and found that both the greater relative presence of outsiders (non-executive directors) *and* of insiders were empirically associated with higher company performance. This curvilinear relationship was then replicated in a further study, and was shown to hold for asset measures of performance (but not for return on equity measures). Another meta-analysis of thirty-seven samples involving 7,644 organizations found that board composition explained less than 1 percent of a firm's financial performance; and that a weak influence on performance occured when there were either relatively more insiders or outsiders on the board (Rhoades *et al.* 2000), a finding consistent with earlier studies.

Dalton and associates (Dalton *et al.* 1998) reviewed the significant body of empirical research findings for these two aspects of governance (CEO duality and board insider/outsider composition) and their relation to organizational performance and found little consistency in the findings. They then carried out a meta-analysis of studies related to these board attributes: for the CEO duality attribute, they identified thirty-one empirical studies with sixty-nine usable samples involving 12,915 organizations. For the board structure attribute, they identified fifty-four empirical studies with 159 usable samples involving 40,160 organizations. Their remarkable conclusion was that:

The results for the board composition/financial performance meta-analyses suggest no relationship of a meaningful level. Subgroup moderating analyses based on firm size, the nature of the performance indicators, and operationalization board composition provide no evidence of moderating influences for these variables as well. The evidence derived from the meta-analysis and moderating analyses for board leadership structure and financial performance has the same character, i.e., no evidence of a substantive relationship. These results lead to the *very strong conclusion that the true population relationship across the studies included in these meta-analyses is near zero.* (Dalton *et al.* 1998: 282, emphasis added)

Why does the research evidence not support suggested "best practices"?

The conclusion of several rigorous studies on the performance effects of CEO duality and of insider/outsider board representation, is thus that these factors do not really make much of a difference.[1] Clearly, these results cannot be ignored by any serious student, practitioner, activist, or regulator of governance. The fact is, however, that they are consistently being ignored by those organizations that purport to know what the "best practices" in corporate governance are, and especially by vocal institutional investors. These findings may go beyond suggesting that we need different practices to suit different contexts. One potential interpretation is that the practices themselves may be irrelevant to organizational performance. There are a number of possibilities (not mutually exclusive) as to why the research does not support suggested best practices in governance. Each of these possibilities has different implications.

Possibility 1: the attributes researched, and related
"best practices," are indeed irrelevant to organizational
performance

Accepting this possibility would, after all, mean only an acceptance of the conclusions of recent meta-analyses of empirical studies that found no meaningful relationships between some of the most strongly advocated "best practices" and organizational performance. The "best practices" that have been shown to have no (or very weak) relationship to performance, as discussed above, relate to the suggestion of separating the CEO/Chair positions, and having a majority of outsiders on the board. If further "best practices" are researched extensively (for example the effects of directors owning equity), and their relationship to organizational performance is similarly found to be insignificant, then this possibility will be strengthened.

Johnson *et al.* (1996) raised possibility 1 in the conclusion to their extensive review of the governance literature:

To our knowledge, there has been no documented evidence of the existence of a unicorn. With tongue slightly in cheek, there can be two general rationales for our failure to "discover" this legendary species. First, this animal simply does not exist. Second, we have not searched in the right place, at the right time, with the right equipment. In many ways an aggregation and summary

---

[1] For critical discussions that seriously question another suggested "best practice," paying directors in equity, see Dalton and Daily (1999a) and Daily *et al.* (1999).

of the boards of directors/financial performance/other outcomes literature has this same character. Maybe such relationships simply do not exist in nature. Or, if they do exist, their magnitude is such that they are not of practical importance. (Johnson *et al.* 1996: 433)

Related to this possibility is the idea that while "best practices" in corporate governance may be irrelevant to performance, "bad" practices (such as a co-opted board that has a low degree of significant external linkages and a low level of relevant and appropriately balanced expertise) may be more strongly related to underperformance; in other words, *good corporate governance may be a qualifier rather than a differentiator*, a proposition that merits further investigation.

This possibility has the most radical implications for the current state of affairs. If it is correct, then a fundamental rethinking of the significance of corporate governance is in order, by all stakeholders concerned. Scholars must start searching elsewhere for the influencing factors on performance; governments, global organizations, and institutional investors must rethink the direction of their regulatory demands on corporations; meanwhile, practitioners will keep hoping that robust and consequential prescriptions can arise from all the research and "best practice" guidelines.

Possibility 2: the operationalization of theoretical concepts and principles has low face validity

One example would be the operationalization of the concept of "board vigilance," with the implication that higher board vigilance would lead to a higher level of organizational performance. Proxies for board vigilance that have been used include proportion of outside board members, and extent of directors' ownership of firm equity. The problem lies in trying to measure an essentially behavioral attribute, however, with indicators that may only have a circumstantial connection to this attribute. Other factors such as personality and a sense of duty may be more important to whether a director is vigilant rather than structural factors such as whether they are insiders or outsiders or whether they own equity. Vigilance is manifested in actual behaviors, however, and accessing and recording board behaviors (rather than enquiring about structural factors in surveys) is thus essential to judging the level of board vigilance.

Daily *et al.* (1999), in addition, found that there is a plethora of operationalizations of "board composition" in empirical research that are not mutually consistent and do not constitute a robust operationalization of the concept of "board independence." Independence is not merely a structural attribute; it is a psychological trait that gives rise to corresponding behaviors. Board composition may therefore be related to, but is not an adequate proxy for, board independence.

What might be useful in this case is qualitative research based on direct observation and in-depth interviewing, on which subsequent quantitative studies can build, to increase both the validity of operationalization and reliability of measurement through triangulation (Jick 1979). Several scholars have called for such field studies (Finkelstein and Hambrick 1996; Gillies and Morra 1997; Heracleous 1999). The fact that such studies are so scarce (for useful exceptions see Pettigrew and McNulty 1995; Roberts and Stiles 1999) may have more to do with boards' unwillingness to be studied in this way than researchers' willingness to undertake them.

The implications of this possibility call for scholars to pay more attention to improving the face validity of their operationalizations; and draw attention to the potential usefulness of behavioral observations and in-depth interviewing of directors and boards in the field, in order to identify behaviors that matter and that point to, for example, higher board vigilance, board independence or other concepts being assessed.

Possibility 3: the influences on organizational performance are too complex to find significant relationships in narrow studies of board attributes

Given that organizational performance is influenced by the organization's strategy (strategic choice – and, most importantly, implementation), and to a lesser extent by various interrelated factors in its micro- and macro-environments (McGahan and Porter 1997; Rumelt 1991),[2] then it is apparent that structural board attributes *per se* may be of little consequence, *except in so far as they influence strategic choice and implementation*. Attempts to correlate board attributes with performance, without an adequate consideration of systemic influences, or

---

[2] See the organizational action (OA) view of strategic management discussed in chapter 2.

of a linkage with their strategic significance, is thus bound to produce weak and inconsistent results.

Possibility 3 implies that scholars need to develop methodologies that can account for multiple, systemic, and multi-directional influences on organizational performance, and to avoid models that attempt to correlate directly board attributes and performance. From this perspective, the implicit assumptions underlying such models (that the factors influencing firm performance are linear and uni-directional) can be seen as too simplistic.

Possibilities 2 and 3 essentially imply that the problem of not finding a significant linkage between corporate governance and performance is a methodological as opposed to a substantive one. According to possibility 2, the operationalization of variables has low face validity and consequently reliability; according to possibility 3, an overly narrow methodological approach is used, that can not do justice to the complexities of the real-world phenomenon. But if the problem is confined to possibilities 2 and 3, the underlying principle that good corporate governance (as generally perceived) leads to better organizational performance is not questioned. Gillies and Morra (1997: 77), for example, have supported this point of view when they argue, "common sense tells us that there is a relationship between corporate governance and firm performance. The fact that various empirical macrostudies in corporate governance have been unable to identify it does not mean that this relationship does not exist."

The fact that the institutional investor community is largely ignoring research findings that question the relevance of "best practices" may be related to these two possibilities. In other words, if institutional investors believe that studies are too narrow and of questionable validity, then from their own point of view they have good reason to ignore them and go on demanding corporate governance reform as if there is no evidence questioning such "best practices."

Possibility 4: different types of organizations require different board practices

This is a concern expressed by several practitioners, who see the possibility of excessive regulation in corporate governance as restrictive and of limited practical use, especially if it follows the "cookie-cutter" approach. In this view, research results are inconsistent because a particular board attribute or structure might be appropriate for one type of organization, but inappropriate or even detrimental in another.

While companies such as Intel or General Motors have paid much attention to aligning their corporate governance processes to suggested best practices, publishing extensive details on their web sites and wishing to be seen as leaders in corporate governance practice, others, especially dot.com companies, ignore most of the suggested best practices, especially when it comes to board independence from management (*Business Week* 2000a). Some argue that conventional best practices do not apply to virtual firms' fast-moving environments that demand flexibility and fast decision-making, and that stock options granted to executives in these organizations align their interests sufficiently with the shareholders' interests so that there is no real need for monitoring by the board. Critics reply that this is no substitute for good governance based on a diversity of viewpoints and expertise, and on the presence of a strong independent element on the board.

Whatever the merits of this particular debate, the wider idea that organizations should tailor their structures and processes to their task and environment has had a long and well-researched history in management research, in the form of contingency theory (see Donaldson 1995 for a useful collection of key works). Important studies in corporate governance have productively utilized a contingency framework (e.g. Finkelstein and D'Aveni 1994; Pearce and Zahra 1991; Zajac and Westphal 1996). Pearce and Zahra's (1991) study, for example, validated the existence of different board types, and found that "participative" boards (characterized by both high CEO power and high board power) are associated with the highest levels of company financial performance.

This possibility implies that scholars need explicitly to incorporate a contingency perspective in their studies. This would draw attention to addressing not simply the board's monitoring role (as advocated by agency theory); but its expertise and counsel roles (consistent with stewardship theory) and its linkages with external resources (consistent with the resource dependence perspective) (Dalton *et al.* 1999), as well as a more explicit focus on the organizational task and context. It would also mean that relevant contingency variables were proposed, based on theory and empirical findings, and explicitly considered in subsequent theory-building and research design. For example, a prospector organization (Miles and Snow 1986) with a flexible and decentralized structure operating in fast-moving environments may require different board structures and emphasize different director roles than a defender organization with a functional and centralized structure, operating in more stable environments.

A contingency approach may also help to place several conflicting prescriptions of agency and stewardship theories in context. Since conflicting prescriptions for practice exist, it follows that one of these two theories must be less applicable in a given empirical context. The challenge therefore lies in identifying the types of contexts in which different theories are most applicable. Possibility 4 goes beyond suggesting that we need better operationalizations: it suggests that we need better theory. Such theory-building would concentrate on identifying relevant contingency factors and how they influence the empirical applicability of different theories. Addressing multiple board roles and their relative significance in task environments characterized by different contingency factors would potentially lead to a more pragmatic contextual understanding of corporate governance processes, as well as to potentially useful prescriptions for executives and for other stakeholders.

Conclusion: the need for a strategic perspective in corporate governance

We discussed recent research on the importance of selected "best practices" in corporate governance, that has generally failed to find convincing connections between these practices and organizational performance. We then proposed four possibilities for this tenuous relationship, that are not mutually exclusive: first, the possibility that "best practices" are indeed irrelevant to performance; secondly, that the operationalization of theoretical concepts has low face validity; thirdly, that studies are too narrow, aiming to relate board attributes directly to organizational performance and ignoring other systemic factors; and, lastly, the possibility that different types of organizations require different practices in corporate governance. We also addressed the implications of each of these possibilities; the first implies that corporate governance "best practices" need to be radically rethought and that a healthy dose of skepticism is in order regarding such practices; the second implies the need for higher face validity of operationalization through behavioral observation and in-depth interviewing of directors; the third implies the need for research models and paradigms that can account for systemic and multi-directional influences; and the fourth implies that a contingency perspective needs to be incorporated in studies of governance.

In discussing possibility 3, it was suggested that corporate governance can be highly influential on organizational performance in so far as it is related to the strategic management of the corporation. This is a proposition theoretically grounded on the findings of several studies that a company's strategy is highly influential on organizational performance (e.g. McGahan and Porter 1997; Rumelt 1991). Even in very tough industries characterized by intense competition and slim profit margins, there are organizations that consistently deliver superior returns to their shareholders, chiefly as a result of effective strategy development and execution. Examples include Dell in the PC industry, Microsoft in the software industry, and Singapore Airlines in the airline industry. Careful study of these companies reveals that they have developed distinctive competencies to support innovative competitive strategies that set them apart from their competitors. Boards, sitting at the apex of organizations, are ideally the bodies that should help to develop and ensure the successful implementation of sound competitive strategies.

Even though directors do take their strategic responsibilities seriously (Dulewicz *et al.* 1995), an extensive review of the role of the board in the strategic management of organizations finds that "the virtually uniform conclusion that comes out of this research stream is that boards of directors are not involved in strategy formation" (Finkelstein and Hambrick 1996: 228). Boards are usually at best involved in strategy ratification rather than formation, and avoid "rocking the boat," especially when confronted with a powerful CEO. Director and board evaluation is rarely if ever carried out, and there are usually no systematic processes for identifying and selecting suitable candidates to serve as directors, but instead reliance on the personal networks of the chairman, CEO or other directors (O'Neal and Thomas 1996).

An effective board would need to ensure productive board processes, including the creation of a climate of trust and candor at board level, fostering a culture of open dissent to enable contrary points of view to emerge, ensuring that directors are actively engaged in important issues that the company faces, and evaluating the board's and individual directors' performance (Sonnenfeld 2002).

Given the importance of strategic management for organizational performance, it is necessary for studies of governance, as well as boards of directors in carrying out their role, to have a clear strategic focus. This would draw attention to the fact that a director's role is not simply to be a monitoring mechanism over management (as advocated by agency theory), but also to offer expertise and advice in strategy formation (consistent with stewardship theory) and to offer linkages with external resources (consistent with the resource dependence perspective) (Dalton *et al.* 1999).

Thus, useful future methodological directions for research on corporate governance would include (1) a higher concern with the validity and reliability of measurements, (2) employment of methodological triangulation, through the use of fieldwork primary data as a rich resource for improving the operationalization of concepts, (3) the explicit incorporation of a contingency perspective in both theory-building and theory-testing, (4) a strategic focus on how boards influence (or don't influence) various aspects of the corporation's strategic management process, (5) a focus on factors related to productive group dynamics as part of a higher concern with board process than simply with board structure. These factors would hopefully lead scholars to a deeper understanding of the "territory," through more accurate mapping techniques and maps; and improve the dialogue between the various stakeholders, through the production of robust descriptions and consequently sound prescriptions.

Bibliography

Baliga, B. R., Moyer, N. C. and Rao, R. S., 1996. CEO duality and firm performance: what's the fuss?, *Strategic Management Journal*, 17: 41–53

Bhagat, S. and Black, B., 1999. The uncertain relationship between board composition and firm performance, *Business Lawyer*, 54: 921–963

Brickley, J. A., Coles, J. L. and Jarrell, G., 1997. Leadership structure: separating the CEO and chairman of the board, *Journal of Corporate Finance*, 3: 189–220

Business Week, 2000a. Dot.com boards are flouting the rules, January 17
2000b. The best and worst corporate boards, January 24
2002. The best and worst boards: how the corporate scandals are sparking a revolution in governance, October 7

Cadbury Report: The Financial Aspects of Corporate Governance, 1992. London, Gee

Coombes, P. and Watson, M., 2000. Three surveys on corporate governance, *McKinsey Quarterly*, 4: 74–77

Daily, C. M., Certo, S. T. and Dalton, D. R., 1999. Pay directors in stock? No, *Across the Board*, November–December: 46–50

Daily, C. M. and Dalton, D. R., 1997. CEO and board chair roles held jointly or separately: much ado about nothing?, *Academy of Management Executive*, 11(3): 11–20

Daily, C. M., Johnson, J. L. and Dalton, D. R., 1999. On the measurements of board composition: poor consistency and a serious mismatch of theory and operationalization, *Decision Sciences*, 30(1): 83–106

Dalton, D. R. and Daily, C. M., 1999a. Directors and shareholders as equity partners? Handle with care!, *Compensation & Benefits Review*, 31(1): 73–79

     1999b. What's wrong with having friends on the board?, *Across the Board*, March: 28–32

Dalton, D. R., Daily, C. M., Ellstrand, A. E. and Johnson, J. L., 1998. Meta-analytic reviews of board composition, leadership structure, and financial performance, *Strategic Management Journal*, 19: 269–290

Dalton, D. R., Daily, C. M., Johnson, J. L. and Ellstrand, A. E., 1999. Number of directors and financial performance: a meta-analysis, *Academy of Management Journal*, 42: 674–686

Davis, J. H., Schoorman, F. D. and Donaldson, L., 1997. Toward a stewardship theory of management, *Academy of Management Review*, 22: 20–47

Donaldson, L. (ed.), 1995. *Contingency Theory*, Aldershot: Dartmouth

Dulewicz, V., MacMillan, K. and Herbert, P., 1995. Appraising and developing the effectiveness of boards and their directors, *Journal of General Management*, 20(3): 1–19

Eisenhardt, K. M., 1989. Agency theory: an assessment and review, *Academy of Management Review*, 14(1): 57–74

Fama, E. F. and Jensen, M. C., 1983. Separation of ownership and control, *Journal of Law & Economics*, 26: 301–325

Finkelstein, S. and D'Aveni, R. A., 1994. CEO duality as a double-edged sword: how boards of directors balance entrenchment avoidance and unity of command, *Academy of Management Journal*, 37(5): 1079–1108

Finkelstein, S. and Hambrick, D., 1996. *Strategic Leadership – Top Executives and their Effects on Organizations*, Minneapolis: West

Fortune, 2001. The dirty half-dozen: America's worst boards, May 14

Garratt, B., 1996. *The Fish Rots from the Head*, London: HarperCollins

Gillies, J. and Morra, D., 1997. Does corporate governance matter?, *Business Quarterly*, Spring: 71–77

Heracleous, L., 1999. The board of directors as leaders of the organization, *Corporate Governance: An International Review*, 7: 256–264

     2001. What is the impact of corporate governance on organizational performance?, *Corporate Governance: An International Review*, 9: 165–173

Jick, T. D., 1979. Mixing qualitative and quantitative methods: triangulation in action, *Administrative Science Quarterly*, 24: 602–611

Johnson, J. L., Daily, C. M. and Ellstrand, A. E., 1996. Boards of directors: a review and research agenda, *Journal of Management*, 22: 409–438

McGahan, A. M. and Porter, M., 1997. How much does industry matter, really?, *Strategic Management Journal*, 18, Summer Special Issue: 15–30

Miles, R. E. and Snow, C. C., 1986. Network organizations: new concepts for new forms, *California Management Review*, 28: 62–73

O'Neal, D. and Thomas, H., 1996. Developing the strategic board, *Long Range Planning*, 29: 314–327

Pearce, J. A. and Zahra, S. A., 1991. The relative power of CEOs and boards of directors: associations with corporate performance, *Strategic Management Journal*, 12: 135–153

Pettigrew, A. and McNulty, T., 1995. Power and influence in and around the boardroom, *Human Relations*, 48: 845–873

Rechner, P. L. and Dalton, D. R., 1991. CEO duality and organizational performance: a longitudinal analysis, *Strategic Management Journal*, 12: 155–160

Rhoades, D. L., Rechner, P. L. and Sundaramurthy, C., 2000. Board composition and financial performance: a meta-analysis of the influence of outside directors, *Journal of Managerial Issues*, 1(12): 76–91

Roberts, J. and Stiles, P., 1999. The relationship between chairmen and chief executives: competitive or complementary roles?, *Long Range Planning*, 32: 36–48

Rumelt, R. P., 1991. How much does industry matter?, *Strategic Management Journal*, 12: 167–185

Sonnenfeld, J. A., 2002. What makes great boards great, *Harvard Business Review*, September: 106–113

Wagner, J. A., Stimpert, J. L. and Fubara, E. I., 1998. Board composition and organizational performance: two studies of insider/outsider effects, *Journal of Management Studies*, 35: 656–677

Westphal, J. D., 1999. Collaboration in the boardroom: behavioral and performance consequences of CEO/board social ties, *Academy of Management Journal*, 42: 7–24

Zajac, E. J. and Westphal, J. D., 1996. Who shall succeed? How CEO/Board preferences and power affect the choice of new CEOs, *Academy of Management Journal*, 39: 64–90

11 | *Types of inter-organizational networks and the strategic roles of directors*

This chapter develops a typology of inter-organizational networks based on the key dimensions of organizational interdependence and network durability. This helps to place the network literature in context by suggesting that network features and processes vary in different types of networks, and have different implications for performance. Secondly, there is an extended discussion of "embedded" networks found in East Asia. A "micro-typology" of such embedded networks is developed, based on the dimensions of formalization of ties and networking scope. Thirdly, taking a strategic perspective on the role of the board of directors, it is suggested that in the context of achieving more effective governance, (interlocking) directors' roles should differ[1] based on the type of network in which they are engaged. This chapter represents an attempt to operationalize a key conclusion of chapter 10, on the need to better understand directors' strategic roles rather than the mostly fruitless attempt so far of attempting to relate structural board features to organizational performance.

At the turn of the twentieth century, Max Weber believed that the spread of bureaucratization was largely fostered by increasing competition between capitalist firms (DiMaggio and Powell 1983). Intensifying competition spurred on by new information and communication technologies has been encouraging a different phenomenon: the creation of various types of inter-organizational networks. Whereas the prime objective of bureaucratization was efficiency, network creation can aim towards increasing innovation, gaining access to new markets, sharing network resources, reducing cycle times, decreasing transaction costs, managing uncertainty, or lobbying regulatory bodies. Even though networks are ubiquitous and varied in form, however, there

---

This chapter is based on Heracleous and Murray (2001).

[1] Whether directors' roles in different types of networks do differ is an empirical question that can be addressed by further research on this area.

is little research on the different kinds of networks and their varying impact on organizations' actions and performance. The development of valid typologies or taxonomies would be an important step in furthering our understanding of this critical inter-organizational form.

Networks embody a relational rather than a transactional or atomistic view of the organization and this entails new challenges of improving our understanding of the origins, evolution, and management of inter-organizational relationships, as well as how they can confer competitive advantage. Networks embody and depend on different kinds of ties at various organizational levels. Ties at board level through the mechanism of "board interlocks" have been seen as the principal indicator of network ties (Mizruchi 1996), yet little has been written about the role of directoral interlocks as relational mechanisms of strategic importance within networks.

Research on inter-organizational networks

Inter-organizational networks have been examined from a variety of theoretical fields, including sociology (Emirbauer and Goodwin 1994), structuration theory (Alexander 1998; Sydow and Windeler 1998), organization theory (Kraatz 1998), and strategic management (Gulati *et al.* 2000).[2] From the perspective of achieving competitive advantage in particular, networks have been seen as spurring innovation (Chesbrough and Teece 1996; Powell 1998), aiding adaptation to environmental change (Kraatz 1998), increasing flexibility and efficiency (Lorenzoni and Baden-Fuller 1995), allowing access to critical network resources at low cost (Gulati *et al.* 2000) and ultimately leading to higher performance (Dyer and Nobeoka 2000; Gulati *et al.* 2000). Such effects are assumed to result from structural opportunities for specialization, from diffusion of information, and/or from various types of inter-organizational mimetic processes (Haunschild and Miner 1997).

Gulati *et al.* (2000) note that strategy research suggests five traditional sources of differential returns to the firm: industry structure, intra-industry structure, inimitable resources and capabilities,

---

[2] Even though the extensive strategic alliance literature (Das and Teng 1998; Hitt *et al.* 2000; Inkpen 1998) would be relevant here, the chapter focuses on inter-organizational networks from a multiple participants rather than a dyadic perspective.

contracting and co-ordination costs, and dynamic and path dependent constraints and benefits. Each of these can be affected by organizational membership of networks. Networks influence the nature of competition and the degree of profitability in an industry through their structure, membership, and tie modality (Galaskiewicz and Zaheer 1999; Gulati *et al.* 2000). According to the literature on the resource-based view of the firm (Pfeffer and Salancik 1978), networks can be seen as creating resources beyond the firm's boundaries – "network resources" to which members have privileged access that confers cost- or value-based advantages and that are hard to imitate owing to their complexity and path dependence.

One of the most frequently discussed effects of networks is their potential for lowering transaction costs. Gulati *et al.* (2000) suggest that traditional transaction cost concepts are limited by their transactional interpretation of firm relationships. If one views individual transactions as part of a history of relationships and as being socially embedded, however, then transaction costs can be mitigated by superior information, trust, and reputational effects which reduce information asymmetry and increase the disincentives for opportunism (Carney 1998a).

The relative interdependence of firms in a network, positively associated with density of ties, is important to most discussions of networks. The durability of the network is also important as certain network effects can be produced only as a result of time and learning. Trust and trustworthiness is a related important network attribute that may be seen as a product of interdependence and durability. Finally, the generative aspects of networks are important: both their ability to create and their potential constraints on creativity (Burt 1992; Coleman 1990; Kogut 2000; Uzzi 1996; Walker *et al.* 1997). It seems clear therefore that networks have many bases on which superior performance and profitability for member firms may be built. The decision to participate in a network and the strategy for shaping, maintaining, and developing membership are important strategic commitments. But since networks are far from homogeneous, understanding their impact and the challenges of effective development and maintenance demands some taxonomy that illuminates their variety.

Yet, despite the breadth of research on inter-organizational networks, there has been little effort aimed at developing network typologies (with a few exceptions, e.g. Belussi and Arcangeli 1998). Developing valid network typologies using relevant dimensions would be useful in analytical terms, as it helps to make debates more conceptually sharp and focused, and enables more holistic organizational enquiry (Doty and Glick 1994). The network typology developed here is not aimed simply for classification purposes, but towards orienting debates regarding the nature, potential motivations for, and consequences of networks, as well as the role of directoral interlocks in different types of networks.

Development of a network typology

This section develops a network typology based on two dimensions – interdependence and durability – and relates generative capacity to the resulting types. The dimension of interdependence was used by Contractor and Lorange (1988) to discuss various types of networks on a continuum between negligible dependence and high dependence. "Inter-organizational dependence" refers to the extent to which firms involved in the network utilize each others' outputs (e.g. raw materials) and resources (e.g. market-related information) in their own operations. A high extent of utilization reflects the operational and strategic importance of inter-organizational relationships and constitutes a high level of dependence. It is likely to be associated with dense, redundant ties and the potential for high levels of trust to operate. This can be seen as a key dimension for creating a network typology, given that networks are usually formed for particular strategic purposes, even if these purposes are emergent (Kogut 2000), and given that important strategic outcomes and variations in competitive advantage depend significantly on the extent of inter-organizational dependence.

A network with negligible interdependence other than through independent transactions, and no durability of relationships beyond individual transactions, can be characterized as a market where participants behave atomistically – an *"atomistic network."* Such a structure has been an implicit or explicit assumption of various traditions, for example industrial organization economics and its translation into the strategic management field (Porter 1980, 1985). At the other extreme of this axis, extensive operational and strategic interdependence can exist between organizations but not necessarily persist for very long or require dense ties in order to function. Drawing from the industry life-cycle literature (Hambrick and Lei 1985) and complexity theory (Axelrod and Cohen 2000; Waldrop 1994), this can be labeled the "*edge of chaos network*" because it reflects the conditions usually found in embryonic industries, in industries experiencing the shock of technological upheaval, or in industries coping with de-regulation, for example. The aims of participation in such networks include scanning, information search, idea generation, and option buying. There is high interdependence but low network durability, in the sense that even though the structure of the network may be relatively stable in the short to medium term, the participants change continually and the external forces at work may shift in due course to a less turbulent and uncertain state.

Network durability is the second underlying dimension of the network typology developed. Networks are constituted through inter-organizational linkages, and durability allows the development of dense redundant ties supporting the creation of trust and generative learning. "Durability" refers to the extent to which these networks persist in the longer term, and with broadly similar participants – in terms of both structure and content. A common example of a network type with a high degree of durability but very limited interdependence is an industry association formed for the purpose of regulatory lobbying, of pre-empting the creation of state regulation through the institution of self-regulation, or promoting professional or craft education and regulating a specialist labor supply. Such networks are usually characterized by long-term persistence and relatively stable membership. But even though they have high durability, they typically have a low degree of organizational interdependence. This network form may be labeled the "*association network.*"

Moving to the diagonal between the two axes, and drawing from Granovetter (1985), networks with a high degree of durability as well as an extensive level of inter-organizational dependence are labeled "*embedded networks.*" Granovetter suggested that economic action should be understood not atomistically but in terms of its embeddedness in ongoing structures of social relations. "Embedded" networks can involve such mechanisms as interlocking directorates, cross-shareholdings, personnel exchanges, information exchange, and significant inter-trading. Such ties and the durability of such networks can be exemplified by Japanese *Keiretsu*, for example, that reflect deeply entrenched institutional features that derive from the structure of kinship and family in Japanese history and from intentional actions of members over several centuries to nurture and sustain the social capital that leads to this high level of durability (Bhappu 2000).

High interdependence can be manifested in terms of vertical networks comprising related suppliers, manufacturers, and distributors, or in terms of horizontal networks comprising such firms as financial institutions, semi-state institutions, and manufacturers of related products that are broadly at a similar level in the industry value chain. High interdependence and extended durability are likely to be accompanied by dense redundant ties, high levels of trust, and coherent cliques that define membership. In such structures, generative learning is possible and self-organization becomes feasible (as in, for example, the Toyota production system, Kogut 2000), as distinct from hierarchical organization led by one or more powerful members.

On the diagonal and between the "atomistic network" and the "embedded network," we find the *"brokered network."* Brokered networks include hub-and-spoke network structures and are characterized by intermediate inter-dependence and moderate durability. They often involve a strategic center which acts as a leader and co-ordinator of the network (Lorenzoni and Baden-Fuller 1995). The nurturing of social capital and building of trust are limited features of this type of network as they rely on governance mechanisms to maintain membership and on the self-interest of members to uphold compliance, as long as the cost of opportunism exceeds the benefits of non-compliance. The exchanges are transactional and based on an economic logic. Consequently, if one member is not performing it is forced out of the network by an intentional choice of the strategic center or of other powerful members, who decide not to utilize the inefficient member's output, which leads to a moderate level of network durability. Examples of this type of network are widespread in the biotechnology industry (Powell 1998). Brokered networks are characteristic of many of the networks in international outsourcing and of the production networks that cluster around global brands that now perform only design and marketing functions, such as Nike. Depending on their learning characteristics and their opportunities, they may evolve over time into embedded networks. The five network forms are illustrated in figure 11.1.

The location of networks in this map is not static. Networks can dynamically morph from one type to another over time. Important influences of this process include industry evolution, type of product,

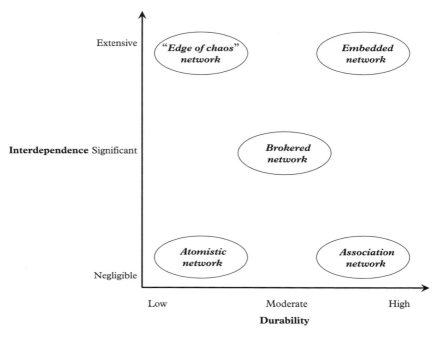

Figure 11.1 A network typology based on organizational interdependence and network durability

or service involved, and technological forces that enable complex inter-organizational co-ordination at relatively low cost, as well as the ambitions and learning of the networks and their constituent firms. In other words, a multiplicity of exogenous and endogenous factors can drive movement between types. For example, *"edge of chaos"*-type networks, can become atomistic types if the structure of the industry matures rapidly around a transparent set of technology standards, markets and competitive options. They can become brokered networks if growth and maturation produce brokerage opportunities (as seen in e-business with the emergence of supply and demand aggregators) and at a later stage define a more stable set of hub-and-spoke relationships and specializations between a few dominant firms and a hierarchy of suppliers. The Toyota production system, for example, has evolved from a brokered network to an embedded network with powerful self-regulation properties and considerable generative impact (Kogut 2000). We should further distinguish between whole networks that migrate from one type to another and migration that takes place at the organizational level as organizations exit a network of one type and enter another. Furthermore, migration in some directions may be more difficult than in others.

These networks are not completely separate, of course. Firms that are competitors and not otherwise connected, as in atomistic networks, for example, often form networks such as research-oriented consortia to develop and hopefully establish particular technologies as industry standards, in this way creating networks that have features of an *"edge of chaos"* type. They have high operational and strategic relevance but are relatively short-term and their members disperse as soon as their task is deemed complete. The constituent members of these networks may at the same time be members of larger hierarchical corporate groups that otherwise behave atomistically and competitively. The network forms identified thus represent analytical distinctions that in practice may not be so clear-cut, resembling in this sense Weber's "ideal-types" (Weber 1922). Firms may, at the same time, be involved in different types of networks, features of networks may change over time, and networks can form at intermediate positions in figure 11.1.

Embedded networks in East Asia

There are three dominant types of business systems in East Asia: the Japanese *Keiretsu*, the South Korean *Chaebol*, and the networks of Overseas Chinese business (Hamilton and Biggart 1988; Lasserre and Schutte 1995).[3] The development of each of these systems has been historically influenced by several dimensions of their institutional context, particularly political and financial factors (Biggart 1991; Whitley 1990, 1991). All three systems constitute embedded networks as described above, as they involve significant interdependencies and ties among the organizations involved, and they persist over the longer term with broadly similar participants (except in the case of Chinese business networks, which exhibit high interdependencies and persist in the longer

[3] This discussion does not imply that only embedded networks can be found in Asia, or that the only types of embedded networks in Asia are the three types discussed. However, these are the dominant types and for space reasons this chapter does not discuss such entities as former colonial trading houses (*Hongs*), or state-owned enterprises (SOEs).

term, but with a relatively lower degree of stability in participants, Redding 1995). As comparative analyses have illustrated, however, the features of these networks are far from isomorphic, exhibiting both similarities and differences among several dimensions that include the extent of personal authority and owner domination, the importance of formal co-ordination and control procedures, management style, type of employee commitment, extent of business specialization, use of evolutionary strategies, use of relational contracting, and presence of long-term inter-sector co-ordination (Whitley 1990, 1991).

Embedded networks are characterized by extensive interdependence through substantial inter-organizational linkages and high durability. Inter-organizational linkages can be of various interrelated types, and include equity ownership, strategic alliances, inter-trading, personnel exchanges, information exchanges, social clubs composed of senior managers, and personal, kinship, or ethnic ties. These linkages differ with regard to extent of formalization (their governance through formal rules and procedures), ranging from low (personal ties), to medium (inter-trading) to high (equity ownership). Formalization of prevalent ties is thus a useful distinguishing feature from an embedded networks' perspective, ranging from informal, personal, and opportunistically formed ties to more formalized ties based on equity ownership and formal authority structures.

An additional distinguishing feature is organizational scope, a central corporate strategy concern (Porter 1985). Organizational scope can help distinguish between networks where organizations involved in different parts of the industry value chain are formally integrated within a conglomerate structure through substantial ownership and control ties, or are kept separate but still involved and interdependent in terms of long-term relational contracting and other types of co-operation. Drawing on relevant literature, an additional "micro-typology" of embedded networks can be developed that is able more finely to distinguish between the three main types of Asian networks. This is presented in figure 11.2.

Japanese Keiretsu

Japanese corporations (*Kaisha*) exhibit a relatively high degree of specialization and a higher extent of use of relational contracting within wider business systems (*Keiretsu*) that are vertically or horizontally

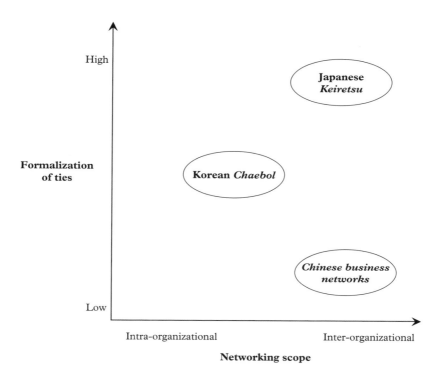

Figure 11.2 A typology of Asian embedded networks based on formalization of ties and networking scope

oriented and characterized by high degrees of interdependency. These interdependencies include equity ties, interlocking directorates, inter-trading, and information and personnel exchange. *Keiretsu* also exhibit significant ties with state agencies. Strategic decision-making is rela-tively decentralized, and consensus-based. It is driven more by existing competencies and strategic commitments than by unrelated opportuni-ties that present themselves opportunistically. Management has a high degree of autonomy from shareholders and exhibits a relatively high stakeholder orientation, illustrated in implicit lifetime employment sys-tems and long-term, seniority-based advancement. The main source of authority is the holding of office; formal rules and procedures are more important in the *Keiretsu* than particularistic, personal ties. Thus, in terms of the embedded network typology above, the Japanese *Keiretsu* exhibit multiple, dense formalized ties, and extended scope based on extensive inter-firm networking (Bhappu 2000; Gerlach 1992; Whitley 1990).

South Korean Chaebol

The *Chaebol* incorporate a wider variety of activities than either the *Keiretsu* or Overseas Chinese Businesses within their authority structures and organizational scope. The degree of relational contracting and other co-operative activities is therefore much lower in these network types. In marked contrast with the *Keiretsu* (and similar to Overseas Chinese Businesses) is a strong connection between ownership and control, with the *Chaebol* being tightly controlled by owner-founders and their families. Strategic decision-making is highly centralized to founders and family members, where personal, particularistic connections are more important than formal rules and procedures. In a similar fashion to the *Keiretsu*, employment is still long-term and advancement is seniority-based, but within a much more centralized climate that may stifle innovation and self-initiative. The *Chaebol* are highly geared and dependent on state-owned banks for funding; their strategic direction has often been influenced by state policies and objectives. The *Chaebol* thus exhibit a mixture of formalized, equity ties with informal, personal ties and a low level of inter-firm relational contracting since they incorporate a higher variety of activities within their organizational scope (Biggart 1991; Whitley 1990).

Chinese family business networks

Chinese business networks are based on personal, kinship or ethnic ties, rather than more dense, formalized ties. As with the *Chaebol*, the patriarchs of Chinese firms are almost worshipped and their beliefs permeate the organization's culture. There is a high level of specialization in individual firms owned by Overseas Chinese (but a significant level of diversification within families). The stability of actors is lower in Chinese family business networks than in both the *Chaebol* and the *Keiretsu*. The participants in different deals change depending on its nature and what they can offer to its successful execution. Thus, strategic decision-making is relatively more opportunistic than planned. As in the *Chaebol*, control is strongly centralized and associated with ownership; but the personal element features much more prominently. The holding of office is less important than relationship to the founder-owner; role and task definitions are much less formal and more protean than in either the *Chaebol* or the *Keiretsu*. The potential longevity and successful internationalization of Chinese family businesses are matters for considerable debate. Chinese business networks tend to depend more on finance from savings, relatives, and business contacts than banks or state-controlled agencies. Individual firm specialization means that the extent of sub-contracting and relational contracting is high within a web of informal, personal connections. Thus, the Chinese business networks are largely constituted of informal, personalized ties with low formalization, and exhibit extended scope through a relatively high degree of inter-firm interactions (Carney 1998b; Redding 1995; Whitley 1990).

Pressures for change

In Japan, as the long-awaited economic recovery began to "look anaemic at best and endangered at worst" (*Economist* 2000b), public debt has been mounting and corporate restructurings have been proceeding very slowly. *Keiretsu* cross-shareholdings and relational contracting have been reducing, banks central to the network have been becoming financially weaker, and some have been forced to merge with banks belonging to other *Keiretsu* (*Economist* 2000d). In Korea, the state has been largely unsuccessful in its attempts to get the *Chaebol* to reduce debt and focus on a limited amount of core businesses. The relative (and uncertain) economic recovery after 1999, according to some commentators, has encouraged the *Chaebol* to "hew to the discredited ways of pre-crisis Korea Inc. Profitable affiliates are dragooned into pouring money into weak ones. *Chaebol* chairmen lose millions on unilateral investment decisions. Suggestions of insider trading by Chaebol families persist" (*Far Eastern Economic Review* 2000b: 64). The 1999 collapse of the Daewoo *Chaebol*, however, and the collapse of Daewoo Motors in 2000 as the state-owned Korea Development Bank refused to provide any more funding, may be indications of more lasting change (*Economist* 2000c). As many patriarchs of ethnic Chinese businesses prepare to hand over power to their children, moreover, several traditional characteristics of these businesses are also in transition. Their children's Western business education and life experience introduces different ways of thinking about and doing business (*Far Eastern Economic Review* 2000a).

All three embedded network types, therefore, are under pressure for change, deriving from interrelated factors such as the global movement towards more transparent and effective corporate governance; the inclinations of global capital towards shareholder value; the effects of the Asian crisis; government demands for slimmer, more efficient, and less monopolistic conglomerates; the Western Business-school education of many of the patriarchs' children; the new competencies required for successful global strategies; and the demands of more flexible workforces that now seek more autonomy and the chance to make real contributions (*Business Week* 2000; *Economist* 2000a, 2000b, 2000c, 2000d; *Far Eastern Economic Review* 1998a, 1998b, 1999, 2000a, 2000b; *Fortune* 1998). Whether these pressures will in the longer term lead to more isomorphic systems whose features are congruent with Western-style agency-theory predictions (Phan and Yoshikawa 2000) remains to be seen.

Interlocking directorates

Research on interlocking directorates

Interlocking directors are a central case of interpersonal linkage between firms at board level. Owing to their position and potential to influence firm strategy and to monitor executive actions, they carry a special responsibility with regard to the creation, maintenance, and development of the ties which underpin inter-organizational interdependence and its durability, which embody trust and generate learning at a strategic level. This section reviews the pertinent literature on interlocking directors, explores its relevance to strategic decision-making, and suggests ways in which interlocks can facilitate network effectiveness and thus guard against networks' potentially adverse features.

Interlocks have various functions, that can be seen as complementary in some cases (Palmer *et al.* 1986). They can be used to co-opt environmental resources (Mizruchi and Stearns 1988; Stearns and Mizruchi 1993), to cement ties within the upper capitalist class (Useem 1979), or to further one's career (Zajac 1988). Studies have shown that information transferred through director interlocks does encourage inter-organizational mimetic processes. For example, interlocks can influence firms to imitate related firms' horizontal, vertical and conglomerate acquisition activity (Haunschild 1993), or to adopt anti-takeover defenses such as "poison pills" (Davis and Greve 1997). The features of a specific practice also influence diffusion. For example, observable practices and practices that accord with prevailing social norms spread faster than non-observable practices and practices challenging social norms (Rogers 1995). Further, both interlocking and its influence on the diffusion of practices are influenced by geographical or spatial factors (Davis and Greve 1997; Kono *et al.* 1998).

The significance of inter-organizational interlocks for firm strategy is further illustrated by findings that interlocks help to shape strategic choices in ways that conform to industry norms, and that extra-industry interlocks are associated with the adoption of non-conforming strategies (Geletkanycz and Hambrick 1997). Board interlocks can be used to cope with increasing levels of environmental uncertainty and particular types of resource dependencies (Lang and Lockhart 1990). They can also be used as control and co-ordination devices in the context of inter-organizational networks (Maman 1999). The influence of interlocking directorates varies, however, depending on the situation. Interlocks are less influential for large firms, for firms that are central in a network, or firms whose CEO has alternative sources of information, such as by belonging to professional associations. They are more influential with issues that receive substantial press coverage and when ties are between similar rather than dissimilar firms (Haunschild and Beckman 1998).

From the perspective of investors, interlocking directorates are often criticized for enabling incumbent CEOs to co-opt the members of their remuneration committee and thus receive significantly higher remuneration than would be the case with a truly independent committee. Research has indeed shown that CEOs who lead interlocked firms do earn significantly higher compensation than those who don't (Hallock 1997). When juxtaposed with findings that interlock activity is higher in lower-performing firms, and that a higher level of interlocking is not necessarily associated with higher profitability (Mizruchi 1996), then the remuneration findings above give an even greater cause for concern to investors.

Other research based on exchange theory has helped to explain how outside CEO-directors can change their orientation from one of mutual support and deference towards the firm's CEO to one of independence and control if they have experienced such changes themselves in their own organization (Westphal and Zajac 1997). In addition, CEOs used to passive boards will tend to appoint new directors with prior experience in such boards in order to perpetuate their power, whereas active, powerful boards will tend to appoint directors with prior experience in similarly active boards in order to maintain their own power (Zajac and Westphal 1996). The structure and composition of boards can have significant effects on intra-organizational control strategies, corporate strategies and strategic choice (Baysinger and Hoskisson 1990). Board involvement in strategic decision-making, in addition, is associated with improved financial performance (Judge and Zeithaml 1992; Richardson 1987).

Mizruchi's (1996) review and evaluation of the interlock literature identified six main potential reasons for interlocking, and evaluated the evidence relating to these, as shown in table 11.1.

It seems safe to assert that interlocking directors can and do have a significant impact on strategic decision-making, although these effects vary according to the situation. The nature of the impact of interlocks in terms of firm performance is not widely researched and, to date, reports show conflicting evidence. Given that interlocks have a significant impact on strategic decision-making, the next section addresses their potential impact within networks.

The strategic role of interlocking directors in different network types

Firms' participation in networks can contribute to their competitive strategies and potentially to competitive advantage. The motives for entering into networks are often explicitly linked to the achievement of specific strategic goals. Directors, as leaders of the organization, should be closely involved in its strategic management (Heracleous 1999; Judge and Zeithaml 1992). From a normative perspective, boards should not only monitor and discipline top management, but should also be actively involved in strategy formation, for example deciding on such issues as diversification, resource management, and strategic change (Finkelstein and Hambrick 1996). The decision about firm scope is a central corporate strategy commitment and is intimately linked with network participation in so far as this affects vertical and

Table 11.1 *Potential reasons for interlocks and research-based evaluations*

Potential reasons for interlocks	Research-based evaluation
Collusion: interlocks represent intentional attempts by organizations to engage in practices that restrict competition	Plausible but unlikely; no systematic evidence that collusion is a motivation for interlocks or that interlocks would be effective in this regard
Co-optation: interlocks are used by organizations to co-opt sources of environmental uncertainty	On balance, the evidence supports the view that a minority of interlocks is associated with inter-organizational resource dependence
Monitoring: interlocks are used for the purposes of exerting inter-organizational control	Empirically, it is not possible to distinguish between co-optation interlocks and monitoring or influence-driven interlocks
Legitimacy: interlocks are used to increase an organization's environmental legitimacy through prestigious connections	Conceptually expected, but little empirical research by interlock researchers, this model is difficult to test and is closely related to the co-optation model
Career advancement: from the perspective of the individual director, interlocks are ways to advance one's career	Supported empirically, this view is complementary rather than opposed to alternative views, however
Social cohesion: interlocks are in effect social ties among members of the upper capitalist class	Evidence indicates that interlocks can partly represent intra-class ties in addition to inter-organizational ties

horizontal relatedness. Directors themselves appear to take their strategic responsibilities seriously (Dulewicz *et al.* 1995), notwithstanding the fact that actual board functioning and processes have often been found wanting when compared to normative expectations (O'Neal and Thomas 1996; Patton and Baker 1987; Whistler 1984).

The discussion here extends the line of thinking proposed by Geletkanycz and Hambrick (1997), that it is "generally beneficial for executives' external ties to align with, or fit, the firm's strategy" (1997: 673). The type of network in which the firm is embedded has important implications for the value of interlocks and for the roles of interlocking directors, and the emphasis of interlocking directors' role changes (or should change) in different types of networks. This conceptual direction is aligned with directors' role of creating useful linkages with external resources, which is consistent with the resource dependence perspective (Pfeffer and Salancik 1978). Directors still have to perform their basic and essential governance functions, however, which include their monitoring role (as advocated by agency theory), and their expertise and counsel roles (consistent with stewardship theory) (Dalton *et al.* 1999). This discussion does not assume that only interlocking directors can fulfill boundary-spanning roles, but does suggest that more effective corporate governance can be achieved if (interlocking) directors are sensitive to how their strategic contributions can be improved based on the particular networks of which their organization is part. This requires that the strategic functions of interlocks in different types of networks be clarified. Table 11.2 summarizes propositions for further investigation, that formalize and clarify the implications of the discussion. These propositions assume that if (interlocking) directors carry out the proposed functions effectively within each type of network, beneficial consequences will result for the network firms concerned. Even though the propositions do not explicitly refer to higher performance effects, these would be a natural result of the positive consequences discussed.

In the *atomistic network*, where organizations are independent market participants, firms act to maximize transactional efficiency with other market participants without aiming to form a durable network with any degree of significant inter-dependence. A key aspect of directors' roles in this case, is informative: bringing into the organization information about environmental trends and competitive conditions, especially on best practices in their industry. There are no relational duties or responsibilities concerning network management.

In the *brokered network*, organizations will still aim to maximize transactional efficiency, but within more durable networks that exhibit significant inter-dependence between firms. As opposed to vertically integrating, firms retain their flexibility by engaging in semi-durable networks that can be altered swiftly by the powerful brokers or hub firms in the network. Firms in the brokered network tend to comply with the governance rules in operation and do not defect as long as the cost of opportunism is greater than the benefits of defection. In brokered networks, governance has market, contractual, and social dimensions. Interlocking directors can help to support these governance mechanisms and maintain their currency by signaling reputation and assuring legitimacy. In so far as a firm makes judgments about a related firm on the basis of the behavior of an interlock director, the latter's

Table 11.2 *Propositions on the roles of (interlocking) directors in different network types*

Proposition 1
In the context of an *atomistic* network, if (interlocking) directors carry out their informating roles effectively, organizational efficiency will be increased owing to higher timeliness, accuracy and use of relevant environmental information

Proposition 2
In the context of a *brokered* network, if (interlocking) directors carry out their co-ordinating and governance-related functions effectively, the central firm can influence network structure and functioning to its own strategic advantage and accumulate a higher level of "Burt rent" (Burt 1992)

Proposition 3
In the context of an *embedded* network, where (interlocking) directors carry out their social capital and trust-building functions more effectively, a higher degree of co-operative strategic behavior and generative learning will result

Proposition 4
In the context of an *edge of chaos* network, if (interlocking) directors carry out their scanning, innovating and diverging functions effectively, network firms will exhibit a higher degree of adaptiveness to complex environments

Proposition 5
In the context of an *association* network, if (interlocking) directors carry out their guarding functions more effectively, the network will have a higher impact on network-relevant regulation, public opinion, and legislation

actions may be powerful and very tangible signals of reputation, trustworthiness, and legitimacy. An additional and more general role of a director is to ensure a high degree of compliance with network rules of governance so that the flow of materials and services within the network is as efficient as possible.

In the *embedded network*, dense, path dependent ties are institutionalized, although being part of such a network may not always reflect conscious strategic decisions by executives. This is partly the case, for example, in the Japanese *Keiretsu* and the Korean *Chaebol*. A key aspect of directors' roles in such networks is to build and sustain the social capital of the network. This may take place with or without conscious intent, as many executives go through long periods of cultural socialization and internalize the significance of nurturing social capital.

The dense, persistent ties of embedded networks are capable of producing strong trust and generative learning leading to self-organizing capabilities in the network. Interlocking directors may be important agents or "carriers" of such trust and learning characteristics. The emergence of "principled trust" (Barney and Hansen 1994), for example, may lead to exchange opportunities beyond the reach of organizations relying solely on market mechanisms, potentially creating significant competitive advantages that are very hard to imitate.

The tacitness of many of the bases of *embedded networks* may blind directors to responsibilities that are necessary for sustainable competitive advantage. An important strategic weakness of embedded networks for the firms concerned, for example, is that since many transactions are not based on a strictly economic rationality, but on a socially conditioned rationality, relative inefficiency may creep in. This is exemplified in the persistent high debt-to-equity ratios of Korean *Chaebol* and the unprecedented (by Japanese standards re-structuring interventions that have had to be carried out on large Japanese companies to bring their efficiency levels to globally competitive standards. The emphasis on getting the best deal even in the context of largely personal and informal ties (rather than formalized ties) within Chinese business networks has not led to such problems.

In *"edge of chaos"* networks, interlocking directors should be able to provide diffuse access to a broad range of experience and knowledge in many other organizations while also providing the potential for intense interaction with a few. Learning, in this context, is (at least initially) more related to search, scanning, information-gathering, and understanding of diversity than to specialization and deepening of knowledge. Board interlocks can be seen as an embodiment of an adaptive search strategy in a complex, ambiguous environment where experimentation and option buying may be the most robust policy. Hence, interdependence is quite high but based on temporary ties.

In such circumstances interlocking directors may serve as awareness creators, as agents in the scanning process, as idea-generators for novel strategies, technologies, or technology applications, and as creators of further potentially useful loose ties. When such networks, or some of their member firms, find a valuable and protectable niche, they are likely to transform into another type; to begin the creation of an embedded network, contribute to a brokered network as broker or client, or evolve into an atomistic network if the market, competition, and technology move rapidly towards maturity and commoditization.

Finally, in *association networks*, durable ties exist without any significant degree of inter-organizational dependence, but reflect collective interests in issues that can affect all members' fortunes in a more or less homogeneous manner. A key role of directors in this context is proactively to guard their industry from inappropriate outside regulation through instituting self-regulation, to act as representatives of the industry in public debate, to advance the industry's best interests in standard-setting fora and international conventions, and to engage in industry-level promotion of education and training. This has become more important with environmental concerns being high on the agenda of state and international bodies, and with the rise of consumer interest in environmentally friendly and resource-efficient products (Hoffman 1997). One example of network-forming from a profession's perspective is the development of various director organizations, such as the Institutes of Directors that can now be found in most countries. While there may be several reasons for their development, one important reason is the institution of self-regulation to maintain the standards of the directoral profession and to pre-empt potential state regulation, especially given high-profile examples of fraud and disaster cases that clearly point to directors' culpability.

The key aspects of (interlocking) directors' roles in different types of networks are summarized in figure 11.3.

This chapter has drawn on relevant literature to develop a typology of inter-organizational networks based on the key dimensions of organizational interdependence and network durability, identifying five "ideal-types" of networks: atomistic, association, brokered, "edge of chaos," and embedded networks. It was argued that the characteristics and strategic consequences of each type of network differed considerably, and therefore a more explicit and nuanced categorization of such networks was required. This development helps to place the network literature in context by explicitly suggesting that network features and processes vary in different types of networks and thus affords a more elaborate and structured way to research and understand these different types. For example, further research could explore the comparative importance of the two underlying dimensions of organizational interdependence and network durability, or whether there is a third

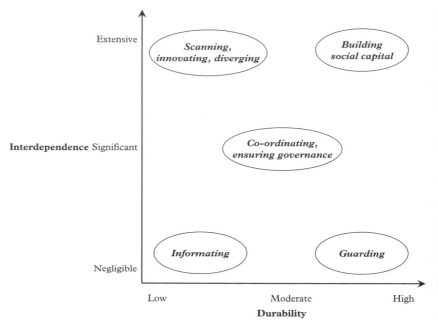

Figure 11.3 Key aspects of directors' roles in different network types

underlying dimension that could prove more useful for understanding such processes.

The chapter also includes an extended discussion of the network type most relevant to East Asia, the "embedded" network, and develops a "micro-typology" of embedded networks based on the dimensions of formalization of ties and networking scope. The three dominant network types in East Asia (the Japanese *Keiretsu*, the Korean *Chaebol*, and Chinese Business Networks) are then located in this typology. Further research can focus on improved understanding of the embedded type of inter-organizational networks, perhaps with an emphasis on issues that are relevant to the Asian region. For example, is there a relationship between low levels of corruption or more transparent and reliable operation of the rule of law, and the efficient and effective operation of these types of networks? Which type of network is more able to withstand environmental volatility such as that related to economic crises, and improve the adaptiveness of its constituent organizations to such volatility? Which network types can best address important strategic imperatives such as globalization for the firms concerned?

It was suggested that in the context of achieving more effective governance, key aspects of (interlocking) directors' roles should differ based on the type of network in which they are engaged. In this connection, the strategic functions of interlocks in different types of networks were clarified, and it was suggested that the strategic role of directors, would be more effectively fulfilled if directors consciously created and exploited interlocks to ensure that networks delivered the highest possible strategic benefits to their organizations and to their network partners. Specific propositions for further investigation were developed, that linked different types of networks, functions of interlocking directors, and positive outcomes if these functions were fulfilled.

The analysis of how (interlocking) director roles vary in different types of networks contributes to a literature on interlocking directorates that has not sufficiently addressed this issue. In addition, traditional perspectives in corporate governance have tended to follow a universalist approach, proposing "best practices" that are intended to apply in all contexts (for example, the separation of the Chair/CEO roles or having a balance of inside/outside board composition). Assessments of whether such "best practices" can lead to improved performance, however, have been disappointing, raising the possibility that what is required are "best practices" in particular contexts, with an emphasis on strategic outcomes (Heracleous 2001; see also chapter 10). Important directions for future research include more detailed empirical exploration of the characteristics of the network typologies proposed; testing of the validity of the dimensions used to construct the typologies; investigation of the empirical variation in roles of directors in general and interlocking directors in particular; and relating these factors to organizational- and network-level performance.

Bibliography

Alexander, E. R., 1998. A structuration theory of interorganizational coordination: cases in environmental management, *International Journal of Organizational Analysis*, 6: 334–354

Axelrod, R. and Cohen, M. D., 1999. *Harnessing Complexity*, New York: Free Press

Barney, J. B. and Hansen, M. H., 1994. Trustworthiness as a source of competitive advantage, *Strategic Management Journal*, 15: 175–190

Baysinger, B. and Hoskisson, R., 1990. The composition of boards of directors and strategic control: effects on corporate strategy, *Academy of Management Review*, 15: 72–87

Belussi, F. and Arcangeli, F., 1998. A typology of networks: flexible and evolutionary firms, *Research Policy*, 27: 415–428

Bhappu, A. D., 2000. The Japanese family: an institutional logic for Japanese corporate networks and Japanese management, *Academy of Management Review*, 25: 409–415

Biggart, N., 1991. Explaining Asian economic organization: toward a Weberian institutional perspective, *Theory and Society*, 20: 199–232

Brown, S. L. and Eisenhardt, K. M., 1998. *Competing on the Edge: Strategy as Structured Chaos*, Boston, MA: Harvard Business School Press

Burt, R., 1992. *Structural Holes: The Social Structure of Competition*, Cambridge, MA: Harvard University Press

Business Week, 2000. Korea's digital quest, September 25: 68–76

Carney, M., 1998a. The competitiveness of networked production: the role of trust and asset specificity, *Journal of Management Studies*, 35: 457–479

  1998b. A management capacity constraint? Obstacles to the development of the overseas Chinese family business, *Asia Pacific Journal of Management*, 15: 137–162

Chesbrough, H. W. and Teece, D. J., 1996. When is virtual virtuous? Organizing for innovation, *Harvard Business Review*, January–February: 65–73

Coleman, J., 1990, *Foundations of Social Theory*, Cambridge, MA: Harvard University Press

Contractor, F. J. and Lorange, P., 1988. *Cooperative Strategies in International Business*, Lexington, MA: Lexington Books

Dalton, D. R., Daily, C. M., Johnson, J. L. and Ellstrand, A. E., 1999. Number of directors and financial performance: a meta-analysis, *Academy of Management Journal*, 42: 674–686

Das, T. and Teng, B.-S., 1998. Between trust and control: developing confidence in partner cooperation in alliances, *Academy of Management Review*, 23: 491–512

Davis, G. F. and Greve, H. R., 1997. Corporate elite networks and governance changes in the 1980s, *American Journal of Sociology*, 103: 1–37

DiMaggio, P. J. and Powell, W. W., 1983. The iron cage revisited: institutional isomorphism and collective rationality in organization fields, *American Sociological Review*, 48: 147–160

Doty, H. D. and Glick, W. H., 1994. Typologies as a unique form of theory building: toward improved understanding and modelling, *Academy of Management Review*, 19: 230–251

Dulewicz, V., MacMillan, K. and Herbert, P., 1995. Appraising and developing the effectiveness of boards and their directors, *Journal of General Management*, 20(3): 1–19

Dyer, J. H. and Nobeoka, K., 2000. Creating and managing a high performance knowledge-sharing network: the Toyota case, *Strategic Management Journal*, 21: 345–368

Economist, 2000a. The end of tycoons, April 29

2000b. Asia's so slow express, November 4

2000c. South Korea dumps the past, at last, November 11

2000d. Regrouping, November 25

Emirbauer, M. and Goodwin, J., 1994. Network analysis, culture, and the problem of agency, *American Journal of Sociology*, 99: 1411–1454

Far Eastern Economic Review, 1998a. Bonds of convenience, June 25: 48–50

1998b. Creative cooking: how Japanese companies dress up their books in order to survive, April 9: 64–65

1999. Father of industry: Robert Kuok, November 25: 68–70

2000a. Pulling away, February 10: 42–46

2000b. Lessons unlearnt, September 21: 64–66

Finkelstein, S. and Hambrick, D., 1996. *Strategic Leadership – Top Executives and their Effects on Organizations*, Minneapolis: West

Fortune, 1998. Korea's comeback . . . Don't expect a miracle, May 25: 120–126

Galaskiewicz, J. and Zaheer, A., 1999. Networks of competitive advantage, in Andrews, S. and Knoke, D. (eds.), *Research in the Sociology of Organizations*, Greenwich, CT: JAI Press: 237–261

Geletkanycz, M. A. and Hambrick, D. C., 1997. The external ties of top executives: implications for strategic choice and performance, *Administrative Science Quarterly*, 42: 654–681

Gerlach, M., 1992. The Japanese corporate network: a blockmodel analysis, *Administrative Science Quarterly*, 37: 105–139

Granovetter, M., 1985. Economic action and social structure: the problem of embeddedness, *American Journal of Sociology*, 91(3): 481–510

Gulati, R., Nohria, N., and Zaheer, A., 2000. Strategic networks, *Strategic Management Journal*, 21: 203–215

Hallock, K. F., 1997. Reciprocally interlocking boards of directors and executive compensation, *Journal of Financial and Quantitative Analysis*, 32(3): 331–344

Hambrick, D. C. and Lei, D., 1985. Towards an empirical prioritization of contingency variables for business strategy, *Academy of Management Journal*, 28: 763–788

Hamilton, G. and Biggart, N., 1988. Market, culture, and authority: a comparative analysis of management and organization in the Far East, *American Journal of Sociology*, 94: S52–94

Haunschild, P. R., 1993. Interorganizational imitation: the impact of interlocks on corporate acquisition activity, *Administrative Science Quarterly*, 38: 564–592

Haunschild, P. R. and Beckman, C. M., 1998. When do interlocks matter? Alternate sources of information and interlock influence, *Administrative Science Quarterly*, 43: 815–844

Haunschild, P. R. and Miner, A. S., 1997. Modes of interorganizational imitation: the effects of outcome salience and uncertainty, *Administrative Science Quarterly*, 42: 472–500

Heracleous, L., 1999. Boards of directors as leaders of the organization, *Corporate Governance: An International Review*, 7: 256–265

  2001. What is the impact of corporate governance on organizational performance?, *Corporate Governance: An International Review*, 9: 165–173

Heracleous, L. and Murray, J., 2001. Networks, interlocking directors, and strategy: toward a theoretical framework, *Asia Pacific Journal of Management*, 18: 137–160

Hitt, M., Dacin, T., Levitas, E., Arregle, J.-L. and Borza, A., 2000. Partner selection in emerging and developed market contexts: resource-based and organizational learning perspectives, *Academy of Management Journal*, 43: 449–467

Hoffman, A., 1997. *From Heresy to Dogma: An Institutional History of Corporate Environmentalism*, San Francisco: New Lexington Press

Inkpen, A., 1998. Learning and knowledge acquisition through international strategic alliances, *Academy of Management Executive*, 12(4): 69–80

Judge, W. Q. and Zeithamel, C. P., 1992. Institutional and strategic choice perspectives on board involvement in the strategic decision process, *Academy of Management Journal*, 35: 766–794

Kogut, B., 2000. The network as knowledge: generative rules and the emergence of structure, *Strategic Management Journal*, 21: 405–425

Kono, C., Palmer, D., Friedland, R. and Zafonte, M., 1998. Lost in space: the geography of corporate interlocking directorates, *American Journal of Sociology*, 103: 863–911

Kraatz, M. S., 1998. Learning by association? Interorganizational networks and adaptation to environmental change, *Academy of Management Journal*, 41: 621–643

Lang, J. and Lockhart, D., 1990. Increased environmental uncertainty and changes in board linkage patterns, *Academy of Management Journal*, 33: 106–128

Lasserre, P. and Schutte, H., 1995. *Strategies for Asia-Pacific*, London: Macmillan

Lorenzoni, G. and Baden-Fuller, C., 1995. Creating a strategic centre to manage a web of partners, *California Management Review*, 37(3): 146–163

Maman, D., 1999. Interlocking ties within business groups in Israel – a longitudinal analysis, 1974–1987, *Organization Studies*, 20: 323–339

Mizruchi, M., 1996. What do interlocks do? An analysis, critique and assessment of research on interlocking directorates, *Annual Review of Sociology*, 22: 271–298

Mizruchi, M. S. and Stearns, L. B., 1988. A longitudinal study of the formation of interlocking directorates, *Administrative Science Quarterly*, 33: 194–210

O'Neal, D. and Thomas, H., 1996. Developing the strategic Board, *Long Range Planning*, 29(3): 314–327

Palmer, D., Friedland, R. and Singh, J. V., 1986. The ties that bind: organizational and class bases of stability in a corporate interlock network, *American Sociological Review*, 51: 781–796

Patton, A. and Baker, J. C., 1987. Why won't directors rock the boat?, *Harvard Business Review*, November–December: 6–18

Pfeffer, J. and Salancik, G., 1978. *The External Control of Organizations: A Resource-Dependence Perspective*, New York: Harper and Row

Phan, P. and Yoshikawa, T., 2000. Agency theory and Japanese corporate governance, *Asia Pacific Journal of Management*, 17(1): 1–27

Porter, M., 1980. *Competitive Strategy*, New York: Free Press
1985. *Competitive Advantage*, New York: Free Press

Powell, W. W., 1998. Learning from collaboration: knowledge and networks in the biotechnology and pharmaceutical industries, *California Management Review*, 40(3): 228–240

Redding, S., 1995. Overseas Chinese networks: understanding the enigma, *Long Range Planning*, 28: 61–69

Richardson, J., 1987. Directorship interlocks and corporate profitability, *Administrative Science Quarterly*, 32: 367–386

Rogers, E. M., 1995. *Diffusion of Innovations* (4th edn.), New York: Free Press

Stearns, L. B. and Mizruchi, M. S., 1993. Board composition and corporate financing: the impact of financial institution representation on borrowing, *Academy of Management Journal*, 36: 603–618

Sydow, J. and Windeler, A., 1998. Organizing and evaluating interfirm networks: a structurationist perspective on network processes and effectiveness, *Organization Science*, 9: 265–284

Useem, M., 1979. The social organization of the American business elite and participation of corporation of directors in the governance of American institutions, *American Sociological Review*, 44: 553–572

Uzzi, B., 1996. The sources and consequences of embeddedness for the economic performance of organizations, *American Sociological Review*, 61: 674–698

Waldrop, M. M., 1994. *Complexity: The Emerging Science at the Edge of Order and Chaos*, New York: Simon and Schuster

Walker, G., Kogut, B. and Shan, W., 1997. Social capital, structural holes and the formation of an industry network, *Organization Science*, 8: 109–125

Weber, M., 1922. The nature of social action, in W. Runciman (ed.), *Weber: Selections in Translation* (E. Matthews, transl.), Cambridge: Cambridge University Press (1978)

Westphal, J. D. and Zajac, E. J., 1997. Defections from the inner circle: social exchange, reciprocity, and the diffusion of board independence in US corporations, *Administrative Science Quarterly*, 42: 161–183

Whistler, T. L., 1984. *Rules of the Game: Inside the Corporate Boardroom*, Homewood, IL: Dow Jones-Irwin

Whitley, R., 1990. Eastern Asian enterprise structures and the comparative analysis of forms of business organization, *Organization Studies*, 11: 47–74

    1991. The social construction of business systems in East Asia, *Organization Studies*, 12: 1–28

Zajac, E. J., 1988. Interlocking directorates as an interorganizational strategy: a test of critical assumptions, *Academy of Management Journal*, 31: 428–438

Zajac, E. J. and Westphal, J. D., 1996. Director reputation, CEO–board power, and the dynamics of board interlocks, *Administrative Science Quarterly*, 41: 507–529

12 | *Organizing for the future*

This chapter begins by addressing the characteristics of the shifting competitive landscape, significantly influenced by the forces of globalization and information and communication technologies (ICT). It expands on the crucial role of leadership for guiding organizations towards competitive success, especially the ability effectively to balance strategic and organizational tensions and paradoxes. The implications of the new competitive environment for organizational design are then addressed, especially how firms can develop strategic flexibility. Intensified competitive churning leads to higher levels of uncertainty and risk. The chapter suggests that even though structured tools exist to help managers deal with such risk, the most effective defense at a strategic level is building sound strategic thinking and implementation capabilities. The chapter ends by suggesting that notwithstanding the hype and popular assertions that the old rules of strategy are not applicable any more, the opposite is true. Strategic clarity based on established principles is now more crucial than ever.

The new competitive landscape and its strategic implications

The competitive environment of most industries has been influenced or even restructured by the two key forces of globalization and technological advancement (Hitt 2000; Hitt *et al.* 1998). Globalization has been spurred on by world-wide economic development, the opening up of overseas markets to global competition, and the advancement of ICT. Even though such technologies can have some positive effects on industry structure, they are often detrimental to industry profitability because they lead to intensified competition. The internet, for example, can lower entry barriers for many industries and geographies, can increase buyer power by raising the availability of information, can lower customer switching costs, and can create pressures for homogenization and commoditization of offerings and therefore for price competition (Porter 2001).

Intensified competition makes product and process innovation even more crucial for firms, so that competitive differentiation can be sustained, in turn leading to strategic discontinuities and disequilibriums in the competitive environment, and accelerating the temporal dimension of competitive processes; timing and speed matter more than ever. Industry boundaries are blurring, and new entrants in established businesses can originate from not only neighboring but largely unrelated domains (Lei and Slocum 2002).

One key competency for success in this new environment is the development of "strategic flexibility" (Hitt *et al.* 1998). This entails a focus on not only developing core competencies that can distinguish the firm from competition in the eyes of customers, but also constant investment in updating, developing, or changing these competencies. Core competencies that remain static run the danger of becoming core rigidities with detrimental consequences for the organization. Focus on human capital also becomes crucial. Firms, in addition, increasingly outsource non-core activities and at the same time focus on developing the knowledge base and learning capabilities of their core employees. Knowledge, as an intangible asset, becomes the key competitive resource. Firms need to be more attuned to the potential and effective utilization of new technologies, become more active in pursuing globalization opportunities and initiating co-operative strategies, and should aim to configure their organization structure to achieve the often competing goals of flexibility and efficiency.

Some actions that firms might take to improve their chances of competitive success include continuously developing new products and services that could even cannibalize their existing ones; make acquisitions of small and promising entrants and learn from them; and encourage parallel product development teams that can innovate faster and more effectively than sequential teams (Lei and Slocum 2002).

The role of leadership

Leadership is crucial in achieving strategic flexibility. Effective leaders of the future will be able to develop strategic visions that can motivate and inspire employees, develop true empowerment based on a culture of trust rather than control, develop learning organizations that can manage and employ effectively both internal and external knowledge, and challenge the status quo to enable continuous creativity (Dess and Picken 2000).

Higher competitive intensity highlights the ability to deal effectively with tensions and paradoxes: for example, balancing innovation with efficiency, cultural coherence with productive levels of conflict, large size with agility, and global integration with local responsiveness. One apt example of a company that balances innovation with efficiency is LVMH, that "only hires managers so respectful of the creative process that they will endure its necessary chaos. Yet when it comes to getting its creativity onto shelves, chaos is banished. The company imposes strict discipline on its manufacturing processes, meticulously planning, for instance, all 1,000 tasks in the construction of one purse" (Wetlaufer 2001: 118).

Another paradox that effective leaders have to balance is simultaneously focusing on the top-down maximization of economic value, as well as the participative development of organizational capabilities. Maximization of economic value involves the configuration of organization structure and systems through programmatic planning; while the development of organizational capabilities involves a focus on cultural values through an emergent process (Beer 2001). It has been shown that a single-minded focus on economic value, for example through downsizing, can destroy the social fabric of the organization and violate the psychological contract with employees, leading to disastrous long-term consequences (Mirvis 1997). On the other hand, focusing on capability development without attention to efficiency can also render the company uncompetitive in terms of cost base. Beer (2001) has argued that effective leaders can balance theory E (economic value) with theory O (organizational capabilities) in the context of change, by viewing organizations as socio-technical systems and managing capital market expectations to reduce the time pressure in delivering the numbers to the market while capabilities are being developed. Effectively managing such tensions and paradoxes would entail sensitivity to both the conservative (caring yin) and interventionist (aggressive yang) aspects of leadership and organization (Mintzberg 2001).

Trends in organizational design

At the same time, organizations have been adapting to their dynamic context by altering their structures, processes and boundaries (Pettigrew *et al.* 2000; Ruigrok *et al.* 1999). Pettigrew *et al.* (2000: 259–260) outline the factors that have spurred the emergence of more innovative forms of organizing; the twin forces of globalization and technology feature prominently in these factors:

heightened international competition in a globalizing economy . . . efficiency drives to reduce costs, pressures to concentrate manufacturing resources regionally and to simplify complex matrix structures . . . Internationalizing firms are strengthening internal networks . . . in order to speed the transfer of knowledge and skill and are investing in alliances and other partnerships to compete through co-operation. Technological change is shortening product life cycles in many industries and pressurizing firms to build organizations with greater flexibility. Advances in information and communication technologies are enabling network formation and utilization.

Ruigrok *et al.*'s (1999) research on European firms has found that in terms of organization *structures*, firms are flattening or delayering, making more use of project-based structures, and increasing decentralization in operational and strategic decision-making. In terms of internal *processes*, there is higher utilization of information technology (IT) and electronic data interchange, higher levels of internal networking both horizontally and vertically, and increased use of HR practices such as internal labor markets, management development, mission-building, cross-company learning, and development of internal knowledge networks. Lastly, in terms of organizational *boundaries*, there is increased incidence of downscoping to achieve higher focus on dominant and related businesses; more extensive outsourcing to facilitate this focus; and higher incidence of strategic alliances. The authors are careful to note, however, that contrary to some popular rhetoric, all of these trends do not represent any rise of the "new organization" (Ruigrok *et al.* 1999: 59); the multi-divisional form still remains the dominant organizational form, albeit with increased incidence of the organizational arrangements described above.

These trends in organizational design are consistent with the pursuit of strategic flexibility; as Nadler and Tushman have aptly suggested, "historically, the purpose of organizational structures was to institutionalize stability; in the organization of the future, the goal of design will be to institutionalize change" (1999: 49). They argue that the successful organizations of the future should be able to increase their "strategic clock speed" (1999: 49), the ability to monitor and interpret key environmental trends swiftly within a context of compressed product life cycles; be more focused in terms of competitive scope and on well-defined customer segments rather than the mass market; and lastly enhance their innovative capacities and in so doing engage in "purposeful cannibalism" (1999: 52) to try and pre-empt competitive incursions.

In terms of organizational design, Nadler and Tushman identify eight core competencies that firms will have to develop to respond to these strategic imperatives. First, the capacity to increase the speed of internal organizational functioning so as to be consistent with faster "strategic clock speed." Second, the ability to "master the art of designed divergence" (1999: 53), the capacity to create productive links or synergies among units with divergent designs, tasks, and strategies. Thirdly, the ability to alter organizational design swiftly and effectively when required, based on pre-existing modular design principles rather than taking the long time periods traditionally required for developing a completely custom design. Fourth, given the need to approach the market in terms of distinct segments, firms should develop the ability to employ diverse channels of distribution (including internet channels) simultaneously and effectively. Fifth, firms will have to employ multiple and divergent innovation streams and processes simultaneously to address the needs of fragmented markets and of different industry situations. Sixth, organizations will have to become adept at creative conflict management that can foster flexibility and innovation. Seventh, organizations will need to develop a sense of organizational coherence across divergent business units, through cultural values that are internalized by employees. Lastly, as discussed above, executive teams will have to develop their own competencies in effectively managing strategic and organizational tensions and paradoxes.

Dealing with strategic uncertainty and risk

The path for profitable growth is laden with danger. Deregulated geographic markets with high potential are uncharted territory characterized by shifting unknowns, where many foreign entrants crash and burn (Heracleous 2001). Corporations, in addition, often undertake major investments by jumping on bandwagons, or for defensive reasons, rather than based on a clear strategic rationale designed to deliver competitive advantage. To compound matters, there is often no clear separation between what is legal and what is ethical in both business practices and company reporting, which can encourage risky and inappropriate company actions.[1]

Uncertainty and risk are thus endemic in strategic management. They cannot be eliminated, but at least they can be monitored and managed. Uncertainty can range from low levels, in relatively stable, transparent, and sedate environments, to extreme ambiguity where key features such as the players, technological standards, customer demand, and institutional direction are as yet undefined, and environmental movements are impossible to predict. In between these poles, there are situations where trends can be discerned, key variables can be identified, and a limited set of likely scenarios constructed (Courtney *et al.* 2001). Within these uncertainty levels, companies can either adapt to the competitive situation and take reactive measures, can take an active "wait-and-see" attitude where they make relatively small investments that can grant them the "right to play" when the competitive situation becomes more patterned and predictable, or they can ideally attempt to re-shape their industry and change the rules of their competitive game (Courtney *et al.* 2001), even if such a task seems next to impossible given current resources. This last stance is what Hamel and Prahalad (1989) have called the pursuit of "strategic intent," and the organizations that achieve this are what Slywotzky and Morrison (2001) have labeled the "re-inventors," companies that re-invent both themselves and their industries.

There are tools that can help managers gauge the levels of strategic risk that their company faces. A useful one, for example, is the "risk management calculator" (Simons 1999) based on three main types of internal pressures: those due to growth, culture, and information management. There are also risk management tools that follow structured processes to identify risks, evaluate and rank them, make action plans, monitor risks, and take relevant actions. The evaluation and ranking of risks is usually based on the two dimensions of risk impact and risk likelihood. Such processes may be effective in more structured contexts where there is a relatively limited number of variables to consider, and thus higher levels of predictability. In strategy and business, however, this luxury does not exist.

---

[1] A survey by *CFO* magazine has found that 17 percent of senior financial officers in the USA have felt pressured by their CEOs to overstate company performance over the last five years (Fink 2002).

The most effective way to deal with strategic uncertainty and risk is to develop sound capabilities in strategic thinking and implementation. Senior managers have to function well as a team that can balance coherence with real debate. They should continually ask difficult and often unsettling questions such as: What are our core competencies, if any? Do they meet the tests of being valuable, rare, inimitable and non-substitutable? Do they match customer demands (actual, potential, and latent), or create new ones? Do we have a unique organizational architecture that supports our competencies, and do we understand the difference between operational efficiency and unique organizational configuration and positioning (Porter 1996)? In what way are customer demands changing, and how can we influence that?

One can of course go too far with customer orientation (Brown 2001). For one thing, a company has to be clear about which types of customers to serve and which types are merely drains on resources and should be avoided. In addition, incremental improvements can often be made based on customer feedback, itself an essential process. But when it comes to radical or discontinuous innovations, insights can come from virtually anywhere, and customer focus groups can be unreliable. New Coke, for example, got the thumbs up from focus groups but flopped in the market. According to Bernard Arnault of LVMH, for example, "some companies are very marketing driven; they follow the consumer. And they succeed with that strategy . . . But that approach has nothing to do with innovation, which is the ultimate driver, we believe, of growth and profitability. You can't charge a premium price for giving people what they expect, and you won't ever have break-out products that way – the kinds of products that people line up around the block for" (Wetlaufer 2001: 119).

The invariance of strategic principles

Many have argued that the new competitive landscape invalidates es-tablished strategy principles and a lot of the learning that has taken place in the past. For example, Harvey and Buckley (2002) suggest that "we are witnessing what Thomas Kuhn . . . referred to as a paradigm shift – a situation in which older ways of thinking no longer apply" (2002: 368). We have to be careful, though, in distinguishing when such statements apply and when they don't. In more fluid, unpredictable and ambiguous contexts, strategic clarity becomes even more crucial. As

Porter has aptly phrased it, "the specifics of competition change every day, but I don't believe that the fundamentals of competition change very much at all" (Porter 2002: 46).

Porter, in his seminal article, "What is strategy?", differentiated between mere operational efficiency vs truly unique configurations of the value chain, and stressed that competitive success comes from the latter, from firms that have both a unique positioning or value proposition in the market, as well as unique organizational configurations to deliver this positioning. He criticized managerial tendencies to latch on to fads without a clear rationale of how such actions can deliver sustainable competitive advantage. In the context of recent trends towards alliances and partnerships, he argued that they must be based, first and foremost, on company strategy rather than on the fact that everyone else is doing it: "There's a prior set of choices that have to be made about what advantages a company is going to offer to what set of customers, and with what unique configuration of activities. Partnering and alliances are somewhere down the logical chain, contingent on the strategy. There is a tendency in management to not see the logical chain but to latch on to a fad in the guise of strategy" (2002: 48).

Porter has summarized his thinking on strategic positioning in terms of six principles (Porter 2001). First, a firm must put superior long-term return on investment as its key goal (rather than simply share price increases, for example, an approach that has led to several companies' demise because it encourages short-term thinking and unsound investments). Secondly, strategy must be designed to deliver unique and well-defined value propositions to specific sets of customers, rather than trying to be all things to all people. Thirdly, this value proposition needs to be supported and operationalized in unique configurations of the value chain, not because the company has latched on to an obsession with "best practices" that most other companies are also following and that result in homogenization and the absence of uniqueness. Fourth, effective strategies necessarily involve trade-offs, tough decisions about what not to offer and what customer segments to forgo; this is in turn reflected in value chain choices that result in true distinctiveness. Fifth, the strategy should define not only the choices of organizational configuration, but also the levels of fit, coherence, and synergy among the choices. This is what makes a strategy hard to copy by competitors, because they would have to copy the whole business system rather than just parts of it. Attempting to copy a whole business system, however, can involve high risks for competition because several of its elements would come into conflict with their own established processes and strategy. Lastly, strategy involves a constant direction in the value proposition that the company should stand for in the longer term (Porter 1996, 2001, 2002).

Hambrick and Fredrickson also argue that "strategy has become a catchall term used to mean whatever one wants it to mean" (2001: 49), and that executives' assertions about their company's strategy are at best statements about limited aspects of a more complete notion of strategy. They suggest that the strategy concept should be clarified, and that strategy is in fact the answer to five key questions: First, in what market arenas will we be active (products, market segments, geographies, technologies, value-creation stages)? Second, how will we get there (internal development, joint ventures, franchising, acquisitions)? Third, how will we be differentiated in the marketplace (image, customization, price, style, product reliability)? Fourth, what will be our speed and sequence of moves? Fifth, how will we obtain our returns (scale advantages, scope advantages, unmatched service, proprietary product features)?

There are, of course, no recipes that can guarantee competitive success in turbulent environments. Effective strategies are products of creative insights combined with tough choices about strategic scope and organizational configuration. Importantly, leaders should not lose sight of the fact that organizations are living social systems, which have not only to be efficient but also meaningful and engaging places to work. Bases of sustainable competitive advantage, beyond unique organizational configurations and market positioning, are ultimately rooted in the stocks of knowledge, culture, and social practices of the organization.

* * *

In the preface, I noted that the genesis of this book was rooted in my interest in how organization theory can engender a new paradigm in strategic management, that takes seriously such issues as the role of agency, how the world is meaningful to organizational actors, a longitudinal focus on process rather than on static cross-sectional analyses, and pays due attention to organizational facets such as strategic choices, culture, discourse, and learning. I have labeled this an "organization action" view of strategic management. I would hope that the work reported here provides students of strategy, strategy scholars, and reflective practitioners with a more organizationally informed view of strategic management; and with the impetus to pursue and perhaps contribute further to such an understanding.

Bibliography

Beer, M., 2001. How to develop an organization capable of sustained high performance: embrace the drive for results–capability development paradox, *Organizational Dynamics*, 29: 233–247

Brown, S., 2001. Torment your customers (They'll love it), *Harvard Business Review*, October: 82–88

Courtney, H. G., Kirkland, J. and Viguerie, S. P., 2001. Strategy under uncertainty, in *Strategy in an Uncertain World: A McKinsey Quarterly Reader*, New York: McKinsey & Co.: 5–14

Dess, G. G. and Picken, J. C., 2000. Changing roles: leadership in the 21st century, *Organizational Dynamics*, 28(3): 18–33

Fink, R., 2002. The fear of all sums, *Chief Financial Officer*, August 1

Hambrick, D. C. and Fredrickson, J. W., 2001. Are you sure you have a strategy?, *Academy of Management Executive*, 2001(4): 48–59

Hamel, G. and Prahalad, C. K., 1989. Strategic intent, *Harvard Business Review*, May–June: 63–76

Harvey, M. and Buckley, R. M., 2002. Assessing the "conventional wisdoms" of management for the 21st century organization, *Organizational Dynamics*, 30: 368–378

Heracleous, L., 2001. When local beat global: the Chinese beer industry, *Business Strategy Review*, 12(3): 37–45

Hitt, M. A., 2000. The new frontier: transformation of management for the new millennium, *Organizational Dynamics*, 28(3): 7–16

Hitt, M. A., Keats, B. W. and DeMarie, S., 1998. Navigating in the new competitive landscape: building strategic flexibility and competitive advantage in the 21st century, *Academy of Management Executive*, 12(4): 22–42

Lei, D. and Slocum, J. W., 2002. Organization designs to renew competitive advantage, *Organizational Dynamics*, 31: 1–18

Mintzberg, H., 2001. The yin and the yang of managing, *Organizational Dynamics*, 29: 306–312

Mirvis, P. H., 1997. Human resource management: leaders, laggards and followers, *Academy of Management Executive*, 11(2), 43–56

Nadler, D. A. and Tushman, M. L., 1999. The organization of the future: strategic imperatives and core competencies for the 21st century, *Organizational Dynamics*, 28(1): 45–60

Pettigrew, A., Massini, S. and Numagami, T., 2000. Innovative forms of organizing in Europe and Japan. *European Management Journal*, 18: 259–273

Porter, M., 1996. What is strategy?, *Harvard Business Review*, November–December: 61–78

2001. Strategy and the internet, *Harvard Business Review*, March: 63–78

2002. An interview with Michael Porter (interviewed by N. Argyres and A. M. McGahan), *Academy of Management Executive*, 16(2): 43–52

Ruigrok, W., Pettigrew, A., Peck, S. and Whittington, R., 1999. Corporate restructuring and new forms of organizing: evidence from Europe, *Management International Review*, 39(2): 41–64

Simons, R., 1999. How risky is your company?, *Harvard Business Review*, May–June: 85–94

Slywotzky, A. J. and Morrison, D. J., 2001. *The Profit Zone. How Strategic Business Design will Lead you to Tomorrow's Profits*, New York: Three Rivers Press

Wetlaufer, S., 2001. Bernard Arnault of LVMH: the perfect paradox of star brands, *Harvard Business Review*, October: 116–123

Index of names

222

Index of subjects

3M, 50
action
    frame of reference, xii
    research, 128–131
adaptive
    learning, 44
    model, 26
administrative behavior, 26
Aenias Tacticus, on strategy, 3
agency theory, 13, 15, 171, 172, 178,
        179, 181, 200
Asia-Pacific Telecommunications Index,
        158
association network *see* networks
atomistic network *see* networks

bad practice, in corporate governance,
        175
balanced scorecard, 82
barriers to change 114, *see also* change
        management
behavioral event interview, 58
best practice, in corporate governance,
        168, 169
    conventional definition, 170
    and organizational performance, 169,
        170, 174–177
    see also CEO/chair duality ,
        insider/outsider composition,
        McKinsey Consultants
BMW, 12
Boards of Directors
    academic research on, 171, 176
    different practices for different
        organizations, 177–179
    effectiveness, 169
    pressure from periodicals, 170
    vigilance of, 175
    see also best practice, CEO/chair
        duality, directoral interlocks,
        insider/outsider composition
Boston Consulting Group, 6–8
brand repositioning, 78
bureaucratization, spread of, 184

Burke–Litwin model, 82, 131
business process re-engineering, 113
Business Week, 125
    and corporate governance, 170, 178

Cadbury Code of Best Practice (*Cadbury
        Report*), 171, 172
Campbell Soup, 170
cash cows, in BCG growth-share matrix,
        5–8
CEO/chair duality, 169, 171–174, 205
Chaebol, 191, 193–195, 201
    debt-to-equity ratios, 202
change management
    and cultural web, 100
    failure, 113
    at Hay Management Consultants,
        104–106
    literature, 113
    need for, 112–115
    and organizational culture, 115
    and organizational discourse,
        117–119
    and privatization, 153
    structural and cultural barriers, 114
charismatic leadership approach, 61–64
Chinese business networks, 191,
        193–195, 202
client focus, at Hay Management
        Consultants, 92, 93, 102
cognitive resources theory, 60, 61
communication, and change
        management, 105
    see also organizational discourse
Compaq, 170
competencies, research, 58, 63
competition, 73–74
competitive advantage, 5, 11, 15–16,
        82
    and organizational culture, 88–89
    "Red Queen" effect, 112
complementors, 10
conditioned rationalities, 29
consolidated industries, 11

228